HEMP CONSPIRACY

A True Story of State Corruption
and Individual Consequence

Paul T. Wylie

Rhino Publishing S.A.
Panama City, Panama

© Copyright 2004 Paul Wylie

All rights reserved. No part of this publication may be reproduced, stored in a retrieval system or transmitted in any form or by any means electronic, mechanical, photocopied, recorded, or otherwise, without the prior written permission of the publisher.

Published by
Rhino Publishing, S.A.
2483, World Trade Center
Panama City, Republic of Panama
00832-2483
admin@rhinopublishing

Design and Layout
BlackEye Publishing

Cover Design
David Wilhelm
Juju Web Design
http://www.jujuwebdesign.com

International Standard Book Number (ISBN)
cloth: 9962-636-66-3 Published in Republic of Panama
electronic: 0-9733121-0-6 Published in Canada

This book is dedicated to

Ivonne Lopez Gomez, the love of my life.

"Esta es la historia de neustra vida de amor, de los tiempos dificiles quevivimos, el vinculo de amor que latiri por siempre nosotros."

Te Amo, Mi Amor.

Acknowledgments

To my mother. Who has showed her continued support throughout this project.

A true survivor

To my family, whose prayers were finally answered. Their continued support throughout this agonizing ordeal brought untold hardship upon them all. It was this support and the spiritual strength it provided that

saw me through.

To the two people who together quite possibly saved my life: Grant Sanders, who provided financial aid and who relentlessly worked to gain my freedom, never giving up until I was home. And Ivonne Lopez, who translated that financial aid into the necessities that allowed me to live tolerably, bringing them to the prison

at great consequence to herself.

To Marc Deeley, colleague, whose contribution in editing the Hemp Conspiracy book and writing chapter thirteen goes acknowledged,

to which I am indebted

I would like to thank Marg Gilks of Scripta Word Services. Pete Brady, Investigative reporter. Don E. Wirtshafter, Patrick Goggin lawyers for their work in gaining the documentation necessary for my release. Jose D. Talavera Nicaraguan lawyer, friend, on going crusader   -
all professionals -

Nicaragua — the land of lakes, volcanoes and natural disasters. But some disasters are not natural. They are man-made.

Nicaragua is a beautiful, bright, sunny country darkened by politics!

Religion and morality are the cornerstones of mankind. We have morality, but lack religious faith. In Central America, there is great faith in religion but little morality. The country is plagued by a political system that promotes immoral, sometimes unlawful behavior. Those in power have no interest in the public welfare. They are not confronting the real problems that come with power. In the guise of public service, they use whatever comes to hand for personal gain. This political chaos encourages corruption, a necessary ingredient for greed and a hunger for money, which drives the system.

- Paul Wylie - "Views of Arnoldo Aleman's Government"

Chapter One

"THE JOURNEY STARTS"

THE AIRCRAFT'S VOCAL address system interrupted my daydream, crackling into action as the pilot informed us in a laid back, vocal tone typical of the region,
"Ladies and gentlemen, this is your captain speaking, please fasten your seatbelts, we are now beginning our descent to Managua Airport".

I sighed and stretched, smiling as I remembered stepping off the plane into the heat on my previous visit to this beautiful country. That was in February, Nicaragua's summer season, this was July, or winter - carrying none of the connotations it does in Canada and elsewhere.

Clasping my seatbelt together I glanced over at my nephew, Grant, who was sitting two up and across the aisle in one of the few seats that could (barely) contain his large frame while providing a not completely uncomfortable space for his legs. Seating professional hockey players was obviously not a design consideration on these planes. I found his presence reassuring; Nicaragua is not exactly the average holiday destination of choice.

And neither was it for us. Grant had been doing business here for a while, so in addition to knowing which seat to book on the plane he also had some excellent connections here.

These were exciting times. On our last trip we had developed a good relationship with an indigenous cigar manufacturer in the historic city of Granada, whose method of curing the tobacco gave it a uniquely dark colour and wonderfully rich flavour. We had also been overseeing Grants crocodile skin business. These were industries typical of those remaining in this economically impoverished country and we were now involved with both on this occasion, having recently gone into the cigar business.

It was on this earlier visit to Nicaragua that greater ambition had begun to manifest itself in my grey matter. More significant than the ingenious wrapper leaf of the cigars was the extraordinary richness of the volcanic soil they were grown in. This combined with the year round climate was every horticulturists dream. Not one but two growing seasons! For a country like Nicaragua, so rich in nature's resources, it is easy to see that like so many other places they owe much of their poverty to conflict and those who have made it financially possible at the expense of constructive development.

Like the majority of human beings, I prefer creation and had dedicated a large portion of my life to cultivating the Cannabis plant. An enjoyable pursuit, I'm sure many of you would agree. In the early days my sole purpose in this endeavour was to breed plants that were high in their concentrations of delta-9-Tetrahydrocannibinol – THC – the reason we smoke it. Or alternatively, only one of the many features this plant is blessed with that has helped secure an enduring relationship between it and humanity for several thousand years! I took great pleasure in selectively breeding the plant in order to maximise some of these desired characteristics, although with some caution given this particular varieties unfortunate legal status.

We need it more than it needs us. And so like all other species on the planet it does not need man or indeed woman to survive. Cannabis does, nevertheless, respond well to cultivation and selective breeding, for which we should all be thankful. One day I am sure we will be. There was a time when at least a majority of people familiar with the Cannabis species were very optimistic about its future relationship with us. I had done a lot of reading and it was apparent from the old science journals that Cannabis at one point was far more valued for its properties of bearing fruit (seed) that could be pressed into valuable oil either for direct consumption or in a plethora of industrial processes. Also, the quality of Cannabis fibre enabled the plant to be used to make commodities from rope and fine lace to particleboard strong enough to be used in the construction industry. To be absolutely sure, even before the 1930's there were over twenty-five thousand documented uses for this incredible plant. Now, in the late 90's, we had access to the technology to replace many of the commodities presently relying on petrochemicals - including a fuel comparable to gasoline, ethanol - by using this plant to its full potential. This has actually been a possibility we have been aware of since at least the 1930's but today's technology would make it a far more efficient and refined process.

Many people like myself were either discovering or rediscovering the potential of this humble herb (it is an annual herbaceous crop) and all over the World considerable interest was developing around the entire Cannabis species. The Indica variety, more often known as marijuana – the variety I had cultivated all those years ago - was attracting new interest for its pharmaceutical advantages over dangerous synthetic drugs, such as paracetamol. People overdose on this analgesic regularly. None to my knowledge have done so on 'pot'. But more importantly, the Sativa variety, commonly referred to as hemp, was receiving an all-together new lease of life. Actually, as well as India and China, most European countries have always cultivated a certain amount of hemp. During the 1990's, on the basis of yet more research, several new commercial and/or research companies had begun to form in Eastern Europe, Scandinavia, back home in Canada and in the vast majority of European Union Countries. 36 countries around the world are exploiting this renewable industrial resource. Hemp was once again (since Henry Ford's initial usage) being used in the manufacture of automobiles, albeit only in BMW door panels!

The economic potential of this crop is phenomenal, especially for agriculturally based regions, which are often considerably poorer than the so-called developed countries. We just eat the food. I was in no two minds about it. The time had come to take hemp where it was needed most. Nicaragua, one of the poorest in Latin America, had all the natural resources to make hemp cultivation a success. In return, the Nicaraguans would be rewarded with jobs and a level of economic security never before experienced – it was a very real possibility and I relished (and still do) every minute of it. Going into the hemp business means long hours with little pay. You have to supplement your income with outside work in order to save enough to start researching again. It was a cycle I was all too familiar with having spent four years studying and researching the industry in Eastern Europe. Regardless, this experience had cemented my opinion. I was convinced that if we could successfully introduce and cultivate hemp here in Nicaragua, the benefits would be staggering – and I would be able to pay for more research!

Almost twelve months work sat in my briefcase. Thinking to myself, I considered the response it would get from Grant's business contacts with a mix of confidence and trepidation. Quite often it is how things are approached that makes them successful and the last thing I wanted to do was come across as the 'gringo with a magic wand that would solve all problems'. People have to work their own magic. On the other hand I also believe in rational argument and so I was confident. The idea was to start off quite modestly with some fairly basic research. Given the lack of a pre-existing hemp industry in Nicaragua we would have to import a large quantity of seed, probably from China. Although I am sure the Nicaraguans could have provided some nice Indica varieties had we asked! Marijuana has always been cultivated here, like most places, on small plots of no more than a few manzanas (a Latin American measurement of land area, smaller than a hectare) high up in the incredibly beautiful, mountainous parts of the country.

In all seriousness though, we had a long way to go. There would need to be good results with the test crop at the very least before the enterprise would be commercially viable. The plan was to use the seed from this initial crop to press oil and because it commands a relatively high price given its unique qualities, we would make enough – at the very least – to cover our costs. At best, this crop would provide a very decent return to the investors. A one million (US) dollar investment had the potential to generate six, just from the seed crop. On top of this we could use the fibre for building construction and/or process it to be spun into textiles, which, again due to its quality, also fetch premium rates. It was more than good; and the Nicaraguans would clearly see the benefits that this new industry would bring both immediately and in the future. Considering the prospects of a mature industry, it was all very exciting.

The plane jerked and bounced violently. Tyres screeching on the hot asphalt brought me right back to the here-and-now in no uncertain terms. I wondered where these particular 'Air Taco' pilots got their licenses and if everyone else on the plane shared my relief when all the wheels eventually hit the ground!

One by one we disembarked and were directed through customs. After having our passports stamped, we were allowed to pick up our luggage from the carousel. Passing through the last customs check, we stepped out into the hot, humid winter air – we had arrived safely in Nicaragua. Making our way through the crowd and menagerie of taxi drivers waiting on the lucrative airport trade, we dodged over to the driver standing aside from the crowd, leaning on the hood of his ageing Mercedes with apparently no concern for all the other goings-on. Lacking any fluency in the Spanish language we made do with, "Buenos días" and relied heavily on the universal language of gesture and the name of the hotel we would be staying at.

Checking into the Margot Hotel around three in the afternoon brought some relief from the heat. Nothing fancy, this hotel was affordable, clean accommodation close to all the required services. We were shown to our room, which came complete with Cable TV and the obligatory fifty or so channels of crap and a telephone routed via the hotel switchboard. Once settled in, I went for a shower while Grant made some calls to let the loved ones know we had arrived safely. He had only been married a short time to a beautiful girl in both appearance and personality called Mary Lynn who despite her concern fully appreciated the importance of this trip. You tend to find that once a place has received enough bad press people can't help but be concerned. Nicaragua has certainly had its share of bad press over the years.

Our main concern, however, was the agenda we had in front of us. Buying and shipping crocodile hides while making sure the cigar manufacturing was on schedule - this was always a concern. As soon as you left, the work stopped and the excuses started, so this time I would be staying on to oversee our operations after Grant concluded his business and hopefully see the creation of a new industry. Getting some attention for the hemp cultivation proposal was undoubtedly high on the list of priorities.

As you would expect, doing business in another culture is always different to ones own and language is only one facet of this. Nicaragua is an all-together different ball game. You could say that it accentuates the modus operandi of our own, culturally distinct system of Capitalism; the only difference being it is more obvious given the country's turbulent political history of civil war. As with most places, the people you know are incredibly important if you want to get things done and in Nicaragua, political persuasion is part and parcel of this. One of Grants key contacts here was a gentleman I had heard quite a lot about, whose name was Danilo Oscar Blandon.

Most of what I had heard was not particularly good. In fact, that is a gross understatement – most of it was incredibly bad; some of it fabricated some of it true. Most of it was apparently true. Blandon was the key figure in a non-fiction book called 'Dark Alliance' written – and published without libel action – by San Jose Mercury-News reporter Gary Webb in 1995. United States paranoia at Communism and/or Socialism on its backdoor had seen the funding and organisation of a right wing 'liberal' armed faction known as the

Contras. This CIA-sponsored terrorist group was created in order to overthrow the existing Socialist 'Sandinista' regime and like all Civil Wars, it was a long and bloody conflict. All the while Nicaragua slid further into economic chaos and its people into poverty. War only benefits the people who make the guns.

However, this conflict was not funded directly from U.S tax dollars. Rather the (then) Reagan/Bush Administration preferred to supply weaponry in exchange for narcotics that later found their way onto the streets of the poor and predominately black ghettos of urban America (see Lusane's 'Pipe Dream Blues: Racism and the War on Drugs'). The story is well documented and actually prompted investigations by both the CIA and U.S Justice Department. At that time Blandon had been in the thick of it. In an ironic twist of fate or fortune he was arrested in San Diego but received a short sentence in return for providing information that led to the arrest of one the senior black Americans he supplied with cocaine, Rick 'Freeway' Ross - currently residing at San Diego's Metropolitan Correctional Centre. Apparently Blandon was paid $166,000 U.S tax dollars for his services.

To be sure, the Sandinistas had previously overthrown the dictator Anastasio Somoza in 1979 and Blandon's own drug supplier, Norvyn Meneses, who was closely linked to the family of the ex-ruling dictator, had fled to the U.S after the revolution. However, despite being listed on DEA (United States Drug Enforcement Agency) files as a major drug smuggler, implicated in 45 Federal investigations, he was able to live in peace to acquire businesses and real estate all over the San Francisco Bay area. Politics is a dirty game. A point noted by a Nicaraguan judge who, on sentencing Meneses for Cocaine trafficking, expressed disbelief that he had been free to operate within United States borders.

Isn't hindsight wonderful? At the time we arrived in Nicaragua Blandon was not only a free man in relation to the U.S authorities but because of the 'success' of the CIA backed Contras, he also had the respect of many extremely influential people within Arnoldo Aleman's new Liberal government

- many of whom were, unsurprisingly, ex-Contras or at least sympathetic to the cause. In short, to do business here without the support of these people would have been impossible, no matter how unpalatable and to think otherwise would have been extremely naïve.

What the phrase 'the end justifies the means' meant for Nicaragua was supposedly free enterprise dedicated to the betterment of its citizens who now, through their new leaders, welcomed foreign investors and offered a safe, tax-sheltered environment – in effect, the 'ends'. Whether or not this was worth over a decade of bloodshed – the 'means'- only the Nicaraguan people can decide that and it would appear that a majority did, including Blandon. Grant was aware of Blandon's influence in this country and rightly or wrongly we had decided that contacting him was the most pragmatic course of action. Nicaragua is looking to the future and so are we. The past is always behind us, right?

I came out of the bathroom towel-drying my hair having had an exceptionally cold shower. Most places in Nicaragua don't have hot water tanks so I was expecting to get used to this. Grant had just placed the telephone receiver back onto its cradle.

"It's on", he said.

"What's on?"

"Our meeting with Blandon. He will meet us tomorrow. He will be flying in on the afternoon flight from Miami. You feel like eating? There's that place around the corner - Los Antejitos. They serve good food".

"Yeah", I replied, "that's the place with the filet the size of a roast. You taking a shower?"

"I guess I should". Grant got up from the bed to pick out some fresh clothes.

"The water is cold, Grant", I warned, as he walked into the bathroom. Reaching over to switch on the television and hear some welcome noise, I smiled on hearing him suffer the shock of the cold water: "Son of a bitch! Is this cold or what? I'll never get used to this!"

I could not believe Blandon would be here with us the next

day to review the project – only one day into our business trip. Progress usually takes more time and effort plus people do not usually drop what they are doing overnight. Perhaps he was homesick and this was an excuse to visit for a few days. Unlikely, but who knows? All I knew at this particular moment in time was that Grants suggestion of dinner was most appealing and my stomach was firmly in agreement. The restaurant we were going to was only a block away from our hotel. A short walk from there was the Hotel Intercontinental, the classiest digs in all of Managua and the place where we would be meeting Oscar Danilo Blandon the next day.

Needless to say, our meal was a gastronomic delight, made even more so by the prices. The same meal in Canada would have been five times what we had paid here. I thought to myself, is it that food prices are arbitrary or is it the value of people's labour? Having consumed more than our fair share, we returned to our hotel for some much-needed sleep – the next day would be pivotal.

Our meeting with Blandon was to take place by the hotel's luxurious pool, since July is the off-season there would not be many guests so peace and quiet was assured. The pool area was situated in a courtyard well thought-out in design and laid out with meticulous detail. Lounge chairs were lined up alongside the pool, each with their own clean towel and at the end of the pool, where we had chosen to sit, cabanas with canopied tops gave ample protection from the mid-day sun. From here, we had a commanding view of the entrance to the pool. It could have been a scene from 'The Godfather' had the distant accents been Italian.

The proposal I had put together was 156 pages long, slightly longer than it could have been in so far as I had translated some of the excessive technical terminology into language the layperson would be able to understand. By combining this with statistics, it was a pretty comprehensive read. Looking over the document, I noted parts that might need some revision after Blandon; a native Nicaraguan, critiqued it.

As is customary, he was late in arriving. Punctuality is not part of the Nicaraguan mindset and so frustration is part of doing business here. When he did finally appear at the entrance to the pool area, he did not match the image I had conjured in my mind. He was in his early fifties, suffering a little mid-aged spread from too many calories and not enough exercise. Right from the start he was likeable. During our introduction, his manner was courteous and his handshake was firm. We spent the first while talking about inconsequential topics and I did most of the listening, putting in my two cents worth when asked, just waiting for my cue to start the pitch. My anticipation – and the pitch – proved unnecessary. He loved the idea!

"Paul, this is great", he said spot-reading the document. "What you are proposing here would provide much-needed jobs for the people. I have people here who would certainly like to hear this. They are high up in the Liberal Party. Do you have any copies?"

"No, that's the only copy. I wanted you to review it first before we make any changes. Do you know how far the government will go in providing us with support? Also, we need support from a University; involving them directly in the project would be extremely beneficial for the industry, as we require knowledgeable personnel". I spoke slowly; trying to contain my growing enthusiasm but the questions still came out in the same breath.

Danilo's own enthusiasm was obvious in the tone of his reply. "My cousin can help us" he replied, "He is in charge of the Catholic University. I will make appointments to see him and my friends in the government. I will call you both this evening".

The meeting had been brief and to the point. We stood up and shook hands before Danilo left us. As he passed back out through the pool entrance I asked Grant, "He's a likeable guy. Do you think he can do what he says he can?"

"Oh yeah, and more", Grant replied. "As I said, he is well-connected around here. If anybody can help us, he can".

I felt elated; the meeting had gone better than I'd hoped. It wasn't a hard sell; it was there in black and white - the benefits of this proposal were mind-boggling for his country.

What we proposed would put Nicaragua at the forefront of the world's hemp agri-business and put much-needed cash into the economy. The number of jobs created, directly and indirectly, could eventually make the hemp industry Nicaragua's number one employer!

Danilo had picked that up immediately and from his language, spoken and otherwise, I knew he would work with us on it. Regardless of what was said about this man, he could not pass up an opportunity that would benefit his people to such a great extent.

"Let's go and see about our quota with CITIES", said Grant. This is the organisation charged with the protection of endangered species. If exporting crocodile or, for that matter, any of the other species (plant and animal) that are under their protection, registering your business with them is mandatory. This institution strictly regulates all permits, and hides or skins are also inspected to ensure control over the species' harvest. This is essentially sustainable business in practice. What man takes, man then puts back and monitors - a simple yet effective compromise between Mother Nature and people.
"Okay; I'll run off a couple of copies of the project for Danilo while we're at it", I replied getting up to leave.

Later in the afternoon, we met with Danilo to give him his own copy of the proposal and discuss how to structure the company. During the first phase of the operation, we would grow a seed crop at a research and development site somewhere near the city of Managua. It was necessary to be close to the University and the Ministry of Agriculture as both would hopefully be working closely with us. From this seed crop, - in affect a large scale breeding project - we would then develop a fibre hemp crop perfectly suited to the Nicaragua's ecology for end market usage in textile manufacture, in addition to the oil seed that alone was capable of returning an income for investors.

In our second phase, we would begin building an infrastructure to support the cultivation of more extensive fibre cropping. This would involve co-operation, not just from the relevant institutions but also the farmers themselves.

We would control all the seed and in partnership with the Ministry, distribute the seed to be cultivated by area farmers. They in turn would be required to sell their fibre crop to the company. Since harvesting for textile manufacture occurs before seed maturation, the farmers would need to obtain more seed for the next crop.

The low cost of hemp cultivation, plus the ability to grow two crops a year, would be a great boon to area growers. Because hemp is a hands-on agri-business, the use of expensive equipment is not needed, making this very attractive to the growers, regardless of the size of their land holdings. By controlling the seed supply, we could control the type of plant grown and therefore THC levels, ensuring strict control regulated by both the company and the government.

Danilo had made an appointment with his cousin at the University for the next morning in order for us to discuss the possibility of working together. We would also be able to have my document translated into Spanish and distribute copies to the required government ministries. Danilo was as excited about this as we were. During dinner, we dissected the proposal at great length, listing all the pros and cons. After weighing the differences, we had infinitely more pros than cons. All three of us were satisfied. Grant would handle the financing, Danilo would take care of the government liaison, and I would grow the crop. It was also agreed upon that the three of us should attend the appointment with Danilo's cousin at the University.

That day, Danilo picked us up in his hired car and took us there. His cousin, Roberto Rivas Reyes, who was Rector of the University, also had close ties with the Catholic Church, professional and otherwise, which made him a very strong potential ally. We arrived on time and were ushered into the anteroom to wait for our interview. Rivas came out of his office to greet us a short time later. He was a large man who looked like he didn't miss too many meals, with a jovial nature that belied the fact he wielded considerable power. Grant had met the man on previous occasions with Danilo and so they were already acquainted.

After a brief conversation, Danilo introduced the hemp proposal to him. One thing I noticed with regard to business here was a refreshing lack of bullshit. People are very 'to the point' – that was my experience anyway. Rivas was interested immediately and asked how he could be of assistance. I explained the outline to him and requested that his institution be an active partner. Looking over the proposal, he suggested that a member of staff translate the material into Spanish. I produced a floppy disk and in a few moments the young man responsible for doing the translation came into the office to pick it up. While we waited, our talk turned to how the project would benefit Nicaragua. I was glad to have replaced some of the more technical language. Had this not been done the translation may have taken several hours. As it happened, this young man had whistled through it in about three, very impressive.

With the translated disc in hand, we promised to return with a Spanish copy for him and stepped out from the comfort of his air-conditioned office. It was nearing lunchtime, which in Nicaragua starts at noon and ends very roughly around two o'clock. More often than not, the trick is to get your appointments done in the morning because the afternoons tend to be a write-off. If you miss the morning, the best that you can hope for is to set an appointment for the following day. After lunch, we had copies made of our Spanish-language package and went to the office of Jorge Montealegre, Vice-Minister of the Economy. After our prescribed wait, we were given an audience.

It turned out that Danilo and Jorge were childhood friends. This fact alone had allowed us into his office after lunch! Jorge was very influential. The Ministry charged with running the Economy is obviously an important portfolio and professionally close to the Presidential Office. Educated at Stanford University, he had an excellent reputation and a sharp mind for detail. When he looked at our proposal, I could tell he was impressed. He asked if we could meet at a later date in order to give him time to review it properly. Thanking him for his time, we left his office with a unanimous feeling of accomplishment.

"Jorge will help us!" said a jubilant Danilo. "Through him, we will get the permission".

"Let's make a list of who should receive a copy of the project", Grant suggested. "We don't want everyone running around with a copy, or someone might beat us out of our advantage".

"I'll take care of that", Danilo replied. "I know who should be given a copy and who we can see. These are my people; they listen to me".

Danilo Blandon had done more in one day than I had ever imagined possible. Things are going very well, I mused. Grant informed Danilo that we were required to go up to Granada the following day to check in on the cigar manufacturing and would get back to him in a day or two. In the meantime, Danilo said he would work on some more contacts for the hemp project. We were already working together.

That night, Grant and I planned out a strategy. We had a lot to do in a limited amount of time. Grant needed to go to the frontier and then swing over to the Atlantic coast to pick up crocodile skins in order to fulfil our quota obligation and make sure there would be no discrepancies in upcoming cigar orders. We had a huge customer now and it was important that completion times were adhered to, so we decided to start in Granada, the place where I would be living.

In Granada, we toured the facilities and went out to the plantation to view the growing tobacco crop, confirming with the factory that I would be remaining here to oversee the orders that were due for export. While here we would also make a start on getting my new home in order. In the morning we set out again. It took us over a week to conclude our business trip around Nicaragua; collecting hides from contacts in San Carlos and Bluefields, then packaging them up with the proper paperwork for export. Danilo had been a busy man in our absence, compiling a sizeable contact list that we could start working on. He was happy to see us when we met in our hotel room at the Margot.

"Where were you guys? I have meetings lined up all over

town!" he exclaimed with absolute passion and enthusiasm.

We described to one another all the work that had been going on since we had seen each other last.

"I have to get back to Canada; I've been down here too long as it is", Grant said. "Paul will be staying on in Granada; you two can work together getting everything set up. I'll arrange the financing in Canada. It's going to take money to get this project going!"

"When do you plan on leaving" Danilo asked.

"Tomorrow", Grant replied. "I'm going to phone and arrange it right now".

Danilo told him we would handle it, and return the rental car after dropping him at the airport. Grant phoned the front desk and asked them to contact the airport. A moment later, he had his confirmation. He would be flying out at ten a.m.

Saying good-bye to Grant at the airport was especially difficult. I enjoyed his company as much if not more so than that reassuring presence. With merely the prospect of being alone, I could feel the heavy burden of responsibility. Being in a foreign country, not speaking the language, not understanding the cultural differences, running two businesses and trying to launch one of the most enterprising endeavours of my life was not an easy situation to be in!

"You'll be okay. If you have any problems, phone", Grant said as we shook hands just outside the flight entrance.

"Yeah, I'll be fine, brother", I replied, smiling.

"Stay safe". With that, he turned and in an instant he was gone, lost among the early morning travellers. I turned to Danilo and we walked back outside to the car.

"We have to turn this car in and rent another", I said.

"Yeah, we will take it back this afternoon; we can still use it today to get around", Danilo replied as he unlocked his door, flipping the switch to open mine. "We have a meeting with Jorge this morning".

We drove straight over to Jorge's office. I was glad that the appointment was early; I was so tired of "hurry up and wait", it was driving me crazy. But as usual, we waited patiently outside his office. Jorge finally summoned us inside to say that he had reviewed the project and found it very exciting. The first and most important thing we were to do, he said, would be to take the project over to the Ministry of Agriculture. With one phone call he arranged for the Ministry chiefs to meet with us on Wednesday - two days away - to present our brief. I thanked Jorge for his help; getting this appointment at the Ministry of Agriculture was paramount to the project's successful beginning. Without the Ministry's approval, it was all over. I needed their assurance that they would not only grant us licensing but also work with us in developing the industry.

Danilo's close friend José Gonzalez was the general manager of CEI (Centro de Exportaciones e Inversiones). I pictured it as a government think-tank, populated by all the young, bright stars of this new style of government, many of whom had been educated in the United States. They returned now to their homeland, ready to put the past behind them. These ideologists were the future of the country and it was to here that we were now going. José was in his early forties, well educated and from a good family. His work here covered every industry in Nicaragua, providing detailed support for businesses. From the start, he impressed me as a genuine individual; I liked his easy manner.

Danilo had introduced Grant to José on a previous visit, not to discuss hemp, but to talk business in general in relation to Nicaragua. José was obviously very knowledgeable and among this knowledge was a particularly unique understanding of the cigar business, and so our talk inevitably drifted in that direction. I had brought some of our cigars and gave him a few to try. He, in turn, gave me some cigars from a new operation that had just started in Managua. We pitched him our proposal and he was immediately interested, sensing the value of the hemp industry to Nicaragua. If there was any place that was most suited to agriculture, it was here. Hell, we all knew the future for Nicaragua lay in agriculture! That was the greatest certainty. Danilo produced a copy of the information package while José let out a slow whistle when he saw its size. He promised to review it and invited me back, any time. Danilo asked José to continue working with me after he returned to the States. We exchanged business cards and promised to remain in contact.

I left before Danilo, leaving the two of them to talk in private and catch up with each other. I leaned against the outside wall with a great sense of relief. Everything was coming together nicely. We still had to meet with the agriculture people, but I remained positive. The economic versatility of hemp combined with its various practical and environmental benefits would speak volumes.

Danilo appeared, smiling. "We're gonna do it!"

"You have done a great job", I said. "I could never had done this without you. But we still have to meet with the Ministry of Agriculture".

"Jorge likes the project; he will talk with them. This is a beautiful project - Nicaragua needs this!" Danilo's excitement showed. It was hard to contain and I shared his feelings completely. "Come on, Paul, I will take you home. But first, let's drop off the copy we promised to Roberto at the University. It's on the way to Granada".

All we could talk about was hemp and where we were going with it. Our conversation had particular emphasis on the benefits farmers could expect and how much money were we going to pay them for cultivating it. This was not just self-interested business. I waited in the car while Danilo ran in to see Roberto. He was gone maybe fifteen minutes. When he got into the car, he exclaimed, "Everybody likes it!" Our trip to Granada was full of even more excited talk. We were actually standing on the brink of revolutionising the agriculture industry in this country. When he dropped me off, I asked Danilo to phone me - I would be expecting his call. We shook hands and I watched him drive off before entering my house.

It was nicely done over with fresh paint, a new kitchen and bathrooms that looked like they had never been used. A back yard held banana trees and an orange tree with a path leading to servants' quarters by way of the laundry facilities - no washer or dryer, just a concrete washstand where the clothes were cleaned by hand and left to dry in the morning sun. Sharing my solitude with only the birds in the sky, this was a paradise I could get used to. Managua is such a rat race.

I spent the next morning at the cigar factory, checking the production quality for our order. I checked quality control – a delightful smoke - and spent some time out at the plantation. We were producing a quality cigar that demanded a high price. Although the product was excellent, I realised that I would have to spend considerable time here in order to keep the shipments flowing smoothly and to a certain extent, my presence was all that was required. Danilo telephoned and said he would be around to pick me up for our meeting with the Ministry of Agriculture. I was ready when he arrived. I jumped into the passenger seat and threw my briefcase into the back.

"I see you rented a new car", I said, glancing around.

"Only for a day or so. I have to be on my way back to the States soon. I want to make sure we have everything in place before I go".

When we arrived at the Ministry, we met with the Director General, the Vice-Minister, and other notables. I introduced myself and gave them a comprehensive outline of our objectives and described the benefits that hemp agri-business could afford their country. They assured me that they had read the brief but were concerned with regard to the plants' narcotic properties. I told them that we would be importing low THC Cannabis Sativa or hemp seed stock with the sole intention of developing a similarly low THC variety for industrial use here in Nicaragua. I explained the botanical aspects of the species and added that the United Nations Single Convention on Narcotic Drugs allows industrial Cannabis production for fibre and seed. It is a legitimate industrial activity that does not fall foul of the Convention. I provided examples showing that most if not all nations on the planet are signatories to this legislation, designed, as it was, to synchronise the global 'war on drugs', not prevent industrial development - a fact, easily observed in terms of the many countries developing the plant for industrial use.

The meeting lasted an hour or so and I had mixed feelings as we left. It was difficult to decide if the meeting had been successful or not; we would have to wait and see. I could tell Danilo wasn't sure either.

"We gave them a lot to digest. They can't make decisions on the spur of the moment. They will have to talk this out", I said, as we emerged from the building.

"Yes, it's a good thing that we have Jorge on our side to help us. Paul, I have to get back to the States but I have asked Jorge and José to help you while I'm gone. I should be back in two months, but if you need to reach me I'll give you my home phone number. Come on, I'll give you a ride". Danilo tapped me on the shoulder and I followed him over to the car.

"Just take me over to the bus station. I'll take a bus to Granada", I told him.

"Okay, man. You're becoming Nicaraguan, taking public transport".

"No, just taking my life in my hands!"

Anybody who has been to Central America understands the dangers involved in the public transport system(s). Needless to say, laughter went some way to releasing the tension following our meeting. At the bus station Danilo assured me the project would go forward, "These are my people; I know how they think. Leave it to me", he said in a most sincere tone.

One thing was absolutely certain. He had done one hell of a job in getting us this far. Our next step was money. We now had to register as a corporation and get the project up and running with all of the necessary permits.

"I will see you in a couple of months. Keep in touch with José. Okay, see you man". Danilo smiled as I got out of the car, briefcase in hand.

"In a couple of months, Danilo", I said before closing the car door and plunging into the crowd.

Chapter Two

"THE SITUATION UNRAVELLS"

Now I was really on my own and the bus ride back to Granada gave me time to reflect on what the last week had brought. There had been a flurry of activity and I was confident that the direction we had taken was correct. Danilo had done a marvellous job in getting the proposal to the right people. If his parting words were anything to go by and Grant could organise the financing, I had no doubts that the project would work. There was nothing for me to do now but follow up with José Gonzalez at CEI; perhaps we could raise some money here. The possibility did exist. Granted, the country was very poor, but money would be available through various multi-lateral organisations, especially for sustainable agriculture-related projects. I would have to research further into the possibilities of raising capital here.

The bus ride didn't take long. My mind was in need of a bit of rest and relaxation so I opted for a cold beer and English conversation at Granada's Alhambra Hotel, where the expatriate Americans hung out to watch Monday night football and enjoy each other's company. In fact, most foreigners could usually find someone to talk to here in his or her native dialect. I came to look forward to these nights; they offered a diversion from the tedium of business as I settled into the day-to-day affairs of the cigar business with occasional forays into the frontier for crocodile skins.

I am very aware of how immigrants feel when they first arrive in a new country, trying to learn the language and the culture, constantly reminded that they will never be regarded any differently despite their efforts. The experience made me very aware of my Canadian identity and I thought it somewhat amusing that I had perhaps discovered the answer to the age-old 'Canadian identity question' in Central America. Since we are a young nation without any real cultural heritage of our own, I think we find Canadian uniqueness in each other. For unlike any other nation on earth, we are composed - at every generation - of people from around the World. The sum of this melting pot is the Canadian identity, multiculturalism. Perhaps this is where the Canadians gain their passive reputation, tourism commercials aside.

The hemp project was always on going as I continued to network with José, spreading the word wherever I found a suitable audience. José offered the use of his resource library and Internet access, which we used to search out prospective organisations to approach for funding. We even went to the Canadian Consulate, hoping for assistance in some form, whether informational or financial. I was totally embarrassed; we were first directed to a waiting lounge where we sat, feeling like complete idiots for an unacceptable period of time. We were not even offered a glass of water and eventually got up to leave without having seen anyone. I apologised to José for the curt treatment and vowed not go back; the visit had been a complete waste of time.

José obviously had a good knowledge of his country and during one of our many discussions we decided to write an information bulletin explaining the business to the public that we could perhaps include as a newspaper insert. We agreed that public awareness might help attract investors, just the thing if this project was to get off the ground. I talked with

Grant and Danilo about this but they thought that it would be premature; someone could come along and take off with our idea. We had no protection from this and I had to agree with them. We were in a vulnerable situation and the last thing I wanted was to have the project stolen. They assured me that the money would come shortly. I would have to be patient for a little while longer.

Christmas came and went and I entered into 1998 hungover but feeling positive that it would be a good year. During the Christmas festivities I had met an interesting man of Nicaraguan ancestry who spoke the English language with total fluency. His name was Jorge Vega. He was working for a Canadian mining venture but his family's roots, like the country, were firmly entrenched in agriculture. We talked about the industry in Nicaragua and both agreed that the future prospects for traditional products – crocodile skins and cigars, for example - were not particularly good due to global markets and whims. I explained to him the benefits of hemp agriculture and how the introduction of this plant could put jobs in areas of rural Nicaragua where they were most needed. When this sank in, he was smitten almost immediately.

During subsequent meetings, he wanted to learn more about the hemp plant. I answered his questions and provided him with plenty of reading material. I asked him if he knew of any land that may be suitable for cultivation and if he could look around with the intention to make arrangements for us to view any. He immediately suggested his mother's property in the village of Sabana Grande, a short distance from Managua airport, the University and the relevant government people - perfect! The land had been lying fallow for some time and its last interaction with man was a melon crop. The land was deemed class "A": sandy loam soil with high fertility. It sounded ideal but we would have to wait for my associates to return to Nicaragua before any decisions could be made.

Jorge seemed reliable enough, although he had been on both sides during the Civil War. He told me that he had been trained in Bulgaria and worked in intelligence for the Sandinistas. After the death of his brother, he became disenchanted with their Leftist views and switched sides, going to Langley, Virginia, for training. It may sound like an extreme change of policy but switching sides was not uncommon. It is one of the realities of Civil War - sons fighting fathers, brothers fighting brothers – an ugly reality.

In any case, I informed Grant of the possible site, describing in some detail the location which, being close to Managua, seemed spot on. There were five other sites that I had been considering. I wanted one site to have heavy soils having developed a technique for cultivating under those conditions, but I had not had the opportunity to test it fully in practice. To be truly successful, the hemp would need to grow in a variety of soil conditions without the use of expensive chemicals. Grant said that he would be back in the next couple of weeks, and that he would also have funding in place - we could start. That was music to my ears. At long last, we were to proceed!

When he arrived we immediately got to work, visiting site after site, going through our checklist, narrowing the list of prospective sites further. I saved the best till last since it was close by and an easy drive from Granada. I introduced Grant to Jorge and they seemed to like each other almost immediately. The three of us set off for Sabana Grande. Along the way, Jorge informed us that he had finished his employment with the mining consortium in Bonanza and that he would like to work for us. Jorge had a good solid background in agriculture, especially in and around the Sabana Grande area where his family had farmed for generations.

He was a good salesman, but the property sold itself. The soil appeared very fertile. Over the centuries, nearby volcanoes had rained organically rich ash, creating a loamy soil. A family lived in a concrete building in the middle of the property. The head of the family would come as part of the agreement, as hired hand and watchman, if we decided to lease. By Nicaraguan law, you can't just order an inhabitant off the property; a reflection that the Sandinista influence was still alive and well. It can be said that some people 'win' and some 'lose' but all endings to conflict (at least where the population is in control) are borne out of compromise.

Besides the ramshackle dwelling stood the hydro pole. I noticed that the power was not in service and discovered that the transformer was in need of repair. A fire caused by an electrical short had damaged the inside of the power panel. Closer inspection revealed that the fuses had also been removed. Jorge asked the watchman what had happened and when a lengthy conversation ensued, Grant and I walked out into the field to assess the size of the property, which totalled 120 manzana, or 82 hectares of flat land. There wasn't a rock in sight. To a farmer, it was a beautiful piece of land.

"Well, what do you think of this, Grant?" I asked, spreading my arms to encompass the expanse of the land.

"It's great, but I wonder how much money Jorge's mother would want", he replied.

"If we use Jorge as a bargaining chip, we may be able to get a reduction on a long term lease", I answered. "Offer him employment in exchange for him talking to his mother. Jorge understands that failure would mean no job".

"He seems to be a nice guy. I can tell he likes you, and he does know his stuff", Grant said.

"You know as well as I do that nothing here seems to be what it is, but yeah, you are right about that. Jorge and I get along well and I will need someone with me who speaks the language. We could do a lot worse hiring some other guy we don't know".

"Let's see if he accepts our offer". Grant nodded in the direction where Jorge stood and I turned to follow his gaze. "I hope he can get us a deal here".

As we walked back to the concrete shack, Jorge and the hired hand were drinking glasses of water and reminiscing about the old days when Jorge used to work on the farm. Jorge showed us the best-selling feature on the property: the irrigation system. It was a drop feed system powered by a huge pump that transported the water underground through large diameter feeder pipes. Piping could run from the feeder pipes to anywhere on the property. This system was costly to install, but once it was running, it offset the cost by efficiently delivering water exactly when and where it was needed. After a few moments of idle talk, we decided we had seen enough. On the way back, we told Jorge that there would be a job for him if he first delivered a long-term lease agreement with his family. He promised he would talk with his family that evening. The next morning, Jorge telephoned to say that an appointment had been set for ten o'clock and asked if that time was satisfactory. I assured him that we would be there.

Jorge greeted us and invited us into his mother's home when we arrived. It was filled with antiques; artwork covered every square foot of wall space. I had never before seen so many paintings in one house. We were escorted to the salon and, as was customary, Jorge asked if we would like some refreshments while waiting for his mother. We both declined, anxious only to get on with the negotiation. We didn't have to wait long. She came into the room and was very business-like as she introduced herself and explained that, since her husband's death, she had been handling the family business on her own. Any decisions she made would be final – in no uncertain terms!

She listened as Jorge translated our proposal to her and then turned to translate her reply to us. This process took some time. There is always some discrepancy in translation, no matter how good the translator is. Two hours later, after some tricky negotiating, she was still adamant about the hired hand. To be honest, we didn't really want him, but she insisted that he came with the property and we would have to pay his salary. In turn, she gave us a two-year lease, renewable after the second. The irrigation equipment would be included and we were expected to fence the property. Jorge telephoned their family lawyer to draw the contract up and made an appointment to sign the lease. We were rolling now, but we couldn't do any work on the property until the lease was ratified, so we decided that we would have a large sign made up reading, 'Hemp-Agro Nicaragua S.A'. Very satisfying.

The next morning we all met to sign the lease at the offices of Humberto Arana Marenco, the Vega's family lawyer, and welcomed Jorge as the first proper employee of the company.

There was a serious clean up needed. We had to set fire to the land, burning all the dry, dead weeds that stood shoulder high – there was little else we could do with them here at that time. We had the hired hand, Chepe, clean around the site, burning the combustibles and piling up the metal to be taken and scrapped. This arrangement had worked out for the best, I thought. Lastly we got hold of a tractor to disk plough the fields. In the space of a week the site was beginning to take shape. After the equipment received a lick of paint and the sign was erected, it looked great. The two investors, arriving in Nicaragua on February 20th, would at least see that work was in progress.

When they arrived, Grant showed them around Managua, introducing them to officials at the Ministry of the Economy. When they were satisfied with the legitimacy of the project, we went on a tour of the potential sites that could immediately be put under cultivation. We saved our jewel, Sabana Grande, for last. They could see the potential and being venture capitalists, decided to invest. We introduced Jorge to them as our translator and returned to the Granada office of lawyer Humberto Arana to legally constitute Hemp-Agro of Nicaragua. The corporation's purpose would be the development of numerous agricultural products whose import and export would both industrialise and commercialise hemp. I was to receive ten percent of the shares. Danilo was also to receive ten percent; and when he returned from the States, be incorporated into the company. The rest of the shares would be divided between the two investors and Grant. We left the registration of the corporation for Humberto to look after.

Outside the office, I said my farewells to the two new partners of Hemp-Agro who would be flying back to Canada that evening. Tomorrow I could meet up with Grant to plan for the coming months. Jorge and I had much to prepare.

In the morning, Grant drove up to Granada and the three of us discussed what needed to be done at Sabana Grande, what equipment we required to finish in order to prepare it and the land for seeding. Most importantly, Grant and I needed to address Jorge's salary. We excused ourselves momentarily while we decided on a wage

Our top priority was getting the seed in the ground, something Jorge could do, as he understood agriculture and the farm machinery. Above all else, he would be my translator. Thus far, he had been indispensable. We decided on a figure of six hundred dollars (US) a month. This was an upper level wage in Nicaragua, but not high enough to be considered obscene. He would be putting in enough hours to earn every penny. We called him back into the room and I explained what we had come up with and put it to him as regards suitability. He agreed, and asked that the salary be paid in two instalments, one at the first of the month and the second at midmonth. We sealed the agreement with handshakes. Jorge asked if he could borrow three hundred dollars for his children's school supplies, saying he would pay the loan back out of his wages, a little at a time. Grant asked him to wait until arrangements had been made with the bank in Granada, but he could see no problem with that as long as it was okay with me. Everyone was happy.

While we awaited Danilo's arrival, the three of us worked around the property. Grant was ready to return to Canada by the time Danilo arrived, so the two of them went to the Seed Management office at the Ministry of Agriculture to get the proper authorisation for the importation of seeds. On the third of March 1998, the Office of Agriculture issued a transcript stating that Hemp-Agro De Nicaragua. S.A. Company could import hemp seeds, as long as the company complied with the requisites of their import law. With permission in hand, Grant and Danilo returned home. Grant had work to do to get me the seeds. Jorge and I were now very busy in Nicaragua. It does say something significant of the project that Grant was able to find the venture capital required before myself and Jorge even got to a stage of regular communication with other funding bodies.

Besides work at the Sabana Grande Research site, I had a mandate to develop more land. Jorge and I became inseparable. Our workday began early and didn't end till late in the day. His language skills were invaluable, especially when negotiation was called for. Everyone tried to take advantage of the gringo, but Jorge was there to put a lid on it. The days sped by at an alarming rate. One day, Jorge announced that 'all work and no play' was not good for your health, and I had to agree with him. His family owned a beach house in San Juan Del Sur, so he suggested that we invite a couple of girls to accompany us for a day of fun in the sun. His girlfriend had a sister and Jorge said he would arrange for the four of us to go - I consented readily. Jorge had also told me how beautiful the sister was, which I mistakenly took with a grain of salt. When she came out of the house, I couldn't believe my eyes. This woman was unattached? How could that be - she was gorgeous!

Jorge introduced her as Ivonne. She was demure; with her hands clasped neatly in her lap, she looked at me with soft brown eyes and showed a delicate smile that immediately melted my heart. It was awkward at first. I stumbled with the words. My Spanish was terrible and her English was no better, so we experienced long moments of silence. Jorge had to translate everything. The day turned out marvellously, though. We ate until we couldn't swallow another shrimp and swam at our own deserted beach. It was fantastic. Communication between Ivonne and I improved on the trip home, and I asked to see her again. Her warm kiss was answer enough. Jorge glanced at me and winked while saying goodnight to his girlfriend.

Over the next few weeks we immersed ourselves in our work and in the evenings I set time aside to see Ivonne. We were developing an obvious feeling for each other. Jorge, seeing that we were becoming involved, had taken Ivonne aside and told her to stay away so when Ivonne told me, I naturally confronted him.

"Jorge, Ivonne has told me that you told her to stay away from me", I said.

"Yes, I told her that", he replied. "She is no good for you, my brother".

"Don't make any personal decisions for me, Jorge, or you'll be looking for another job!"

I thought perhaps that Jorge was jealous of the time I spent with Ivonne; he considered her a threat. We'd become too close, no longer differentiating between business and friendship. Long hours together had bonded us, although I still thought his attitude was less than desirable. If it wasn't for the damn language problem, he could stay out at Sabana Grande and I could do my own thing, but for now, I needed him with me. I had just entered into negotiations for another property in Malacatoya, a small farming village near Granada.

The short distance belied the difficulties involved in traversing it. The road following the contours of Lake Nicaragua could best be described as hellish, suitable only for four-wheel drive vehicles in good condition. Depending on the time of year, driving on the lake's sandy shore would be preferable. The road culminated at a ferry crossing, then continued toward the village on the river's far side. The property was located some twenty kilometres past Malacatoya, and involved fording a river and travelling through no man's land to reach the site. If you got a flat tire out there, you could consider yourself in serious trouble. At night, the mosquitoes were so thick that they drove you mad. This was rural Nicaragua - beautiful in a wild, exotic way. The acres of rice fields stretched to the horizon where the land met the sky.

The Malacatoya property was four times the size of Sabana Grande, bordered on one side by the lake. Canals led from the lake to the property, providing an efficient, extensive and inexpensive irrigation system. I had found our second site.

I telephoned Grant to tell him about the Malacatoya property and to ask the status of the seeds. The seeds were on their way and he would be arriving the first week of May. I smiled as I hung up the phone. All our hard work and diligence was beginning to pay off. We would have a crop in the ground.

Ivonne and I decided to set up house together. When she moved in, I felt very happy for the first time since arriving in Nicaragua. Jorge and I resolved our differences over the relationship. We understood that work was top priority and our private lives would just have to fit in where they could.

Grant and Danilo flew in on the May 10th. It was good to

see them. It had been a long time and talking on the telephone just didn't cut it. Grant checked into the old standby, the Margot Hotel, while Danilo opted to stay with his sister.

We elected to have a meeting in Managua. When we were grouped around the restaurant table, Grant looked at me and asked, "How is everything going; are we ready to plant?"

"As soon as we have the seeds, we can put them in the ground. When will they arrive?"

"Don Wirtshafter from The Ohio Hempery is brokering the deal. He's over in China right now", Grant told me, continuing,

"We must have the proper documentation from the Ministry of Agriculture", Danilo said, "I will get the necessary permits tomorrow". Grant interjected,

"We need to draw up a proposal tonight for you to take to the Ministry". I took a notebook out of my briefcase and wrote while Grant dictated. The note stated that the company, Hemp-Agro, showed interest in promoting the cultivation of hemp in Nicaragua, and for this purpose, we needed to import the seed for cultivation. As was described in the study we'd presented to the Ministry, cultivation would be for the purpose of obtaining textile fibres, industrial oil, paper pulp and other industrial products. As I put the pen down on the tabletop, I asked Grant how many tons of seed were being shipped. "Fifteen", he replied.

The next day, Grant and Danilo delivered the signed note to the Ministry. They were told that they must present a formal petition. The following day, Grant and Danilo returned to the Ministry. Grant presented a petition for the import of fifteen tons of industrial hemp seeds of the Zolguanica 95 variety (Cannabis Sativa L). The Seed Management office analysed the petition and then reviewed the legislation on "Narcotics Psychotropic and Other Controlled Substances". Article 36 established that the controlled seed was Cannabis Sativa. On May 14th 1998, the Seed Management office issued to Hemp-Agro Nicaragua Certificate No. 000009 for the import and marketing of seeds and plants. The next day, the Seed Management office authorised entry of the seed into

Nicaragua. We confirmed with the Ministry that we had met all the terms of commitment and we were assured that no other permits were required, other than the Phyto-Sanitary certificate.

We had developed a good working relationship with the Ministry of Agriculture, something that we had nurtured since the start, so when Victor Leon of the Seed Management office asked if I would speak with the technicians to familiarise them with the plant, I readily agreed. I gave the first lecture to a packed hall. The audience exhibited a keen interest and I left feeling like we were making headway. I told Victor Leon that I would like the technicians to come to the site and observe the cultivation process and he showed much enthusiasm.

Grant and Danilo had to leave the country again shortly after the lecture.

"Paul, the seeds left China on the third of last month", Grant told me before they left. "Expect them soon. We have to get them in the ground".

"I'll be ready", I assured him. "There's no need for worry".

"All the paperwork is looked after. Everything is in order. If you run into problems, go to Jorge Montealegre; he will help", Danilo added. "I will be back as soon as I can, but I have to get my Visa straightened out". He put his documents back into his briefcase, snapped it shut and then turned to look at me. "Do you think Jorge is doing a good job? I have another man who could work". I wondered about these comments. Firstly, a native Nicaraguan would not surely need a visa to return home and since he lived in the US, he presumably had the correct documentation. As for the comment about Jorge, this really made me nervous. Was there a history here connected to the Civil War, both had been active on the same and opposite sides?

"Yes, Danilo, Jorge is doing an outstanding job", I answered, then added, "but, taking on Malacatoya is spreading us a little thin. Perhaps we can use another man regardless".

Danilo seemed pleased to hear that. We said our good-byes standing out in the parking lot. I waited till they'd driven off before climbing into my truck. Jorge and I continued to ready Sabana Grande for the arrival of the seeds. When work there was complete, we spent our time in Malacatoya, working long hours under extreme conditions to prepare that particular site. I finally telephoned Grant to find out if he knew where the shipment of seed was. I needed the seed immediately; otherwise, I would have to keep the tractors disking the land - an added expense we didn't need. Grant told me he would try to find out where the shipment was and call me back that evening.

It was nice to arrive home after a long day to find Ivonne there. We had been getting along famously. Her fluency in English was improving more than my Spanish, a point to which I was slightly embarrassed; she would translate any calls I received into English with the aid of a dictionary, and have my messages all laid out for me to view when I got home! We had just concluded our supper when the phone rang. I was relieved to hear Grant when I answered the phone; perhaps he had positive news.

Instead, I listened intently while Grant told me we were in trouble - the United States authorities had seized the seeds! Treasury officials boarded the vessel Maesk Toyama at the Port of Los Angeles in Long Beach, California and were holding the cargo for examination. I was thunderstruck and stood riveted to the floor, my mind formulating a series of questions. Why had the seeds gone to the United States from China? Who was handling our affairs at the Port? We needed those seeds released and sent here on the double!

Grant had located Don Wirtshafter and contacted Sealand, the shipping company; both would be doing whatever was necessary to get the seeds released. Danilo would be returning to make sure there were no further problems with the seed at Nicaraguan Customs - good news in an otherwise upsetting call. I told Grant to phone the minute he heard any news concerning the seeds. When Danilo arrived on the afternoon flight from Miami, he looked tired. He said the Americans were making things difficult for him to leave the (US) country and that he suspected Jorge of stealing from the fuel accounts we'd set up at a local gas station. Someone had told him that Jorge was taking cash from the attendant and producing a phoney invoice. He wanted to replace Jorge.

I argued on Jorge's behalf, citing his unblemished work record and the effort he had expended on behalf of the company. The allegations had to be untrue. Danilo relented, but said that he didn't want Jorge at Sabana Grande. He could work at Malacatoya. Danilo had a replacement in mind for Sabana Grande, a mechanic named Rudolpho, who also knew agriculture. He could take over immediately. I told Danilo that we needed more tractors out in Malacatoya for Jorge. There was a lot of work to do there in a short time. I suggested hiring a man by the name of Lazaro Urbina, who had three tractors and a crew. Jorge could oversee that operation while the new man and I focused on getting the seed in the ground at Sabana Grande. With any luck, we could move our equipment over and start seeding soon.

Jorge did not like it much when Danilo and I confronted him, but he did understand that it was important that he be in Malacatoya right now. At least he still had his job. I took Danilo to Tipitapa, a small farming community just outside of Managua, to meet Lazaro. When I introduced them, I was surprised to discover that they knew each other from a long way back, and liked each other. Danilo knew Lazaro as a good worker and told me that I had chosen well. We took Lazaro with us to meet with Rudolpho at the Sabana Grande site. On the way, we explained Lazaro's duties to him and told him that he would be working with Jorge. We spent the remainder of the day showing Rudolpho what I expected from him and went over the production reports. It was also necessary to go out in the fields and take soil tests - the idea being to test the soil before planting and then again after harvesting in order to compare soil fertility. Both Rudolpho and Lazaro showed keen interest. As long as that interest remained, they would work out just fine.

The next day, Danilo and I made the rounds of the government offices to ensure that all our paperwork was in order - we did not want further delays. Later in the evening, Grant phoned to say that the American Treasury had approved the seed shipment as industrial hemp seed, put their seal around the shipment and allowed the ship to leave port. The seeds would travel to Puerto Quetzal, Guatemala, where they would be off-loaded and sent to Managua by transport truck. Danilo and I were jubilant - we would have the seeds in the ground and our dream that much closer to a reality! In June, the seeds entered Nicaragua at Guasaule, where the shipment was inspected, sampled for analysis at the Laboratory of Vegetable Sanitation and Seeds of MAG-FOR (government agriculture agency), and finally released at the end of June. Now I had to get them in the ground.

All during June, I had not heard from Jorge. Lazaro revealed that Jorge was not showing up to work. They were lagging behind, and it was clear that Lazaro was fed up with Jorge. When I inspected the site at Malacatoya, I found the equipment in neglected condition and the site well behind schedule. This was the last straw for Jorge; I had given him lots of rope, but he'd chosen to hang himself. I had to remain focused on Sabana Grande and get that completed; if we lost the Malacatoya site, it could not be helped at this point. Planting commenced July 1st, 1998. That very day, I had a confrontation with Jorge. We had been out to Malacatoya and he knew that I was aware of what was going on. Before I could fire him, he quit. That was fine by me; I told him to come by the house to pick up his cheque.

He smiled at me and said, "It's not over yet" before walking away. I shook my head. After all that we had been through, to end our friendship like this was ridiculous, but I think he felt that I was in some way responsible for the situation he had created. Too bad I thought.

During the next three months, work progressed around the research site. It looked successful - the plants were growing. Seeing them swaying in the gentle tropical breeze made for a beautiful sight. There were rumours that Jorge was threatening to retaliate for what he claimed was mistreatment. I was warned to be careful of him. I didn't think much of it; people for whatever reason like to start rumours, no matter how malicious. However, soon after hearing this, Jorge came to my front door asking for money. By law, he said, we were required to pay him holiday pay and two weeks' severance pay. I countered with a demand that he pay back the money that we'd loaned to him when he was hired. He dismissed that and requested payment of $600.00, or he would go to the Ministry of Labour. I told him that he could do whatever he thought fit, but I could not and would not pay him. I would tell the business associates about his demands and if they thought that he should be compensated, then they would pay him.

When I phoned Grant and Danilo and told them about Jorge's demands, Danilo said he would be back to handle those affairs. Grant said that he was thinking about taking on some new partners and wanted to fly down to look at the crop. In mid-October, both Grant and Danilo visited the site and we discussed the business at hand. Danilo said that he would look after Jorge and whatever outstanding bills there were. It was a Godsend to have that lifted from my back - it had become increasingly difficult to juggle finances because of all the delays and problems. Our corporate money was being eaten up fast, and Grant suggested that we take on more partners. Three men from Vancouver had expressed an interest in the project. These people specialised in marketing and what they could bring into the partnership, other than the obvious infusion of cash, was their ability to sell our end products. We would be manufacturing our oilseed in the first of the New Year and we would need to have the product sold in order to pay the investors. Also, taking on these new investors would mean that the slices of the pie would get a little smaller. Besides we original three, there would be five additional investors, all from Vancouver. Grant said that he would return with the investors and left Danilo and me to carry on.

Jorge did not stay silent for very long. I was summoned to a court appearance in Granada. There I was shown a false labour contract between Hemp-Agro and Jorge Vega. No labour agreement had ever existed, and the signature was a poor forgery. I gave this document to a lawyer in Granada to hold in case Hemp-Agro wanted to proceed with a criminal case. I then explained the situation to Danilo and told him that I preferred not to proceed with criminal charges. I would never put someone into prison for such things. For the time being, Danilo said, we would remain silent - we didn't need any publicity. He suggested that we go to the police and have them patrol the Sabana Grande site against theft. If anyone was found stealing, then they could expect prosecution.

The next morning, I met Danilo and his friend, Yuri Cisne, at his house in Managua. Both men were good friends with police chief Carlos Palacios. We had an appointment to meet the chief that morning to discuss police protection at Sabana Grande. Palacios said that we could have the perimeter patrolled on foot. Workers going home would be searched to ensure that nothing left the site. I felt that service was well worth the extra money we would have to pay. I would have felt better if the site had electrical fencing around the perimeter, but the cost and connotations made that idea prohibitive for now.

Jorge Vega's family was becoming a real nuisance. His brother came nosing around the site a few times, and then we received a summons for a suit against Grant for non-compliance with the lease agreement. As if forging documents wasn't underhand enough, he'd cajoled his mother into this action probably thinking we were having money problems and so wouldn't be able to defend ourselves. They hoped to take the property back. I told Danilo that Jorge would go away if we paid him his $600.00. Danilo said he would look after the situation, so I let it go.

Grant phoned to tell me that the new investors from Vancouver would arrive October 25th and stay for a few days while deciding whether or not to invest. I told Grant that this was a good time to see the crop: just before harvest, when the plants were laden with seed. It would give the investors a good idea of how much seed we would harvest and oil that would be pressed. Lazaro Urbina was also preparing another site for planting, so they could observe how we planted a crop as well. A day before the investors were to arrive, Grant flew in to set up an itinerary for the group. Besides showing them the land and explaining the process, we set up a tour of an oil processing facility in Granada and a tour of a laboratory at the University where we were having our lab work done.

The investors stayed for three days and then accepted our proposal; we found ourselves with three new partners. The corporation was growing, with apparently too many hands in the pie. When Grant asked me if I would mind giving up my ten percent to accommodate the new partners, I was reluctant at first, but had faith in Grant's judgement. It would be in our interests, and benefit the company as a whole for him to hold controlling shares. I understood better than anyone that we needed the additional money the new investors brought in order to conclude our first crop; after that, it would look after itself. The marketing ability that these new partners brought was also to our advantage. This partnership was a good marriage, so I gave up my shares and made myself an employee of the company.

The new partners left Nicaragua just in time to miss one of the worst tropical storms of the century. Hurricane Mitch destroyed food crops, washed away whole communities and displaced families, but throughout all this, our hemp crop remained unharmed – an incredible test of its strength. On November 18th, the Seed Management office issued Certificate No. 0000195, registering the cultivation of hemp variety Zolguanica to Hemp-Agro. We had registered the first Nicaraguan strain of industrial hemp! Harvest time was drawing near and some equipment hadn't arrived. If it were not here in time, we would harvest by hand. Danilo and I worked hard at organising the workers and training them in harvesting the crop.

Jorge and his family had realised the futility of the lawsuit; they immediately dropped it when our company lawyers contested. That left us to focus on the harvest and then to produce our first finished product: seed oil. Danilo and I hired an accountant to keep accurate records, as was required by Nicaraguan law. Juan Francisco was highly regarded in his profession and his English skills were a definite asset to us.

He also proved dependable: from many of our experiences, an uncommon trait in Nicaragua. He handled the administrative duties while Danilo and I started the harvest. It went slowly at first, until the workers learned to recognise the mature seed and became accustomed to the routine of collection. This was a monumental task, considering the size of the harvest, but I was confident our workers could do it well.

Danilo would be leaving Nicaragua soon to be with his family for Christmas, and neither of us wanted any problems while he was away. I had been talking with José Gonzalez over at CEI about publicising the successful project and José said that he would help with this. We talked it over with Danilo and all agreed. The business was up and running, now was a good time to start this process.

On a hot, humid day in mid-December, Danilo picked me up at my home in Granada. On the way to Sabana Grande, he looked over at me and said, "I was at the United States Embassy yesterday afternoon - I had to meet with the ambassador. He didn't want me to go public with the project at this time. He said he doesn't want the American public to think that the money coming for the Hurricane Mitch disaster relief fund would be used to promote hemp production. He wants us to put a lid on it till after the money comes".

"Jesus Christ, Danilo!" I said, trying to control my temper, "this is the second time I've been told not to go public, and this time it's bullshit. Look, we have a successful venture here. The people of Nicaragua have a right to know. I fail to see what the Americans have to do with Nicaraguan policy. It is certainly not in the best interest of this company to remain silent!"

As I stared gloomily out the side window at nothing, coming to grips with this new revelation, Danilo added, "That's not all. The DEA have ordered me out of the country - my country! They are squeezing my balls, the bastards. Every day, they want me to phone in and give them my flight information".

"What the fuck do the DEA have to do with you, or this project? We are in Nicaragua!!!"

"Why do they want you to go?" I asked.

"I'm sure it's the ambassador. He doesn't like me. They say I have overstayed and that I did not tell them of my plans. I asked the DEA to come out and look at Sabana Grande so they would realise that I need to stay".

"Jesus Danilo, what the fuck is going on?! Why are you subject to the whims of the DEA? This is a hemp project. The DEA prevent this even in the US!!"

Danilo said nothing. Lifting the cell phone, he punched numbers into the handset. The conversation Danilo had with his DEA "case handler" was loud and tempestuous. He was arguing that there were no flights until the following week. The case handler said he didn't care how Danilo got out of the country - he could walk, for all they cared - but he had to go. Danilo slammed the phone down.

"Those bastards won't leave me alone. I have to go right away, Paul. I will make sure Juan Francisco stays with you through the holiday until I can be back in early January".

"When will you go?"

"First flight, Paul", he said between clenched teeth.

I thought it better to change the subject despite my growing concern and anxiety at this situation. There was no explanation and I suspected that pushing for one would have made little difference, although this had to be explained by Danilo's past but how it was going to affect the future was my immediate worry.

With Danilo gone, Juan Francisco and I had soil samples taken from the site for the comparison study at the University. While we were away, the police had visited and halted work at the site. When we returned from the University, our workers were milling around, confused about what exactly the police were doing here. I reassured them that there would be a reasonable explanation and told them to come back to work the next day. Juan and I tried to find out what was going on, why our work was being curtailed, but the police said nothing.

My fears were heightened when, on December 19th, Rudolpho, Juan and myself were detained at the offices of

DIC (Nicaragua's police HQ) for questioning. Rudolpho and Juan were taken to an interrogation room and I was escorted to a separate room and introduced to two DEA agents and one Nicaraguan narcotic official. The DEA agents, one of whom was Danilo Blandon's "handler" - Joe Petrauska - stated before the questioning that they were there only as translators. They had no official status while out of their own country. Since when do US federal agents act as unpaid translators when abroad?

I knew then I was in very serious trouble. Something had gone terribly wrong. I answered all their questions; after all, I had nothing to hide. I was guilty of no offence. We had all the proper authorisation from the government of Nicaragua. As the questioning wore on, it became apparent that the 'Nica Narco' were grasping at straws, trying to extract a confession that I was growing marijuana. This guy had already made his mind up, no matter how hard I tried to explain otherwise. I left the interview after promising that I would return with our certificate from the Seeds Management office, which would confirm to them that we had permission to cultivate hemp at Sabana Grande. Juan Francisco was waiting out in the parking lot. We'd been there for the last twelve hours. Confused and tired, all we wanted to do was go home and sleep.

The next day, I returned to the Police compound with a mountain of literature and copies of all the legal documents pertaining to our authorisation. I was confident that after examining the material they would validate our documents and apologise for their misconduct. Looking over at Juan afterward, I could not help but notice he was very worried. I had him drive over to the bank as we needed to withdraw money for the workers' Christmas pay. After we concluded our banking and were walking out the door, I noticed a couple of police officers walking in.

"Was that the police, or am I imagining things?" I asked Juan as we got back into the car.

"That was the police, Paul".

"Go back in there, will you, and ask our friend the teller what the police are doing at the bank".

I waited in the car while Juan went back inside. Something told me the police were there to investigate our bank accounts.

Juan returned and jumped into the driver's seat. As he started the car, he looked over at me and said, "They were there to seize the bank accounts!"

"Shit, take me home, will ya?" I said, shaking my head, trying to find some kind of logic in this apparently ludicrous situation. I lit a cigarette and inhaled hard. I was very worried. How can they just seize the accounts? I thought. Not only have we committed no offence but we have co-operated fully and been charged with nothing. This is very bad indeed.

Chapter Three

"LA LOMA DE TISCAPA"

AS WE DROVE into my laneway, I had the dreadful feeling that something terrible was going to happen - the last two weeks had not gone well. The interview with the Nicaraguan narcotic officers and the DEA had certainly not gone well, the whole experience had been bad in the extreme and now our accounts had been seized without reason. I was glad to have Juan Francisco with me. He was more than the company accountant; he was my primary translator and confidant. In the last couple of days, he'd helped steady my nerves. We'd provided the authorities with everything they requested, and then some. I was satisfied we could do no more but wait and at least try to go about business as usual.

"Doctor, I think we've got more problems", exclaimed Juan, using the title given most professionals in Nicaragua. "The military are on the highway, checking vehicles".

" Don't worry about them. They're just looking at car documents, Juan". I tried to sound convincing, but failed. "Try to relax, okay?"

I couldn't help smiling as we drove into the yard. I really

liked it here; it was not only beautiful, it was my home, my peace of mind. During the last month, Ivonne and I had painted the old plantation house. The yard was immaculate, with towering mango trees providing some welcome shade. As it was Christmas time, all the shrubs were flowering. I was truly proud of my home, and Ivonne, who did the lion's share of the work around the house. We were going to have the best Christmas together, just the two of us.

"Juan, how about coming in and having a drink? You can see Ivonne and talk some Spanish while I fix us some munchies", I said, trying to lighten up the situation. After all, Christmas is not the time to feel depressed over problems that you can't do anything about. It's a time for rejoicing the birth of Christ, a time when family and friends come together, shed past differences and celebrate the season. This was to be a happy time!

"Doctor, I'm going home", Juan replied. "It's been another brutal day, amigo. Say hi to the missus for me, and I will pick you up at the same time, in the mañana. Oh, by the way - get some sleep, you look like shit".

"Thanks, amigo", I said. "Esta es un bueno idea! If I were you, I would take a different route home. I don't want any bad phone calls tonight".

"Oh, don't worry about that, boss. You don't get any phone calls here. You just go missing!" Juan quipped.

Ivonne stood in the doorway, smiling. Our two toucans stood guard beside her. It looked like a photo for Better Homes and Gardens.

"Hi, sweetheart", I greeted her, "and how was your day in paradise? You look terrific; anybody tell you that today?" I tried to sound like everything was normal, concealing my feeling of impending doom.

"Just fine, amor", she replied. "Now that I've got you home at a decent hour, we can spend some time preparing for Christmas. Today's the twenty-third, if you haven't noticed. Tomorrow is the Christmas party with my family and you haven't picked up the presents yet! What am I going to do with you!?"

"For starters, you can give me a great big kiss. Then, after that, we take it from there".

"Hold your horses, lover boy; you've got phone messages. Some very strange ones, Paul. We aren't in any trouble, are we?" inquired Ivonne.

"Why would you say that, Ivonne?"

"Well, Danilo phoned and he sounded worried, Paul. That tells me something is wrong". There was a slight tremor in her voice.

"No, it will be okay", I assured her. "We're under investigation, that's all. When they've had time to review all the material we've presented to them, they will see how ridiculous all this has been, and everything will be back to normal. Why don't you go and get me a huge glass of lemonade while I sort out these phone calls, okay? Thanks, amor".

I hoped I was reassuring enough but I could feel that dread return - a cold, unmistakable feeling you get when you realise that no matter what you do, the inevitable will happen. Later on in the afternoon, after a light supper, Ivonne listened to music while I worked on the computer. A vehicle pulled into the driveway. I recognised the car immediately; it belonged to the company lawyer. What is he doing here at this time? I wondered, and absently checked my watch: 6:15. It could only be bad news.

I told my security man to open the gate to let the car pass through and went out to the patio to greet Leonel Espinoza and José Talavera. I could tell by their expressions that things were bad, and both lawyers coming to see me at this time in the evening only confirmed this. These guys just don't make house calls.

"Good evening, gentlemen. What brings you to my home tonight? I don't believe this is a social visit", I stated.

"Paul, can we go inside?" Leonel looked worried and harried. "Paul, turn on your television, right now", he ordered.

"What channel?" I asked, not yet fully digesting this.

"Any channel; it's on all of them", towering José Talavera declared nonchalantly. He looked down at me and smiled. He was a guy who liked trouble – I suppose the more there was the richer he got. I complied, and there before my eyes, on national television, the police were announcing that our research site at Sabana Grande was growing marijuana! I stood transfixed, staring at the screen, not believing any of this. The police went on to say that arrest warrants had been issued for the Hemp-Agro associates and myself.

"You must leave here immediately, Paul", Leonel said, snapping me out of my shock. He stared intently at me. "I'm your lawyer; I will advise you of what must be done. First, take all the company documents and files to a hiding place. No matter what happens, the police must not seize those original documents. Tomorrow José will hold a press conference with you, explaining your side of the story. We'll have you home for Christmas".

One look at Ivonne, and I saw the whole picture. I expected to see disbelief, but seeing her look of shock and mind-numbing panic was like being hit by a Mack truck.

We held each other tight and she whispered in my ear, "I'm scared, Paul".

"I am too, sweetheart".

I raced around the office, collecting all the files and my brief case, which still contained the employees' Christmas money. I took a last look at my office. At the door, Ivonne gave me a hug and a kiss. I assured her that everything would be okay and that I would phone later in the evening. I hurried over to the lawyers' car without looking back – it was hard enough leaving as it was. I climbed into the back seat, anxious to be underway – my heart was pounding.

"Where to, Paul? We cannot be taken into custody with you, so we will have to drop you off somewhere safe. You will have to make your own way. In the morning, telephone José to come to pick you up so you can turn yourself in", Leonel said.

"Take me to Yuri's house", I replied. "I'll keep the documents there until they're needed".

"Lay on the floor till we get out of here", José told me. "They will be watching the house to see who is coming and going".

I lay on the floor of Leonel's car, thinking, this can't be

happening to me! Snap out of it, Paul! I told myself, you've got to think this through clearly. Listen to your own words of advice - get a game plan together, stay focused, take one step at a time.

We reached Yuri's house and no sooner had I got out of the car and said good-bye - Leonel sped off, probably as panic-stricken as I was. I felt certain that the documents would be safe with Yuri, who was not only a close friend of Danilo but was also a very powerful figure in the military. Earlier in the day I had given his brother my passport and $1200.00 in cash to have my passport updated and stamped. I needed my passport now. If need be, I could escape back to Canada. At the door a furious and extremely nervous Yuri confronted me. I tried my best to calm him down, but he was adamant.

"Get out of here, now!" he kept saying.

"Yuri, where is my passport?" I asked calmly. "I need my passport now, and then I will go, okay?"

Yuri had lost all composure. "My brother has your passport and he is not home. You must leave now!"

"Tranquilo, amigo. Esta es bien", I said.

Turning away from the door, I glanced around to see if there were any parked cars with curious occupants. Satisfied that there weren't any observers, I moved off, walking in the shadows. I was truly alone and gripped by an overwhelming fear of the unknown. Perhaps I would wake up and find myself at home. I needed desperately to get to a phone to call Grant and tell him of the trouble; between the two of us, we could surely come up with some idea. At this moment, just to hear his voice would have been reassuring. The owners of the Margot Hotel were okay; Grant and I had stayed there often enough. If I could make it there, they would be discreet. I would be safe, at least for a night. Grant could call and we could make plans. As I walked I thought of Canada. Man, I thought, would I ever like to be there now.

Reaching the major thoroughfare, I hailed a taxi. The taxi had another occupant so remembering that some taxi operators were police informants, I told the driver I wanted to go to the Intercontinental Hotel. From there, it was only a short distance to the Margot Hotel. I could travel that far undetected. The taxi driver dropped off his previous fare and continued on. We made no conversation and that was fine with me; all I wanted was to get to a phone. We'd nearly reached the military hospital two blocks from my destination when a Toyota pulled in ahead of us and parked broadside across the road. Motorcycles pulled up to the taxi windows, their riders wore balaclavas and were obviously heavily armed.

Just the sight of them put the fear of God into the taxi driver. He yelled, "Robbery! Get down!" and drove the car up over the curb onto the sidewalk and around the Toyota. I heard rapid gunfire and the back window shattered, raining glass on me. The gunfire continued until the back tires were hit, disabling the taxi. The driver managed to make it to the military hospital parking lot. I tried to open the rear door to make a run for it, but when I pulled on the lever, it came off in my hand. I looked up to see guns pointing at me from every direction. Trying to resist would be foolish. These guys meant business. I had no other option but to raise my hands.

"Get out of the car, keep your hands in clear view", shouted one of the masked marauders. "Where is your pistol, we know you are carrying. Where is your pistol?" he kept repeating.

"I don't have a gun! For fuck's sake, take it easy!"

"Get out of the car", he said with an intensity that would melt steel.

"Okay, I'm getting out, and I'm unarmed". I opened the window so I could reach outside to open the door, all the while keeping my eyes riveted on the gunman.

When the door was fully open and I had one foot on the pavement, they came at me from every angle, lifting me into the air and slamming me down on the trunk of the car. Now they had all the company documents, the workers' Christmas money and of course, me.

Sitting in the back seat of the Toyota, sandwiched between two gorillas with my hands cuffed behind my back was not the most comfortable position to be in. As luck would have it, I was not going to be riding very far with my abductors. I suspected where they were taking me - back up the hill to the offices of DIC for interrogation. The last time I was there, I knew I would be returning home. This time I wasn't so sure. As we approached, the guard at the gate shone a flashlight onto my face, trying to catch a glimpse of who I might be.

"Open the gate; we have a transport", the driver said.

"Where are your papers, señor?" asked the guard with a smile that showed off his missing front tooth. You could tell by his uniform, which was two sizes too big for him despite the belly that hung out over his belt, that this man was destined to be a gatekeeper for a very long time.

"If you phone, you'll find we are expected", the driver said, demonstrating the typical Nicaraguan patience. Even the simplest tasks are carried out with unnecessary difficulty.

"Yes, I will. It will take a few moments", the guard muttered over his shoulder as he shuffled over to his post. Before the guard could check, out of the dark came a figure dressed in a black US-style S.W.A.T. team uniform. His eyes took in the situation for a second and his gloved hand brought a walkie-talkie to his mouth. He spoke a few words; immediately, the gates swung open.

Our cavalcade sped up the narrow, twisting road that led to the Police compound. At the interrogation offices, I was let out of the car and told to wait beside it. Everyone dispersed in two's or three's, leaving me standing there with my hands cuffed behind my back. I knew I was being watched and was going nowhere. My last time here at La Loma de Tiscapa, I'd noticed that, straight ahead of me across the parking lot, some one hundred meters past the commemorative artillery piece, the ground dropped off. You could probably clamber down the bank, but after negotiating the treacherous slope, you faced a fence, beyond which lay residences that probably housed police families. No, I would need an accomplice and two free hands to escape, neither of which I had at the moment.

A long line of offices extended fifty meters on my right. Across from these offices was another building where the chiefs of staff were located. This was where I'd had my interview with the DEA and the Nicaraguan narcotic officer. To my left were interview rooms and beyond those were the infamous jail cells that used to house Somoza's political prisoners. If those walls could talk of the horrors that went on in there; it didn't bare thinking about, especially in this situation. Even if only a small percent of the rumours were true, it would be enough to give most people sleepless nights. Past the cellblock, the roadway led to the guard kiosk. Behind me, a small courtyard contained a sitting area. The police barracks were on the right side of the courtyard and an interview room was on the left; behind there was the embankment. Tempting as it was, I would have been a fool to try. Perhaps even a dead fool.

I stood inhaling the cool night breeze and trying to collect my thoughts. Why was this happening? Who was behind this? I had so many questions and no answers. Only a few days ago, I'd been here supplying these bastards with enough literature and legal documentation to keep them reading for a month. I gazed down at the volcanic lagoon, Tiscapa, under the watchful eye of the immense steel statue of Sandino, ironically - the freedom fighter. If he'd only known that the oppression he fought against would be replaced with oppression in another form! Left wing politics all sound great, in theory. However, in practice, their policies only become a menace to the people they are enforced upon.

"Bring the gringo in here".

Hearing this snapped me out of my thoughts. Two guards were heading in my direction. I knew my time was up. I turned and walked toward them, determined not to let them break me. After all, I knew I wasn't guilty of anything; I had committed no offence against the Republic of Nicaragua. I was sure when my lawyers came, I would be released immediately to go home to Ivonne for Christmas. I was taken into the interview room and motioned to sit down in a chair that faced an area where ten or fifteen police officers came and went, all in a constant state of agitation. There, on a table, lay my briefcase and documents, the focal point of this frenzy. One of the policemen held up an empty holster and shook it in my face.

"Where is the pistol?" he demanded. "There is no need to lie; we have the holster, now we need to know where the pistol is".

"I told you before and I'm telling you now, I never had a gun!" I retorted angrily.

"Then where did this come from? You will tell us, gringo. The night is early", said the officer.

His smile gave me a cold chill. I knew this guy had planted the holster. What else would he plant in order to detain me? This was nerve racking. Half an hour went by. It was grim. My hands were still cuffed behind my back and had now gone completely numb; my wrists were on fire. It was hard to sit still in the chair, but every time I moved the cuffs would dig deeper, my wrists burning more intensely. When I asked if the cuffs could be loosened, they just shrugged off the request. I think they enjoyed knowing I was in discomfort. I made up my mind that, no matter how much I had to endure, I would never grovel but the whole situation was painful.

A tall, large-framed man entered the room. He carried himself with an arrogant air of authority - this must be my interrogator. He wore no uniform but was well dressed in an expensive designer polo shirt and tailored trousers, clearly not an ordinary police officer.

"Lieutenant, could you please clear the room and bring Captain Cuadra". His booming, authoritative voice resounded throughout the room.

"Yes, sir; at once". The lieutenant gestured for his men to vacate the room.

When only the interrogator and I remained, he sat down behind the desk and motioned for me to bring my chair closer. With great difficulty I slid the chair over to his desk. For a few moments he sat looking through a file, seemingly lost in thought.

"I don't see anywhere here in this pile of papers that you are a violent sort. No need for you to be in handcuffs. Would you like a glass of water or a coffee, perhaps?" he said in perfect English. I was astounded. I guess the look on my face gave my astonishment away. "Yes, I speak English. I was raised in Bluefields". He said.

Bluefields is the largest Nicaraguan community on the Atlantic coast. It was a British colony at one time, settled by pirates and a base for the slave trade. The coast of Nicaragua is a hodgepodge of culture comprised of Miskito-speaking native Indians and English-speaking Afro-Caribbeans, with Spanish as the universal language.

"Superintendent Henry is my name, Mr. Wylie. If you'll excuse me for a moment, I'll go find someone to take those things off your wrists". With that he rose and went to the door to summon an officer with a set of keys.

I could not believe my 'fortune'. For the first time since this ordeal began, I felt a glimmer of hope. When this man heard how preposterous all of this was, he was sure to reconsider the outlandish claims against me and set me free. I could feel my luck turning. He returned with a policeman and a set of keys to remove my manacles. At first my fingers wouldn't move. They remained rigid until the blood started to circulate. I vigorously moved my wrists to get the feeling back.

"Thank you very much, Superintendent", I said with much gratitude.

A knock on the door announced the arrival of Captain Cuadra; he, like the superintendent, had a military bearing. His uniform was neatly pressed; you could tell he'd been a soldier at one time. A subordinate entered with him, carrying a tray with two cups of coffee. What a contrast this guy was to the captain and superintendent! He wore a shirt that I'm sure he'd slept in, and his pants were not long enough for his gangly legs; they came to his shins. I smiled, trying not to laugh.

"Captain Cuadra and I will be conducting this part of the interview", Superintendent Henry stated. "At this point in the process, we are only concerned with compiling a list of the contents of the briefcase. All the documents will have to be listed, as well. May we please have the lock combination for the briefcase?"

"It's not locked. Just set the tumblers to zero and it will open". I took my first sip of coffee. It tasted wonderful. I could feel the warmth flowing into my extremities and I began to feel alive again. I closed my eyes, letting the coffee rejuvenate me.

When the captain opened the case, he whistled, bringing me out of my reverie. "Tell me something, Mr. Wylie. With this much cash on you, were you preparing to flee the country?"

"Captain, that money you see there is the Christmas bonus money for my employees. Tomorrow that has to be given to them for their Christmas!" I pleaded. It was true. Fifty families needed and were relying on that money. In Nicaragua, the labour law states that you must pay workers one-week's pay prior to Christmas. I knew my employees were counting on this money.

"Captain, count the money and document the total, please", said the impassive Henry.

This is how it went. Each item was removed from the briefcase and I was questioned about it, then the article was documented. When they finished with the briefcase, Henry and the captain left the room. I was by myself. This guy never read me my rights, I thought – do people have rights here? He never told me I was being charged with a crime. What gives? I've been shot at, abducted at gunpoint, and now I'm being questioned against my will. This is bullshit! When they returned, I had myself worked up. I needed answers to some of my own questions. I stood to meet them and said, "Am I being charged with anything? Because, if I'm not, then I would like to go home".

"You're not going anywhere unless we tell you that you can", said Captain Cuadra.

"Why do you think you are here?" queried Superintendent Henry.

"I don't know why; suppose you tell me", I demanded.

"Because we have determined that the plants growing in Sabana Grande are marijuana", said Henry.

"That's ridiculous!" I exclaimed. "I want my lawyer present, right now".

"Who is your lawyer?" Henry asked.

"José Talavera. Here is his phone number". I reached into

my back pocket for my billfold and produced his business card.

Henry accepted the card, looked at it for a split second, and retorted, "In Nicaragua, we don't have to notify anyone. Right now, you will be escorted back to your place of residence and we will confiscate any other documents and search for contraband". With that said, Superintendent Henry stood and told Captain Cuadra to gather the goon squad.

"Mr. Wylie, we will talk again when you return. I'm sorry, but you have to be handcuffed; it's regulation". Henry turned to an officer, barked out a command, and strode out the door. I was told to stand up and turn around so they could put the bracelets on. I winced when they snapped them shut; my wrists were bruised from the last episode. I was taken back outside and loaded into a Wasp or Russian army jeep. The Russian military left all their equipment behind after the war, so the government gave the police the Wasps for transport vehicles.

I was seated between two police officers and across from me sat three more. They were making sure I wasn't going anywhere. The driver started the jeep and backed out of the parking space. In the middle of the parking lot, motorcycles and two more vehicles carrying more cops joined us. One man jumped out of the last jeep carrying something I could not recognise in the darkness. He put these items on the roofs of the vehicles. When he approached our transport, I realised he was setting lights on the roofs. After fifteen minutes or so, we were ready to roll. Down the hill we went, through the gate by the guard shack, and out onto the street. The wind in my face felt good. The cool night air pulled the sweat off my body like a sponge. Thoughts of Ivonne came flooding into my mind. How was she coping with this?

I noticed how fast we were travelling. Whenever a traffic light was red, the driver sounded the siren and turned on the roof lights. He sped through each intersection, heedless of anyone or anything in our way. There was no regard for safety. He just kept his foot on the throttle and steered. As our cavalcade approached my front gate, I could see that all the lights were on in the house. We stopped at the front gates. I told the driver I had the keys for the gate and I was told to stand while another cop shoved his hand in my pocket to retrieve them before jumping over the side of the jeep to unlock the gate. The gates swung open and the jeep pulled up in front of the house.

Ivonne stood on the front porch with her arms crossed. She wore a look that said, "make my day" - she was ready to fight, and who could blame her. I just hoped the situation remained calm. As they led me from the jeep, I could hear Ivonne arguing with a police officer over their authorisation to search. When I reached the porch, Ivonne broke off the conversation and ran to hug and kiss me. It felt so good to be in her arms; my tension seemed to ebb away into the night. I could tell she'd been crying, in spite of her fresh application of makeup. To Ivonne, this must have felt like her happy, insulated world was crashing down around her shoulders. The police decided our time for intimacy was over.

As we entered the house, I whispered to Ivonne that she should follow the police around the house to make sure they didn't plant anything - their average wage is not enough to support them, so they are always doing 'favours'. We entered the living room/office area as we came in through the front door, beyond this lay the kitchen and next to it a bathroom. The hall led to bedrooms, each with an en-suite bath. They sat me down in a chair beside my office desk. Ivonne brought me a glass of water to drink, but it was impossible for me to drink with my hands trussed behind my back. She asked if the handcuffs could be taken off. The request was denied, but she did manage to have them loosened, providing me with a little more comfort. Ivonne fed me water a little at a time then jumped up to follow when the officers moved toward another room.

The police were everywhere. Some searched outside in the yard. I had some one-hundred-pound bags of seed that were unusable for cultivation due to poor germination and had just bought new seed bags for our newly harvested crop. The police were engaged loading the lot into their trucks. Some of the police searched my office. They packed the computer into boxes and took any piece of paper that had writing on it. The office desk came with the house and the owner, General Alberto Montealegre Somoza, had some articles of his own in the desk. This caused some consternation! The police were reluctant to confiscate anything with his name on it. Montealegre had been in charge of the dictator Somoza's feared National Guard, and his name still carried considerable weight. The police decided to be careful with their search to avoid any potentially unpleasant repercussions.

Ivonne entered the room and signalled that the search was complete in the back bedrooms. She looked tired and frightened. She didn't know what lay ahead, and no one gave her any answers.

"Lieutenant, my husband is a good man. Don't let any harm come to him", Ivonne pleaded. "He is a professional, not some dangerous criminal! He does not need to be treated like one".

"Señora, he will be detained at the Loma de Tiscapa for questioning", the lieutenant told her. "You can bring him breakfast tomorrow. We will let you talk to him. You will see - he will be fine. Who knows, in a day or two, you may have him back".

The police were occupied loading articles into the transport for several minutes, so I was able to speak with Ivonne. I explained what was immediately necessary, telling her whom to call in order to arrange legal representation. It was imperative that Grant be contacted but Ivonne was at a disadvantage here. She could not communicate directly with Canada because of the language difference, so she would have to use Danilo as a go between until we could set up a proper line of communication with Canada.

The police finished loading the vehicles. At any moment they would be back to take me away. Ivonne wrapped her arms around me and held me tight. All I could do was reassure her that this was only temporary and I would be home in a day or two to celebrate Christmas. We kissed passionately, not wanting the moment to end.

"Gringo, we go now!" barked the lieutenant. Two police officers led me towards the jeep.

"Paul, I will be there in the morning with breakfast", shouted Ivonne. I thought, I'm okay; it's a fuck awful situation, but in a day's time this will all be over. I will be celebrating Christmas with Ivonne, opening presents, eating, drinking, and dancing.

The jeep started up and fell in line with the other vehicles. The cavalcade snaked its way through the gates and out onto the highway. I looked back at my hacienda and the beautiful woman who had made it home. clear. I would just need to hold onto that picture for the time being.

Chapter Four

"INTERROGATION"

Superintendent Henry and Captain Quadra met us when the convoy of police vehicles returned to the D.I.C headquarters. There were no pleasantries exchanged this time, only Henry issuing commands and barking orders at everyone in his vicinity. I was hustled inside and shoved into the chair that I had occupied earlier. As I sat there, I began to think something must have happened while I was gone. Henry's demeanour had changed; I could tell he was upset about something. I hoped he wouldn't agitate the rest of my captors; the last thing I needed was a bunch of maniacs running around yelling and screaming at me in a language I could not fully understand.

When Superintendent Henry entered the room, followed by the larger than life Captain Cuadra, he no longer appeared agitated. Henry strode toward me with that same purposeful military stride. He definitely was a man used to giving orders but he was like a double-edged sword, expressing rage one moment and an almost tranquil persona the next. He sat down, opened a file lying on the desk, and began to make notes. Captain Cuadra set about bringing in all the documents that had been taken from the house. This was how it began; one officer would pick up a document, another would hand copy the document's name, and yet another typed it out on an old machine. It was a laborious task, considering that the only person who understood English was Henry. When they didn't understand something, they would call on me to identify the article.

The hours wore on. I was tired, sore and just plain fed up. I asked Henry if they could remove the handcuffs. He nodded at an officer, who came over and removed them. Man, did it feel good to have my hands free. It gave me renewed vigour; I almost felt awake again. I asked if I could have a cup of coffee, but that was denied. I guess I'd pushed my luck; I would have to be satisfied with whatever concessions I could get. It was well after midnight when they finally finished their documentation of the articles. I was relieved. By habit, I'm an early riser and this was well beyond my bedtime. Henry stood and stretched to release the stiffness associated with sitting for a long time.

"Okay gentlemen, that wraps it up for tonight. Captain Cuadra, before you leave for the night, could you see that we are brought coffee", ordered Henry.

"Yes, sir", Cuadra replied. "It will take a few moments, though. There will have to be a fresh pot brewed".

"Thank you, Captain", replied Henry, and the captain left the room. When the door closed, it ended the cacophony that had indicated a group of people clearly inept at their duties. If this situation had not been so serious, it would have been funny. This was no laughing matter though - it was positively depressing - drug charges in this country are not taken lightly. Henry and I were alone now. There was an uneasy stillness in the room. The air felt heavy despite the frigid air being blown into the room by the air conditioner. Perhaps it was because the two of us sat across from each other without saying a word, eyeing one another, Henry wondering how to proceed with the questioning and me not knowing my future.

We sat staring at each other for what seemed like eternity,

when a knock on the door broke the silence.

"Come in", Henry said. The door opened and an officer brought in coffee. He sat it on the desk in front of us and wordlessly retreated. I was thankful for the timely intrusion. Sipping the hot coffee, Henry spoke to me for the first time.

"I'm going to ask you a few questions about your involvement with Danilo Blandon. When did you first meet Danilo?"

I replied without hesitation, "I first met Danilo on August 1st, 1997, here in Managua".

"Have you been to his house in the United States?" asked Henry.

"No, I have not".

"Is your relationship with him confined only to business or do the two of you socialise?"

"I consider Danilo not only a business associate but also a personal friend", I stated.

"What is your involvement with Yuri Cisne?" Henry asked.

"I have no involvement with him".

"Have you been to his house in Managua?"

"Yes, I've been to his house", I said. "He is a personal friend of Danilo. When Danilo is in Managua he stays with Yuri's family. From time to time, we would meet there to discuss business".

"What is your involvement with Leonel Espinosa?"

"He is the Hemp-Agro corporate lawyer".

Again Henry asked, "Have you ever been to his home?"

"No, my relationship is purely professional".

Henry made notes of my responses to his questions. I had answered the questions truthfully. The only thing I was guilty of was trying to introduce a non-traditional agricultural product to a nation that could ill afford to turn its back on an industry that could provide a more sustainable future.

"You told me earlier that you weren't carrying a handgun, but this holster was found on the ground", Henry said. "There is no reason to lie; it is inconsequential to me that you have a handgun, but I have this report to file and it would not be favourable to have loose ends left unanswered. Now, I ask you again: where is the handgun?"

"Look, I have no reason to lie - as I said before, I don't know how the holster got on the ground; it was probably dropped by one of your own men. I was not carrying a handgun!" I retorted. "Whatever I say, it is only my word against yours, and it is highly unlikely that you are going to believe me".

I was tired. I knew that I was close to losing it. That was what he wanted. I would never give him the chance to frustrate me. From now on, I would smile whenever I felt frustrated. I was determined that, no matter what, I was not going to blow my cool in front of Super-cop.

"Where is your passport?" inquired Superintendent Henry.

"I was in the process of acquiring my residence status, so I turned in my passport to have it updated and stamped", I answered.

"They have your passport at Immigration", Henry pressed.

"I don't know; it should be processed later today".

"Who did you give your passport to?" asked Henry.

"Yuri's brother took my passport and money. He knew someone at Immigration who would look after the processing. For me to go and sit all day at Immigration just isn't practical at this time. I simply don't have the time, Superintendent".

"How much money did you give this guy?"

"Twelve hundred dollars", I said.

"That's a lot of money to be giving to someone, isn't it?"

"Yes, I suppose it is to some people, Superintendent".

With that, he began to tap his pen on the back of his hand while he sized up whether or not what I had told him was the truth. He then turned his gaze back to the papers before him and continued to write. Some moments passed before he spoke again.

"Let's start at the beginning, shall we? Why Nicaragua? What reason was there for selecting Nicaragua to grow hemp?" Henry asked.

So I related to him the benefits of hemp cultivation, and the importance of hemp agri-business in Nicaragua as it related to short and long term gains for the country. I described Hemp-Agro's long-range plans concerning hemp production and how the country would prosper in the future as the hemp industry grew to meet the increasing demand for marketable products. Henry was a good listener, all the while taking notes and asking questions. He asked what each associate's involvement was in the corporate structure. He wanted to know the extent of the government's involvement with Hemp-Agro. He wanted to know as much as he could glean from me. This question and answer period went on into the early hours of the morning. I was nearing the point of exhaustion. All I wanted to do was sleep. Henry would ask another question; I would answer. Finally I'd had enough.

"Superintendent, I am starting to fall asleep in my chair - I can hardly keep my eyes open. I'm not prepared to answer any more questions", I stated flatly.

"I will have them bring more coffee. There are a few points I would like to go over so I can have a clear picture in my mind about the seed that was brought here from China. Is it possible for the seed to gain in THC while in transit?" Henry asked.

And so it was, question after question, going over the same, often ridiculous, points of inquiry several times. Did the seed produce THC while in transit, I thought to myself – fucking hell. It became apparent that he was not going to let me sleep. Time seemed suspended; it felt like it was neither sooner or later. My body craved sleep. Every time my eyelids would involuntarily close I was shaken awake to answer another barrage of questions.

"Have you ever been in a jail before?" asked Henry.

"No".

"You will be held here till you go in front of the judge. The problem is that this is Christmas and the courts are shut down. I do not know when you will go to court, but by law there is a set time in which you must be arraigned. You know, I don't like this. It smells of an international incident brewing. The press will be all over this like a fly on shit. I am only the interrogator; I do as I'm told, I make my recommendations to my superiors, whether they listen or not. The decisions are up to them. I need your signature attesting that the declaration you provided is true. Your signature is also required for the items that were confiscated from you".

Henry pushed the documents to be signed in front of me. I signed them and handed them back.

"You don't believe that Hemp-Agro or I have committed any crime, do you?" I asked.

"It doesn't matter one way or another, but I suggest you pray that the judge believes that you haven't committed any violation. I will have my men escort you to your cell. Later today your girlfriend will be allowed to bring you food, clothes and a towel but you are not to have any reading material for the time being. Understood?"

"Yes, I understand. When do I see my lawyer?"

He rose and smiled in a noncommittal way, then turned away from me and walked toward the door. I heard him summoning the guards who would take me away to God-knows-where, but I was too tired to care, as long as there was a bed. The guards found me asleep in my chair. I was too tired to be awakened by mere noise; they had to shake me to get me up. Once wakened, I was led outside, where the morning sunlight blinded me. After a moment or two, my eyes finally adjusted to the glare of the sun and I determined by its position that it was just after seven. The warm breeze seemed to caress my nerves.

They led me down the concrete walkway to the Casa Cinquenta, or the Fifty House. This was where the political prisoners were kept during the days of Somoza. It had been a place of pain, torture and immense suffering. For many, the hallways I now walked down had been their last. The stories I had heard of the infamous Fifty House never prepared me for this. A light every fifty feet illuminated the passageway just enough to navigate it. I was taken through a locked iron door set into the concrete.

Everything was constructed of concrete. It was like a bunker. Since there was no ventilation, the air was very heavy; just being in there brought sweat to your forehead. Along the walls of the corridor were cells numbered from one to fifty - hence the infamous name. We halted in front of number ten and the guard fumbled with the keys. He finally selected one and opened the steel door. I was pushed into hell. The guard tried to explain to me how the facilities worked in rapid Spanish. I understood nothing, but I got the drift. I nodded to signify my understanding and he turned and closed the door, leaving me in silence.

I took stock of my surroundings. On both sides of the cell, there were two steel-framed bunks attached to the wall. There were no bedsprings or mattresses, only broken pieces of plywood to lie upon. No blanket or pillow, only discomfort. I walked two paces towards the centre of the cell. Above my head, cut out of the ceiling, was a two by three-foot hole with criss-crossed steel bars. Through this opening I could see a wooden shed roof covering the concrete cells. Behind me, just to one side of the door, was the combination shower-toilet. There was nowhere to sit, only a hole in the floor where you squatted to shit. I didn't want to know how it worked!

Forget it, I thought. My lawyers had better get me out of here today; tomorrow is Christmas day. Suddenly I felt an overwhelming wave of fatigue. I took off my shirt and pants and rolled them up into a makeshift pillow. My shoes and socks I neatly placed under the 'bed'. Sitting down to arrange my sleeping area I noticed movement where it joined the wall: a non-stop parade of insects. Where they were going or where they came from, I couldn't have cared less about but I was not going to share my bed with anything that moved so I swept them off, determined that if I couldn't be comfortable, at least I could have some peace of mind. I lay down and closed my eyes to recharge my battery. God knows, it needed recharging; one day had changed into the next under the most extreme circumstances I ever thought possible. Before I could lay my head on the pillow, I was asleep.

I don't know how long I slept for but I know it wasn't long enough. The guard rudely awakened me by banging on the door. Startled, I jumped up. He peered into the cell through a sliding panel in the door and yelled commands at me that

I did not understand. I perceived that he wanted to give me something. When I drew near he thrust a plastic bag through the portal. I grabbed the bag from him and returned to the bed. I was elated - Ivonne had brought me fresh clothes and food! I needed to change - badly - I was beginning to smell myself. Under the clothing in the bag there was toilet paper, soap, my toothbrush and toothpaste - what a bonus! It's funny, these articles didn't amount to much, but without them, being in there would have been that much more unbearable.

I put my food to one side of my bed, taking care to wrap everything in plastic so the insects wouldn't get at it. Next I folded my clothes neatly on the bed and took stock of what I had to wear. Ivonne was thoughtful. She had brought me sandals, shorts, a polo shirt and of course, fresh underwear and socks - perfect attire for this sweatbox. I placed my toiletries beside the shower stall. Looking at the shower made me shudder. It was filthy, but in my present state, I had no other options. Stripping off my underwear and donning my sandals, I walked into the stall. To my left, a concrete holding tank held about three gallons of water. There was a valve at one end for refilling. I inspected the tank and figured out what to do. On the wall, chest-high, was another valve with a spout directly above it. I opened the valve and the water came streaming out. It was cold but refreshing. I let the water cascade down me, hoping to wash my troubles down the drain.

When finished, I towel dried and donned my fresh clothes, feeling more positive again. As I ran a comb through my hair, I thought, in a couple more hours, the lawyers will have me out. I will be home for Christmas, opening presents with Ivonne - I will be able to put this behind me.

"I wonder what Ivonne packed for a lunch - or is it breakfast?" I said out loud. "Whatever time of day it is, I'm hungry".

I opened the plastic bag to inspect the contents. There was a bag of rice and beans and another with fried chicken, two bread rolls and a container of milk. As I sat on my bed eating, I began to piece together the events that had transpired since my arrest. Everything was clouded with inconsistencies. For every question I had, there was not enough information to formulate an answer. There was no sense in thinking of what could be or should be. I had to be free before I could get to the bottom of this unpleasant affair. The food began to lose its appeal. My appetite waned as gloom fell over me once again.

Using my towel and dirty clothes as a pillow, I lay down on the bed. Although I was alone I knew there were people on the outside working diligently to gain my freedom. The best that I could do was at least try not to dwell on the present situation; it would only wear me down. Thinking of Ivonne, I soon fell asleep. Again the jailer woke me up, this time by opening the door instead of the sliding panel. He motioned for me to come out. I stood up and stretched, put on my sandals, and smiled at him as I walked to the door. He gave me a shove; propelling me down the same corridor and through the same door I had entered in by, until he shouted to halt. He opened a wooden door, led me inside, and told me to sit down. I was left alone in the sparsely furnished room.

After fifteen minutes or so, the door opened to admit a man and a woman, both middle aged, accompanied by a guard.

"Fifteen minutes", the guard muttered, and left us alone.

"Hello, Mr. Wylie", the man said. "I'm Jack Adams and this is Marion Chamorrow. We are from the Canadian Consulate. We heard about your arrest and incarceration in the news. I know this sounds ridiculous, but, are they treating you well?"

Adams didn't strike me as the diplomatic type. He sported a two-day beard and wore a t-shirt with a Canadian logo on the front and blue jeans. Chamorrow looked the part, however. She wore a dress, her hair was styled, and her manner was business-like.

"No, I am not being treated well", I replied. "You should see where I'm being kept. There is no toilet facility, just a hole in the floor. I'm not allowed reading material, so time stands still. I don't know what you've been hearing, but this is a complete misunderstanding. I hope I will be released today. I don't want to spend Christmas in here".

"I don't believe they can refuse you reading material",

Chamorrow said, concerned. "That is against the Geneva Convention. It would fall under human rights abuse. I will ask them and see if we can't get some magazines for you".

"What we need is some information", Adams interjected. "The usual - date of birth, that sort of thing".

Five minutes later, the questions done, he looked up from his notepad and said, "I brought a newspaper with me. Here, have a look at what they're saying".

I took the newspaper from him. It was a copy of the El Nuevo Diario, a national paper of left wing persuasion. There on the front page, the headline stated "Taken: a major plantation of marijuana". Along with the headline was a photo of two fatigue-clad narcotic agents standing in front of our Hemp-Agro sign. Other pictures showed the narco officers burning the stored fibre crop. Along with the article describing the estimated four million pounds of 'marijuana' confiscated, a very distraught and nervous Minister of Agriculture, Mario de Franco, used an interview to side-step accusations of his involvement in the project. I was devastated; I could not believe this. It was my worst nightmare come true.

When I looked up from the paper, Adams said, "Who do you have for a lawyer? I think you need one. You have to realise our situation in this matter. We can't interfere with the criminal proceedings in this country, but we can ensure that you receive a fair trial and your rights are protected".

"Understood, Mr. Adams", I said. "Could you please notify my family in Canada, and also get in touch with Ivonne? She would feel better, knowing that representatives of the Canadian government were here to see me. My lawyer's name is José Talavera. You will have to look up his number in the phone book, because these bastards took my notebook away from me.

"When can I expect you back to visit? I could use you to relay messages for me, as I'm not allowed contact with anybody".

"I have to make appointments to see you", Adams answered. "They are making any visitation with you very difficult. Tomorrow is Christmas day, so it will be a couple of days before I can get back to you".

They stood up and we shook hands. On the way to the door, Marion looked at me and said, "I hope you believe in God".

With that they left, leaving me alone once more. This time, though, I felt like I was falling, spiralling downwards with no bottom in sight. Where was the end to this? My lawyer had better be here today with some answers, I thought. The door opened and the guard signalled that I was to follow him. I rose and fell in behind him. This time I knew exactly where we were going. Back in the cell, I lay down on my bed and thought about the newspaper reports. They were calling the crop marijuana - how ridiculous!

This had to be a political play; no one in their right mind could confuse the two plants. Both were Cannabis, but there were no similarities beyond the common name. They didn't even look alike. Why did the Minister of Agriculture not come forward and proclaim our innocence? I was beginning to feel anxious. I couldn't just lie there and wait for them to come and release me from this hellhole. I rose and paced from one end of the cell to the other - all of eight feet. I don't know how long I continued, but dizziness made me stop. I have to strengthen my resolve to beat these bastards. I need exercise and decided that I would do push-ups - as many sets of twenty as I could. What else was there to do in this hole? I blasted out five sets of twenty in rapid succession. While I had my nose close to the floor, I saw a whole new world. From this vantage point, I could see different species of insects scurrying about their daily tasks - fascinating.

Climbing back onto my bunk, I ate the rest of the cold chicken, saving a scrap for my new friends. I tossed it out onto the floor and sat back to watch what would happen: would the ants or the mealy bugs get to it first? I could hear the guard coming down the hall. He stopped at every occupied cell to open the portico. I counted two instances, so there were more prisoners here. When he arrived at my cell, he peered in, then slammed the panel shut and trundled off down the hall. Lying back down, I closed my eyes, but the perpetually burning light shone in my eyes and made sleep impossible. I tried putting my head on the opposite end of the bed, but the broken boards I lay on were uncomfortable and made sleep difficult. I moved back to my original position, rolled onto my side, and closed my eyes. Sleep finally came.

I'd lost track of time when I awoke; it seemed to always be daytime. I wasn't sure, but I thought it was still the day before Christmas. I lay on my iron bed staring at my dirty bare feet and beyond them, the hole in the floor that served as a toilet. I didn't jump anymore when the cockroaches crawled across the floor; I watched them as they watched me. After a while I closed my eyes and breathed slowly. The guard approached again, noisily; this time when he opened the portal, he had something for me. I knew the plastic bag was from Ivonne, my lifeline to the outside world. I opened the bag to find a loaf of bread, milk, cheese, cold cuts and a candy bar. I was in heaven as I opened the bag of bread to make myself a sandwich. In between the bread slices, I found a neatly folded note from Ivonne.

The letter bolstered my hope. She said that although the news reports were damaging, a lot of people were rallying support for me. Ivonne's family supported me, especially her mother, who was working non-stop to gain my freedom. Visiting day was on Tuesday, Ivonne had been told, five days from now, but Talavera thought I would be free by then. Her letter also contained cheery passages of love and from those I drew renewed strength. I spent the next few hours searching out and destroying every cockroach I could find in my four-by-eight lockup. Just when I thought I had exterminated them all, more appeared. My ant friends had a feast; they came out and systematically hauled the dead cockroaches off the floor. The mealy bugs would not scavenge for food; perhaps they were vegetarian. They had a path that ran along the wall where it met the bed but, interestingly enough, they left both the food and myself alone.

At odd periods, the jailer would come by to peer into my cell to see what I was up to. During one particular visit, instead of sliding the portal open, he swung the door open. Again I was going somewhere and down the corridor I was led, but instead of going through the same door where I had met with the Consulate people, I was taken to another interrogation room with a few cops present. I was shoved into a chair and again questioned about my passport. After numerous rounds of questions and several hours of tedium, they asked me to sign the deposition. I refused, stating that until my lawyer was present, there would be no more questions or signing of any documents.

I was taken back to my cell. I was actually happy to be left alone with my insect companions. They weren't very talkative and so didn't ask questions. Lying down on the bunk I read the letter from Ivonne. When finished, I rolled over on my side and took quiet comfort in her words. All through the night I tossed and turned. It was impossible to get more than an hour of sleep at a time. If it wasn't the light shining in my face, it was that guard banging on the steel door. Finally I had had enough. It was time for push-ups. I rolled out of bed and got down on the floor to perform what was to be a morning ritual: five sets of twenty. After a cold shower, I felt refreshed and ready to face another day; the only thing was I had nowhere to go.

Today was Christmas and my chances of getting out of here were slim at best, at least until the break between Christmas and New Year's Eve. It was depressing to think of spending the next few days in here. The jailer came to the cell and yelled through the portal, "Basura! Basura!" I wondered what the fuck 'basura' meant. After a few moments of gesturing, I understood. He was trying to tell me he was collecting garbage. While I gathered up my plastic food bags, the guard unlocked the door and thrust a broom into my face and told me to clean my cell. I gave him my garbage and took the broom from him. While I swept, he left, then returned with a mop. We exchanged tools and I mopped the floor. When he returned again he brought a package and a gallon of water. He smiled at me for the first time when he presented the water.

I thanked him and returned to my bed to examine what Ivonne had sent me. Fresh fruit with Gallo Pinto - fantastic!

Water! Bottled water, what a luxury! I realised I'd had no water to drink in quite some time. Drinking the tap water here would definitely cause problems of some sort. I devoured the fruit and followed it with a drink of water. As I was loading up on the water, I felt a rumbling in my belly. I would have to use the 'facilities' - how I dreaded the thought! I undressed and squatted over the hole. How degrading. I felt like an animal. No, I felt worse - animals were treated better than this. When I had finished I had to flush the excrement down the hole. I gingerly submerged my hand in the tank holding the water, not knowing what was living in there. I felt around at the bottom of the tank for a stopper. The rubber plug had deteriorated over the years so there was a plastic bag wrapped around it. I pulled the plug and water exploded from the bottom of the tank onto the floor, flushing the shit down the hole. I quickly turned the shower on, soaping and scrubbing to wash the residue away.

Afterwards, sitting on my bed, I felt an uncontrollable urge to do something - a feeling that would recur daily. I paced till I was dizzy, and then did push-ups, counting them out loud until I was hoarse. When the guards came by on their rounds and found me frantically doing push-ups, they acted like nothing was strange. I suppose they had seen this before. Finally fatigue overcame me and I settled down to talk to my friends.

I lay on my bunk staring at nothing, recalling past Christmases in Canada. When I heard the guard at my door rattling his keys, I knew I was going somewhere.

"Visita, gringo", snapped the jailer, impatient to get this over with.

"Quien es?" I questioned, hoping to extract any information I could from him, for this was the first time he'd spoken to me.

He shrugged, noncommittal. "Venga", he ordered. So I put on my sandals and walked ahead of him to the door of the visiting room.

I eagerly awaited my visit. It was great just to get out of the cell and talk to someone, even for only fifteen minutes. The door opened and in came Juan Francisco. I jumped to my feet at the sight of him. We embraced and shook hands, then sat down to talk. I knew how difficult it was to arrange this visit so what he had to tell me would be important.

"Juan my friend, thank you for coming today", I said. "Christmas is a time to be with your family, not visiting someone in jail".

"Have you read the newspapers since your arrest?" Juan asked.

"Yes, the Canadian Embassy was here yesterday".

"You must understand, not everyone believes the news; there are a lot of people behind you. The timing is bad; everything is closed for the holiday, but the lawyer Talavera is working to get your release as soon as possible. How are you holding up?"

"I'm okay Juan, but one thing that keeps nagging at me is why Talavera hasn't been here to see me", I said. "I need specific information about what is going on. Have you seen Ivonne?" I added.

"Yes, I was there yesterday. She is standing behind you. She is a strong girl; you are lucky to have a good woman, Paul".

"When will you be talking with Talavera?" I asked.

"Later this afternoon. He is the one who got permission for this visitation. Pretty good connection he's got at the courts", Juan said.

Just then the door opened and the police interrogators waltzed in, demanding that Juan act as an interpreter. One held the declaration that I had refused to sign. Juan looked at the document and told me what I already knew - these guys wanted Juan to witness me signing it. Juan read the document over, explaining it to me as best he could. If I wanted to make any changes, I was free to do so. There was nothing incriminating; it was the same story I had told Henry earlier. I had nothing to hide because I had not committed any criminal offence against the Republic of Nicaragua and I told Juan to tell these monkeys precisely that. When Juan translated, they looked at one another, smiling like they'd heard it before. The cop who was doing all the questioning thrust the document onto the table and told me to sign it. Reluctantly, I decided to sign. Who knew what they would do if I refused? Juan and I said our good-byes and I was once again led to my cell.

I made myself a sandwich and contemplated what Juan had said. The one thing that gave me hope was that Talavera had connections at the courthouse. I felt positive about going home. Tomorrow was a holiday; the court would be closed but the next day was Monday. That would be the day of my release. I paced up and down the cell, planning all the changes I was going to make in my life upon release. When I tired of walking, I did push-ups. The blood racing through my body, oxygenating my brain, felt good. Fatigue set in, forcing me to lie down. I couldn't sleep so I just stared at nothing, thinking of better times. I could hear the guard coming, rattling his keys. Another visit, I thought. I swung my legs off the bed and put my feet into my sandals, anticipating the door opening.

The door opened and in stepped the guard, accompanied by another.

"Otra visita", I said. This time I didn't receive a reply. I chalked it up to some "no fraternising with the prisoners" rule.

Down the hall I went, but when I approached the visitors door, I was shoved past both it and the door to the interrogation room. I was taken to a room I'd not been in before. This room contained weigh scales, photographic equipment, a fingerprint booth and another old, beat-up manual typewriter. The guard on duty asked me my name and where I lived. When he was satisfied that I was who I said I was, he produced a set of leg irons and handcuffs. When they were sure that I couldn't make a run for it, they led me out. I had no idea where the hell I was going or what they intended to do with me, but one thing was for sure - I was headed outside.

The sunlight stabbed at my eyes, temporarily blinding me. Two policemen guided me towards a waiting van. I took a seat on a bench that ran the length of the van. The two cops, both heavily armed with AK47s and pistols, sat across from me. Another jumped into the driver seat and we were off.

It felt good to see the city again and breathe fresh air, even though I was trussed up like a turkey. The van wound its way to the south side of city. I was no more than a couple of miles from home. My thoughts were there; after all, that's where I should have been on Christmas Day.

We drove up to a gated fence. From where I sat, I could see Juan Francisco's BMW in the parking lot. I felt elated - could this mean I was going home now? The side door opened and the police led me out. Standing before me was Talavera, his broad face beaming. As we crossed the tarmac to a building, Talavera tried to explain that I was to appear in front of the Magistrate Orietta Benavides to give declaration in the Second District Court. Juan Francisco was to be my interpreter. We entered the courthouse and were shown seats in front of a desk equipped with a microphone. A photographer was engaged, setting up his equipment. I looked over at Juan Francisco, who was sitting beside me. He was smiling. It was then that I knew I was going home today. What a Christmas present! Imagine going to court on Christmas day, I thought. It must take a lot of political clout to arrange this. I'll have a huge party for the legal staff, especially Talavera, for pulling this one off.

The courtroom door opened and a gorgeous woman walked in. She was dressed casually but tastefully. Her Cartier sunglasses and designer clothes told me she was no court stenographer. Suddenly, I felt a pang of self-consciousness, sitting there in my underclothes. I hadn't shaved and I must have smelled from the hours of confinement. She strode past us and entered her chambers. In a few moments, she called Talavera in. When they reappeared, there were court personnel with them - it was show time. The woman took a chair opposite me and introduced herself, then outlined the purpose of the proceedings. When she was finished, she gave Juan Francisco time to translate.

Now, this task is not as easy as it seems, for not all words have the same meaning in both languages. I could tell Juan was having trouble with the translation into English. The judge also sensed that Juan was not as fluent in English as was thought, but she was patient. This only made Juan more nervous, which caused him to completely lose his train of thought. I smiled at Juan, trying to get him to relax. I told him to tell the magistrate that I appreciated the fact that today was Christmas Day and that I was thankful to be given the chance to be heard. She stared hard at me. If those eyes of hers were bullets, I would be dead. I knew right then that this was a lost cause; this woman did not appreciate being here. I probably broke up her gift-giving party and I was going to pay for it.

For the next two hours, we stumbled through the disposition. The magistrate rapidly lost all patience and was on the verge of losing her temper. I remained calm and wore a smile even through the worst parts. I knew I was going back to Fifty House; it was a fact before the proceedings began. This was a beautiful woman all right, but she was part vampire and today I was giving blood. Juan was only too glad to get this over with. He felt like he was to blame for the outcome of the trial. She had raked the poor man over the coals, belittling him for his ineptitude. She was right; Juan did not make a good interpreter, but he had done his best and he was there for me on a day when he should have been with his family. What did surprise me, though, was that Talavera did not say one word during the proceedings. I thought that strange and it bothered me. The testimony that I gave was the same one I had previously given to the police, twice. Why didn't she just read the report?

I stood up, waiting for her to finish her summation. The photographer was busy snapping pictures while the police prepared me for the journey back. When she finished, Talavera stepped up beside me and said, "We will have you out on Monday". Those words kept ringing in my ears: "out on Monday". Sitting in the police van looking out the window to the parking lot, I could see Juan Francisco getting into his car, dejected by the outcome. It was sad to see.

Back in my cell, I lay on my bunk going over the day's events. This was a Christmas I would remember till the day I die, for all the wrong reasons. What kind of a country would tolerate a judicial system like this? I'd thought this was to be a bail hearing. At least in civilised countries, your lawyer speaks in your defence. It was almost hilarious, being taken to court in your underwear. If it weren't for the fact that this was my life on the line, I would have laughed.

The jailer arrived with another bag of food from Ivonne, my Christmas dinner in jail. Every time I received a package from Ivonne it excited me; it was the focal point of my day. However, this particular package was special because we had counted on our being together this day. I knew this must be very hard for her, being separated with no chance of communication. As I sat back and opened the bag, expecting the usual, I was surprised; she had roasted a chicken! This might not sound like much, but being in here, it was a meal fit for a king. I found a plastic-wrapped letter in the cavity where the dressing should be. I tore open the plastic, starving for any news of a home life that had been taken from me. Reading the letter made me laugh and cry, it was such an emotional release. She was bearing the load that had been thrust upon her. Her family had rallied around her, especially her brother Ricardo, who was staying with her through the holidays. I could relax knowing that, no matter what these bastards were doing to Ivonne and me, they would not destroy our love for each other.

After a thoroughly enjoyable meal, I settled into watching my insect friends going about their daily routines. It dawned on me, watching the insects, that to survive I would also have to adopt daily routines. I started hunting cockroaches, killing them and then leaving them on the floor for my pals to feast on while I slept. Every hour on the hour, the guard making his rounds awakened me. Between that and the constantly shining light, sleep was a series of catnaps. When I had enough of lying on my bed, I got up and paced until I was tired of that. Then push-ups, followed by a shower. Feeling refreshed, I would eat and await my beloved package from Ivonne. She brought food and water three times a day. I could judge the time by the meals that arrived. When I finished eating I would lie on my bunk and read Ivonne's letter until tiredness overcame me. The hours transformed into days.

Once again, outside my door, I could hear the jailer rattling the keys. I was again going somewhere. I was led to the visiting room. I didn't wait there long before Ivonne walked in. My head exploded with a kaleidoscope of emotions. We embraced for long minutes, while I soaked up the warmth and the familiar smells of her body. Our welcoming kiss was long and lingering, neither of us wanting the moment to end. We sat beside each other, holding hands. Ivonne described to me what the newspapers were saying. The Canadian Consul had contacted her and told her they would be in to see me this week with a few magazines. It was a short visit but it did much for my morale. Now I was ready emotionally to face anything they could throw at me. We said tearful good-byes. Ivonne promised to come on the next visitation day, Tuesday - only two more days to wait!

The next day I had a visit with the Canadian Consul. They brought me two back issues of The Economist and current newspaper reports. I was to be allowed magazines, but newspaper reports were prohibited. I was front-page news in every newspaper; it took some time to read and digest the information. There were pictures of me at the courthouse in my underwear, handcuffed. There were pictures of our research site at Sabana Grande, on fire. There were pictures of our documents of authorisation from the Government of Nicaragua. The articles were the most disturbing; in every article they called the plant marijuana. The National Assembly -Nicaragua's legislature - were calling us a "drug Mafia". Even Cardinal Obando was calling us narco-traffickers. Not one article spoke in our defence and that was very unsettling.

When I had finished reading, Adams explained that he was in touch with Canada and also with Talavera, who would be here with an American lawyer later that day or the next. Adams said that Talavera believed that his testimony would clear the air and that I was not to worry; I would be free to go home with complete exoneration. I was optimistic at the news. I knew who the American lawyer was, and if anybody could get me out of here, it was he. Don Wirtshafter was not only a lawyer but also a world authority on hemp, particularly hemp oil. His factory, The Ohio Hempery, is the largest oil extraction facility in the United States. Shit, he was the man who brokered the deal for our seed stock. If anybody could gain my release, he could. I was now going to get the legal defence I needed. His testimony would clear the air of any allegations of wrongdoing! I thanked the Consul representatives for coming to visit and bringing the good news.

"Hang in there, Paul. You missed Christmas but there is a chance you will be out for New Year's", said Adams in the doorway.

"A couple of days more of this, I can handle", I responded.

The next day being Tuesday the twenty-ninth, I waited in anticipation of Ivonne's visit. She came early in the day with news that she had talked with Talavera and met Wirtshafter. Don and José were preparing their defence strategy at that very moment. She was excited, and her excitement was catching. It was an upbeat and relaxed visit. We discussed how we were going to put all this behind us and get on with our lives. We were both laughing. In our hearts, we knew that after Don gave his testimony, the authorities would have no recourse but to release me. Don and José had told Ivonne that they would visit the following day to talk with me, and not to worry. At this point, I wasn't worrying. I was just thankful that now I was finally going to have some kind of legal defence. Ivonne and I held each other; our parting kiss said it all. We knew I would be a free man for our next.

It was sometime in the evening when the guard came to take me out. I was escorted into the room where the fingerprint equipment was. The policeman asked me my age, date of birth, and my residence address and typed my answers onto a card. Normally this is not a difficult procedure, but the man had problems spelling my name properly and suffered countless typographical errors. He would finish typing a card and then realise he'd made mistakes; instead of using deletion fluid to correct the errors, he would rip the card from the machine and start over again. Again, I would have to give him the information. The third time this happened, I lost patience with this nonsense.

"Please give me a pen and paper and I'll write the information down for you", I said.

"No entiendo, hablas español, por favor", he replied.

This was not going to work; a definite language problem existed between us. After more attempts, he became frustrated and called in help. I don't know who was more frustrated, him or me, but when he returned with another officer I was ready to scream. Whatever the new officer explained worked; I was eventually provided with a pen and paper to provide the necessary information.

Next came the fingerprinting. I thought the man had problems with a typewriter, but he was an absolute menace with an ink blotter. It was like a Laurel and Hardy movie. First, he would coat my palm in ink, right up to my wrists, then, while trying to turn my hand over to make the impression on the paper, he would coat his shirt in ink because he still had the roller in the opposite hand. I was laughing so hard I had tears in my eyes, which only provoked him to perform more serious blunders. While attempting to put the roller down, he spilled the bottle of ink on the table. Ink ran off the tabletop onto the floor. As he was grabbing paper towels to mop up the mess, I decided it best not to laugh - I would never get out of there before morning. Two hands later, he was now ready to photograph me. He told me where to stand and to hold a placard in front of my chest. I complied and stood ready for him to take the picture, but he wasn't ready - there was no film in the camera. Back to my cell they took me. It would take some amount of scrubbing to get the ink off me.

The next afternoon, Don Wirtshafter, José Talavera and another man who identified himself as an interpreter came to visit. To me, it felt like the cavalry had just arrived in the nick of time. We got over the pleasantries and began to talk in earnest. Don was here to give expert testimony and give credence to my claim that the plantation was growing hemp and that Hemp-Agro was indeed solely interested in the industry of hemp.

Talavera brought with him a copy of the El Nuevo Dario newspaper. The headlines presented the question "Was This a DEA Operation?" A very good question indeed. Especially since we'd been operating and conducting our business in Cupertino with the government of Nicaragua! President Arnoldo Aleman stated in the article that Hemp-Agro Nicaragua S.A. had demonstrated that the crop at Sabana Grande was not marijuana.

The newspaper also contained an interview with Danilo Blandon, who steadfastly denied any wrongdoing and provided further proof that the government had known of the project since its conception. I thought this was a turning point, because all previous articles had described us as "narco-traffickers, gangsters or mafia". Newspaper publishers must sell papers, and sensationalism accomplishes this, but what they'd done to us was fucked up. Where did their sources come from? Who was providing the information? There must be accountability in the press. Our visit was brief but I was left feeling positive that the next day's proceedings would go well and my ordeal would be over. Later that evening, I was told to pack all my belongings.

Sadly, I was only being moved to another cell. I followed my jailers past cells that I knew were vacant, to those cells at the end of the corridor. Inmates talked from one cell to another - my time in isolation was over. If I was to be housed with another person, I thought, chances were good that he would be an informant or a police officer. I would have to watch what I said; any careless remark could undo our defence. These were dangerous moments. Any little thing that they could use against me, they would. I was a gringo, and gringos were tolerated but not liked.

I entered the cell and met my new cellmate. As we introduced ourselves, it was evident from the start that communication between us would be by gesture; neither he nor I could speak the other's language. That suited me fine; I was in no mood for idle chat. I had grown accustomed to being alone and with all the turmoil in my life; I wanted it to remain that way. I pointed to the lower bunk, demanding that that one be mine. I hoped my brusque manner would convey the message to shut up and leave me alone. The rest of the evening I lay on my bunk reading the magazines the Consul representatives had provided. No light bulb shone in your eyes here; you could turn the light on and off - a small luxury.

I woke in the morning feeling positive. It was the last day of the year and could well be the last day of my incarceration. I wondered what time the proceedings would be over. Early, I hoped, so I could be released in time to celebrate the New Year with Ivonne. My cellmate had awakened as well. Jumping off the top bunk, he motioned for me to follow him to the toilet. Instead of a hole in the floor, there was a porcelain toilet. The only drawback was that there was no flushing apparatus. You had to fill a gallon container with water and pour this into the tank, repeating the process until the toilet was clear. The shower stall was large but the curtain had long ago been torn down. Around the perimeter was a two-inch high concrete retainer to keep the water in.

The double-size cell was certainly welcome after the cramped quarters I had been occupying. The best thing, though, was the sight of treetops swaying in the breeze and the azure skies. A barred window ran the full length of the cell. It was only eight inches wide, but it helped me feel closer to the real world. By being able to discern night and day, my body clock could get back to normal.

Breakfast was served and we performed the daily ritual of cleaning the cell. My cellmate had to rely on the prison food for sustenance. This was my first sight of jail food. God, it was disgusting! It was typical fare - rice and beans - but it looked like it had been left out for some time. A crust had formed on top of it where the grease had coagulated. I had lots of bread so I offered my cellmate some to go with his meal. Talking to me through bites of this mess and swallows of water, he told me his name was Eduardo Silva Mena. A thief of the lowest form, he made his living rolling whoever flashed a billfold at the Mercado Oriental, a cesspool they called a marketplace. He had been behind bars off and on since he was ten years old. I didn't doubt that he was telling me the truth. He had a friendly relationship with all the jailers. He knew them all by name and knew the shift changes. The guards would bring him cigarettes; some would even bring him money to buy the cigarettes. Both cigarettes and money were supposedly considered contraband. Eduardo certainly had things going on in here - a fact that made me cautious.

I noticed the insects in here had different routines and there were a few different species that I didn't know and hopefully wouldn't have to become acquainted with. The hours wore on. I began the cycle of pacing, push-ups and rereading articles, anything to keep my mind occupied. I knew all the while that Don and José were embroiled in a legal battle to gain my freedom. I had everything riding on them. I knew, even though I had done nothing wrong, that this was Nicaragua and things were never what they appeared to be. Ivonne came to visit that afternoon. I was anxious for news of the proceedings.

"I was hoping I would be free by now", I said

"I waited at the house for as long as I could, but there was no phone call from Talavera. I needed to see you; it's terrible, sitting waiting for a call", Ivonne said tearfully. "Visiting hours are over soon and tonight is New Year's Eve - no way was I not going see you before the New Year!"

I held her in my arms and reassured her. We had to remain strong through this ordeal, I told her.

"I'm still positive that in the next couple of hours José and Don will be here with a court order to get me out. No judge, after hearing the testimonies, would keep me in here".

We sat and talked about home, how she was coping emotionally and financially. These were great concerns of mine. Ivonne didn't need any more difficulties. We said our goodbyes, hugged and kissed, vowing our love to each other.

Soon after the jailer delivered the food that Ivonne had brought. There was plenty: meat, salad, fresh fruit, milk and water. I gave Eduardo some fruit in exchange for cigarettes, a good trade - I always had food and he always had cigarettes. After we had eaten, Eduardo was called out by one of the guards. I could hear them laughing as they went down the hall. My suspicions were correct; my new cellmate was a rat! It was long after visiting time. He was obviously talking, the son of a bitch! Someone like that would sell his mother for a pack of cigarettes. I lay on my bed, feeling morose. I knew something had gone wrong today. I was robbed of my Christmas and now New Year, too! I was stuck here till after the holiday. Monday was the fourth of January; that would be the earliest possible release date.

Later on Eduardo returned, all full of smiles, happy that is until I confronted him. I wanted him to understand that I knew what he was up to and he had better not be telling stories about me. Of course, he denied everything. My Spanish was terrible but he caught the drift. He explained that when this shift was working, he got to watch television with the guards. I let it go at that. In the evening two men and a woman who were housed down the hall from us began singing and calling out to each other. The woman sang Christmas carols in English; her accent was Caribbean. At first it was funny, but after several hours of listening to this girl wailing off key, it became irritating. All I wanted was to get this day over with.

Lying on my bunk, I could hear music playing in the distance as the people of Managua brought in the New Year. I fell asleep as fireworks marked the start of 1999.

The next day, the routine of jail had not altered. New Year's Day was just like any other. Eduardo left to watch television in the evening and I was left alone for which I was thankful; being in close proximity to someone you don't particularly like is hellish. But for the next four days I had no visitors, so I had no communication with the outside. I thought that Talavera should have come to explain what had happened at the testimony. Now I could only wait for Ivonne's food packages and changes of clothes. On Monday evening the guard came and took me out to be fingerprinted and photographed again. The idiot had smudged the last set of fingerprints so they had to be done over again. This time it felt good just to get out of the cell for a little while. I let them muck up my hands, took my time answering their questions, and smiled for my pictures - anything to waste some time before being returned to my cell.

The following day - Tuesday, January fifth - after the

guards made the morning rounds, I was notified that I was going to court. This time I had Eduardo talk to the guards. I didn't want to be taken there again without clothes on. They gave me time to get ready. I was glad that Eduardo was in the guards' favour. I was a nervous bundle of energy, bopping around the cell like a tennis ball. This elation felt great after the depression of the last few days. Once again, I felt positive that now I would be set free! While travelling to the courthouse, I continually fought to keep my anxiety in check. I was anticipating a clear "not guilty" verdict. I knew that there would be media representatives at the courthouse, but was unprepared for the throngs of people waiting outside. It was a media circus, all jostling for good angles.

Police officers positioned themselves protectively around me as I emerged from the van. I kept my head high and my shoulders square. I put what I thought was a grim look on my face, to show to the cameras the defiance of a persecuted innocent. As we made our way through the crowd, I noticed many of the Hemp-Agro employees were present, no doubt interested because they were still owed their Christmas money. It made me feel good that they were there. I was whisked into a crowded courtroom. The room was small anyway but with the media equipment, it was standing room only. The police removed my handcuffs and guided me toward the desk where I had sat to give testimony on that fateful Christmas Day. Ivonne made her way over to me and whispered some words of encouragement. I felt immediately calm, knowing that she was beside me; a look from a smiling Talavera also reassured me that everything would turn around now.

After signing in and being introduced to a court interpreter, I was taken to a chair that faced the audience of reporters, where I proclaimed my innocence. Next I answered questions from Judge Orietta Benavides and finally I answered questions from the prosecutor, Alicia Duarte. I thought now Talavera would stand and present our case and provide a defence that would crush the prosecution. That did not occur. Talavera just sat in his chair and passively watched the proceedings unfold. I knew right then that all this was nothing more than an inquisition. They wanted my head, and it was being delivered on the proverbial silver platter. There was no defence on my behalf; this was Napoleonic law at its 'best'.

Returning to the desk where I had signed in upon entering the courtroom, the interpreter and I sat facing the court stenographer.

He leaned over to me and said, "I hope you get out of this one. You are in a lot of trouble".

I simply nodded my head, too numb to speak. Everything seemed to be spinning by me; nothing seemed real. My life had turned into a movie. I didn't listen to the stenographer when she read the disposition, nor did I listen to the interpreter. My thoughts were a million miles away. Just a moment ago I was on top of the world, and now my world had been ripped from its foundation again. The Judge wasn't present to read her decision to send me to prison so a secretary sent me to prison instead. After she finished reading the sentence, she asked if I had anything to say. I said that I thought the court's decision was irresponsible. She then asked if I wanted to retain Talavera. I thought it better to say yes, even though I wanted to fire him and punch him right in the head, as well.

"Do you wish to appeal the sentence?" she asked. I did.

During the reading of the sentence, Ivonne held her hand supportively on my shoulder then kissed my cheek. I turned to see her face. There was a fire in her eyes, but only a soft smile on her lips. I bent to kiss those lips, for I was not sure when I'd kiss them again. She walked by my side until a policeman grasped my other arm and led me out of the courtroom. This time I smiled at the cameras to try and convey my determination. Pointless really. At the police van, I said good-bye to Ivonne and told her that we would see one another on the next visiting day. I had not thought I'd be going back to Fifty House! I'd been sure I was going home. The judicial system in this country is incredible; I fumed silently. The criminal proceedings were fixed from the start; the magistrate, not old enough to be a lawyer let alone a judge, was merely a puppet that the police used to suit their needs. Talavera hadn't said one word in my defence. Why couldn't he have explained to me the system of justice, prepared me for this onslaught of judicial malevolence?

I needed better legal counsel, I decided, someone experienced in criminal proceedings and fluent in English. I also needed to call Grant and tell him what the hell was going on. I knew he was not being told the truth; trouble was how could I get to a telephone? That night I lay in my bunk, going over the events of the last two weeks, trying to find the key that could unlock the door to my nightmare. Instead of being extracted from this situation, I was being propelled deeper into the judicial system. Someone had to put the brakes on this roller coaster before it crashed!

Chapter Five

"THIS AIN'T KANSAS DOROTHY"

THE NEXT MORNING, I woke for the last time at Fifty House. Eduardo and I, along with three other inmates, two men and one woman, were given our personal effects and told to line up in single file and were marched to the police van. During the ride we introduced ourselves. The woman was from Corn Island, a small island off the Caribbean coast of Nicaragua. The inhabitants were very poor, making their living from tourism and fishing, but some were lured into the cocaine trade by the fast, 'easy' money, and she was one. She'd been arrested at Managua airport while transporting two kilos of cocaine. She understood English and spoke with an island slang. She'd been the singer at Christmas. I told her she sang terribly and needed lessons, which brought a laugh from everyone.

One of the men introduced himself as Denis Lopez and confided that he'd been educated in the U.S, returning to Nicaragua when the war was over. He was facing his second incarceration for cocaine trafficking after being found with ten kilos of cocaine in the trunk of his car. The other man, a low-life character, kept hitting on the woman. Our van drove out to the farming community of Tipitapa, about thirty minutes from Managua. It was a pleasant drive until we approached a massive concrete structure whose peeling white surface told of years of neglect. I could see two guard towers rising like sentinels from the perimeter walls, which were topped by both barbed and razor wire. We had arrived at the infamous La Modela - Tipitapa Prison - where only the hardest, most dangerous criminals in Nicaragua were held.

We had to wait inside the van, parked beneath the boiling sun in front of the gate, where all traffic was halted and screened before admission. People passed through on foot, hauling all manner of goods into the prison. I could see each person being asked to produce identification before being allowed through the portal. I thought this peculiar, but I assumed they were the loved ones of those incarcerated behind the walls. Desperados have mothers too; a few had entire families that cared for them, judging by the long line-up. On the other side of the gate, a Coca-Cola truck was off-loading cases of sodas. Men stacked empty bottles by the side of the truck preparatory to loading. Looking at this made me thirsty.

"I sure could use an ice cold Coke", I said to no one in particular.

"Have you been in prison before?" asked Lopez

"No, can't say I have". I shook my head, still not believing that this was for real. "This is a lot better than Casa Cinquenta, where we were", Lopez told me. "They will put me and you in a good gallery - Two Alta - that is where the good people go".

The gates swung open and our van drove inside and stopped where the Coca-Cola truck had been parked. Prison officials emerged from a massive set of doors to greet the new arrivals. They took our paperwork and signed for us like we had just been purchased, then led us through the massive doors into the shade of a portico. We waited on the roadway leading to a huge gravelled yard. Buildings rose on each side. To the left was the hospital and women's dormitory; on the right was Administration, where all newcomers were processed. We drew stares from numerous passers-by. I noticed that all the inmates dressed in civilian clothing; I didn't see any prison uniforms. Denis Lopez saw my bewildered look and explained. "Hopefully they will keep us together; it will be difficult for you here, not speaking the language. In a few days, depending when visiting day is, our wives can bring us clothes. Just make sure that everything is blue".

"What are all those rooms over there?" I pointed to doorways where a number of people came and went, milling about and talking to one another.

"That's the school. See all these buildings around the courtyard? They contain classrooms. On this side of the courtyard, down at the far corner, is a barber shop". Lopez pointed it out to me. I was glad he was with me; he not only spoke English but also knew his way around here. My former cellmate Eduardo knew his way around here as well. He had friends who came and said 'hello' before the guards chased them away. I would watch out for Eduardo and his friends. The woman from Corn Island was taken to the women's gallery as we marched past. It was strange to see bed sheets and clothing hanging from the barred windows, drying in the sunlight.

In an empty concrete garage we were told to strip. Once the four of us were naked, the guards told us to squat, keep our arms out in front of us, and stick our tongues out. When body searches satisfied them that we'd secreted no contraband on our persons, the guards told us to stand away from our clothes. They went through all of our belongings, separating what we could keep from what would be confiscated. I could keep my purple swimming trunks – being as they were, close enough to the requisite blue. Only one polo shirt made it through their check, but they ripped the sleeves off the shirt. I was allowed to keep my shoes, sandals, socks and underwear, and also the reading material, food, and water I had brought from Fifty House. Those accompanying me who wore blue jeans had them cut off at the knees and their shirtsleeves were also ripped off.

After answering questions concerning our health, sexual preference, religious faith and education, we were assigned our dormitory number. I was given Two Baja; Denis was also given Two Baja; Eduardo was given Two Alto and the other prisoner was given Gallery Five. I could tell from the look on Denis's face that he wasn't happy about the posting. When I caught up with him walking back to the portico, he told me we were going to the worst place in the prison. "It's a good thing that we are together", he said. "Where we're going, we will have to watch each other's back". I wondered what could be worse than where I'd just been. The last couple of weeks had seemed surreal; I still hoped to wake up and find my life in order once again.

We walked down a long corridor that ran through the heart of the institution, stopping every thirty meters to be let through locked iron bars. Just past the second set, I spotted the only telephone. A line of inmates waited to use it. I would make it my priority to get to that telephone as soon as I could. Somehow, I had to get a call to Canada. At the third set of iron gates, we were halted at a table in the middle of the corridor. To the left of the table was Gallery One; to the right was Gallery Two. Inmates hung off the iron bars of the cell doors, yelling across the hall at each other. To me, it was indecipherable noise, what I would have expected of a madhouse. Perhaps it was. The guard at the table signed us into a book that everyone had to sign, whether coming from or going to any of the galleries. The guards had to move the inmates away from the door so we could pass through unmolested.

Once inside, the horror of this dungeon hit me like a baseball bat to the head. It was an embodiment of the sixteenth-century prison I'd envisioned while reading a Dickens book! We were led to an empty cell - number seventeen. I had a packet of cigarettes in my shirt pocket, but a hand reached into my pocket and swiped them as I entered the cell. In no time, they'd been handed out to everyone nearby. The guards retreated, sensing the inmates' piranha-like agitation over the cigarettes. Denis and I were left to fend for ourselves.

The cell was appallingly filthy, which didn't surprise me, considering our surroundings. The toilet was broken around the seat; the concrete appeared to have been chipped away, not worn away. An inmate in the neighbouring cell revealed that ours was the worst cell in the gallery. He and Denis continued talking in Spanish, so I investigated the view from the window. I looked out onto a yard strewn with garbage, mostly plastic bags and vegetable scraps. I estimated that our cell was roughly in the middle of the wall flanking the yard. Denis came back to report his grim news. For now, we were stuck with this cell, but the guys next door had offered to help us clean it up. When we went next door to get a broom and some cleaner, the occupant introduced himself as El Conjeo, or The Rabbit. Through Denis, he explained that we should leave our belongings in his cell till lockup, so they wouldn't be stolen. Remembering the cigarettes I'd lost, I agreed, but there was no way to tell if these guys wouldn't rob us too.

We tried to wash away the filth and stench that had accumulated in the cell over time. We directed the dirty, sudsy water into a hole in the floor under the concrete sink but first had to unplug the drain hole, about an inch and a half in diameter, by repeatedly ramming the end of the broom handle down the hole. Denis pointed out that, if we could not free the clog, bathing would be impossible. Since there was no shower in the cell, this was where one stood to bathe with water in the sink. With help, we finally freed the clog and continued our cleaning. There were no beds or mats provided for us to sleep on, only the concrete floor. Of course, such luxuries as sheets or pillows were out of the picture. Again our neighbours next door came to the rescue, lending us each a piece of foam-type rubber to lie on with the stipulation that our makeshift mattresses be returned every morning.

I decided to leave the confines of the cell and explore my surroundings. There wasn't much to explore, only a central hallway that was being used by inmates for exercising; they walked or jogged from one end to the other in a continuous non-stop loop. All fifty cells, opened onto this main corridor. I joined those looking through the gallery door and peered out, trying to discover what they found so interesting. I realised there was nothing interesting; they were all here waiting for something, or just waiting for something to happen. I turned to walk back to my cell and came face to face with a large, well-built black guy with "crazy nica" tattooed on his bicep. His eyes were piercing, yet soft. I knew he was a no-nonsense sort of guy, but he wasn't threatening. He was a little intimidating, I'd say!

"Hey bro, where you from?" He had an East L.A. accent.

"Canada", I replied. "Where did you learn to speak English?"

"I learned in prison, man. I did three bits in California, then I got pinched on a parole violation - three strikes, you're out. They busted my ass all the way back here. Got my family and everything back there". He was trying not to stutter. I found out later that he only stuttered in English.

We walked down the gallery together. He told me there were a couple of gangs in here that would try to rob us, if the right moment presented itself. They would be armed with home-made weapons, he said; I should be careful not to allow people into my cell, because if they were going to do me, that's where it would happen. At his cell, he said he would catch up with me later. I kept on walking. In a room at the end of the gallery, people played board games on a concrete podium; a window ran the length of the room, allowing a cool breeze to enter the otherwise dark, humid interior. I looked out onto another exercise yard, also littered with garbage. The decaying vegetable waste made the air fetid. I hadn't been standing there for long when I was joined by another black man who said he was from Bluefields. His cellmate, he told me, was from the United States; I should come and meet him. I followed the man down to his cell.

A hammock hung between the cell door and the window and a man was stretched out on it, reading a book. He looked up at me. "Come on in here", he said, swinging his legs off the hammock. When he stood up to greet me, he was about six feet tall. He had the size and the agility of a football player.

"Hi, my name is Damien". He didn't offer his hand.

"My name is Paul".

"I know who you are; everybody in here knows who you are. You're the Canadian who was growing all that weed", Damien said. "First thing you got to realise, people in here will be hitting on you. They think that, because this is a big case and you're a gringo, you are rich. Come on and let's go for a walk". We walked down to the end of the gallery and turned to face the way we had come, so Damien could look at anyone approaching while we talked.

"What is the food like?" I asked. "I'm getting kind of hungry".

"God, this shit isn't food, it's worse than terrible. I used to weigh two hundred and forty pounds and now I'm lucky to weigh one-eighty. Sometimes I won't eat. They got this dish called Mondongo; it's made from the lining of a cow's gut - that shit is nasty. When you get your food, look it over real good for shit in it", Damien warned me.

"What kind of shit?"

"The beans always got rocks in it - you have to be careful that you don't crack a tooth. If the rice is off-colour, don't eat it - no telling how old it is".

I was losing my hunger fast, listening to his description of the food. Our talk turned to pleasanter topics, about home. It was nice to talk to someone from North America, even though Damien lived in San Bernardino, California and my home was thousands of miles away, in Ontario, Canada. We were the only two North Americans in the prison.

I could tell when the food arrived because everyone scurried around getting their eating utensils before standing in line to be fed. The highlight of the day, mealtimes!

"Do you have any bowls to put your food in?" Damien asked.

"No. I don't have anything; neither does my cellmate".

"Come over to my cell and I'll get you guys a couple of bowls", Damien said. "When I came here I was in the same boat - didn't have nothing. Nine months later I still got nothing, but I got some books. You like reading, Paul?"

"Yes, I do".

"Good; after dinner, come on over and pick out a book to read. Just remember, guard it with your life - English-language books are hard to come by", Damien warned me, then added, "I'll go and get you those bowls and bring them over to your cell".

I told Denis that dinner had arrived and Damien had offered to lend us bowls. I introduced Damien and Denis while we walked up to the line. When it was our turn to be served, I felt like turning around and going back to my cell empty-handed. I'd never seen food like it in my life. Three men presided over five-gallon buckets. When you presented your bowl the first man gave you a measure of rice - a glutinous mass that still contained the hulls. The next man served a dollop of beans in a watery sauce. I looked over at Denis and no words were needed; facial expressions said it all. The third man was serving a drink of some sort. Since we didn't have cups, we had to pass (thank God). I had brought bread with me from the other jail and, luckily, water as well, but it didn't make the food any more palatable, nor was it easy to wash down. After a few mouthfuls, the rest went into the toilet.

I decided to visit Damien and take him up on the offer of something to read. We went through his books, whose topics ranged from science fiction to self-help. I selected a seven hundred-page historical fiction that was guaranteed to keep me reading for a while. Damien told me lockdown was at seven and they came to let you out at seven in the morning. Bidding him goodnight, I returned to my cell to read my new book. As promised, the guys from the neighbouring cell brought foam pads over for Denis and I to sleep on.

When the guards came in at seven, a call rang up and down the gallery: "La Cuenta". Everyone went to their cells and closed their cell doors, then stood at the door while the guards walked past and took a count for their daily roster. After the count was taken, another set of guards locked each cell by installing a half-inch bolt through the latch and tightening the nuts. No one would be getting out or going in. Making our beds up wasn't difficult, since we didn't have any sheets. It was becoming too dark to read - in the tropics there is very little evening; it's either light or dark. We didn't have a light bulb in our cell, so we talked. Our conversation drifted to what we needed our wives to bring. Top priority was food and water, of course, without which we would surely perish in here. We also needed a lock to keep our belongings safe. We both drifted off to sleep dreaming of the good life that, for the moment, was out of reach.

I woke as the new day dawned. The water had been turned on and was just starting to run out of the faucet that filled the toilet tank. When the tank was full, I plunged my hand into the tank and pulled the plug to flush the previous nights piss from the toilet bowl. I later found out the water ran for only two hours in the morning and would not come back on until the late afternoon, just for a couple of hours. However, this schedule was erratic, I was told. Sometimes there would be no water for days and inmates would resort to collecting the water that ran down the roof in the rainy season. After La Cuenta was called, they fed us breakfast while we stood at the cell doors waiting for the guards to come and unlock them. Boiled Soya beans and rice was the fare that morning.

"Denis, I can't eat this crap", I said. "This is not fit to eat".

"Today my wife will come with food", Denis replied. "I told her when I was moved here to bring barco".

"I hope she comes soon, amigo, because I can't afford to lose any more weight". I walked over to the toilet and dumped the breakfast.

I sat down and thought of what I would require Ivonne to bring for me. Denis began doing leg squats while I opened my book to read, thinking to pass some time. The inmates were starting to get agitated, banging on the cell doors and chanting. I did not understand what they were saying, but I knew they wanted out of their cells. Finally the guards came with their wrenches to open up the cell doors and let the animals loose for another day.

I spent the day getting acquainted with daily life in this hellhole. The hardest thing for a newcomer to get used to was the constant noise; I couldn't bear it after being in solitary confinement. The noise was inescapable. It was everywhere, and what made it worse was that I couldn't understand a word of what was said. It was a jumble of noise many decibels too high for my ears. I decided to walk, burn off some nervous energy. I passed Damien's cell, but he was sleeping.

How in the hell could he sleep through this? I wondered.

The Crazy Nica approached me with a couple of safety razors.

"I got a couple of razors", he said. "One has been used before, but only a couple of times, and the other one is brand new. I figured you would want to get cleaned up a little bit".

"Thanks. It's been two weeks since I shaved last", I said. "Hell, it's been that long since I looked in a mirror".

"Mirrors are prohibited. Man, you get caught with one in here, they send your ass to Gallery Ten for thirty days".

"What's Gallery Ten?" I asked.

"It's like going to the hole in the States, only worse. There's an exercise yard between Gallery Seven and Gallery Five. Ten sits in between them, right in the sun. Only you and the concrete cell that gets real hot during the day and real cold at night. Thirty days sitting in the darkness in those conditions drives people nuts", he said

To me, that didn't sound too bad - thirty days by myself; at least I would be out of this madhouse. I said my "see you later" and went off in search of Denis, to tell him that we could shave. I found Denis talking to a couple of guys so I went on to the cell to shave and have a sponge bath. Maybe being clean would cast a positive light on my dismal surroundings.

Denis returned with a wealth of information, some of it good, some bad. In here, you had to take the good with the bad. If you didn't, you ended up doing hard time and nobody did any more than a year of that before insanity set in. There was a lieutenant in charge of every gallery. In our gallery, the lieutenant was called Freddy. Depending on whom you talked to, Freddy was known as a fair guy. If you had any special requests such as telephone calls, special visits, or trips to the commissary known as The Bar, you got authorisation from Freddy. The drawback was that he very rarely came around. Gallery Two was regarded as high-risk; the guards didn't come in here, and that, unfortunately, included our Lieutenant Freddy. He maintained an office and was supposed to come every Monday, Wednesday, and Friday. The next day was Friday so I planned to be the first one at the office. Somehow, I had to get to a phone and call Grant.

"There is a Cuban guy in here who says he is some kind of lawyer", Denis told me. "He wants to meet with you. He speaks English and says he can help with some things".

"What kind of things?"

"Don't know, Paul, but I'll go and tell him you will see him".

When Denis returned, he said the Cuban was coming down to our cell. While I read, Denis stood out in the hallway talking to passers-by while looking out for the Cuban.

A couple of men accompanied the Cuban. When he entered the cell, they stayed outside with Denis

"My name is Angel", he said. "I just want you to know that if you need any requisitions, I can help. I've got a typewriter and I know my way around here".

"I need to make a phone call to Canada", I told him. "Since I was first locked up, I've been denied access to a telephone and I need to call my family".

"No problem, brother. I can do that; Freddy and I are tight. I'm working on an English program in the prison right now, so I get to see him every day. When he comes tomorrow, I'll go with you to see him", he said, then added, "I see you got a book from Damien. If you want, come on up to my cell and I'll give you some books to read. Everybody is locked down in here on Saturday and Sunday".

"I need a piece of paper and a pen", I said. "I have to make a list for my girlfriend so she can bring me a few things".

"You're gonna need a big mother fuckin' lock for your door, bro, and not a little one, neither. These bastards smash those little ones like fuck-all", said Angel with a wide smile.

After he left, I told Denis that I thought he was way too friendly, but for now we could use his typewriter and his information. Both, if used properly, would make life a little easier. In the afternoon, Denis was called. He returned smiling.

"I got barco - we are going to eat good now!" he exclaimed.

His exuberance gave the day a twist of positive energy. His wife had sent two five-gallon containers of water and a huge gunnysack of food! We decided that, from now on, one of us would have to remain in the cell to protect the food. The procurement of a lock became an immediate necessity. I left Denis to guard his food while I went to Angel's cell. I found him lying on his bed reading. He motioned me in and I sat down on an upturned five-gallon pail that served a dual purpose in life: something to carry water in and something to sit on.

"I have come to ask if you have a piece of paper and a pen", I said.

"Sure thing", he replied. He rummaged through his pile of notebooks and produced an empty one, which he gave to me.

"Look, I got this deal going with the prison officials and I need English teachers", he said. "I thought, since you're from Canada and have an education, you could help by teaching a class. It would get you out of here during the day, out where there is sunshine, and every once in a while, you get to see some girls. And you will be close to the telephone. Everything happens out there", he added. "Nothing happens in this shit hole".

I opened up a packet of cigarettes and offered him one.

"You be careful with cigarettes", he warned as he accepted one. "Never pull a pack out of your pocket like that - a mistake like that could get you shived. Just keep one or two on you; that way, nobody knows what you got".

Since possession of money within the prison was an offence, cigarettes were treated as legal tender among prisoners. I nodded; I had no desire to get knifed for a pack of cigarettes.

"Everybody in here knows your partner got a large barco", Angel continued. "They're going to try to rob you guys. You got to be careful".

He lifted up his mattress to show me an iron bar. "I just whack them with this if they get too close to me", he said with a conspiratorial smile.

"What are you in here for, Angel?" I asked.

"Murder. They say I shot guy. I'm handling my own appeal. The case is looking pretty good - there is only circumstantial evidence. I just need some money".

"Tomorrow you are coming with me to see Freddy, Angel", I stated. "It's important for me to make that phone call".

"Just come and get me, bro. Hey, do you want a book I got? Espionage and murder mysteries - have a look and pick out what you want to read".

I bent over to inspect his collection of five books, found a couple I liked and extracted them.

"Don't give them to Damien because he doesn't give them back. Make sure you bring them back to me!" Angel instructed.

I nodded and left, thinking, this guy wants something from me. What it is I don't know, but I'll find out soon enough!

He did say one thing that was certainly true - everything happened out there. The teaching job could be the answer to a lot of things, one being telephone access.

Before we turned in for the night, Denis and I each wrote a list of items for our loved ones to bring. Besides a lock, we needed a hot plate. Denis had all this wonderful food but no way to prepare it. After La Cuenta, we each did some floor exercises before turning in. Tomorrow, I hoped, Freddy would allow me to phone Canada.

The next morning, I stood at the door waiting to be let out. I would go with Angel to see Freddy, then I would come back to guard our belongings while Denis went to see him. As soon as the door opened, I went down to Angel's cell, but I found it empty and locked. I found out he'd been taken out earlier. That changed things a bit. I would have to try to talk to Freddy without the aid of an interpreter. By eleven o'clock there was still no sign of Lieutenant Freddy. The guys next door told us that if he wasn't here by now, chances were he'd be a no-show.

The call came for "Yard".

"Go on out and get some fresh air", Denis said. "There's no sense in the two of us staying inside".

I agreed. "Yell at me out the window if Freddy shows up", I told him. It would be my luck that he showed up when I wasn't there.

Out in the yard, some inmates ran around the perimeter of the compound, dodging the garbage thrown from the windows. It was January so there was some grass left, but not much. The searing heat combined with the lack of rain killed the grass off and the surface of the yard turned to hardpan. Dust became so thick it could choke a maggot.

Others congregated in little groups on the sidelines to watch the soccer game that was a gallery ritual. This game resembled soccer, but it was murder ball. The game had just started when one of the Colombians broke his arm. Others injured their shins and ankles. I met a guy named Herman Guadamuz. We sat and smoked a cigarette and tried to understand each other. He told me that Damien was his good friend and that when his family came from Rivas to visit, they welcomed Damien as part of their family. When you are a foreigner who doesn't speak the language and you have no family on the outside that can come and give you hope you run the risk of losing your mind. I thought Herman might be a lot of things, but what he was doing for Damien was admirable. I saw Denis waving at me from our window. I thought Freddy had shown up, so I jogged over to the window, he looked upset.

"I was robbed!" Denis exclaimed. "These guys came in here armed with knives. There were too many - I couldn't stop them!"

"What all did they get?" I asked.

"Everything. We don't have anything left. I went and called the guard, but they didn't do nothing", Denis said.

"Denis, we can't do anything about it now. I'll be in soon and we will talk about this".

Sons of bitches! I thought. They waited till everybody was outside and when Denis was alone. I knew recovering our possessions would be hopeless. I hadn't lost much, but I felt sorry for Denis. This, I knew, would hurt him deeply. It wasn't the food they took but the means by which they took it.

I hoped he wouldn't do anything foolish. I rushed in from the yard to see what was going on. Denis was talking to several people who were hanging around in front of our cell. When I approached, Denis came over to me with apologies for my missing things. We went into the cell and Denis re-enacted what had occurred. They'd known he was alone and unarmed, so they stormed the cell, cornered Denis, and showed him their weapons. There was not much Denis could do against five armed men in the confines of a five-by-ten cell. Denis had been right to give them the food. The thieves were serving life sentences for murder; one more murder would not have changed their circumstances much.

What did concern me was that Denis had gone to the guards. It was a jailhouse code of ethics that you never ratted on another inmate. Once you became labelled as a rat, you become a target; everyone knew you couldn't be trusted. Even the guards didn't like rats. I felt that being close with Denis right now made my situation more dangerous. If they were going to do him, then they would have to do me too. In the afternoon they called me out and I was taken outside to the courtyard and escorted down to the barbershop. Beside the barbershop was a booth that sold pop and other sundries. One side of this booth served inmates and guards and the other served the visitors who came for conjugal visits. The rooms for conjugal visits were on the other side of a chain-link fence.

Talavera stood waiting for me here. He was all-smiles as he ordered a Coca-Cola for me. He had brought an interpreter with him, and Ivonne – that certainly got me smiling. Talavera, the interpreter and myself were taken to a visiting room that had only a few people in it, so we could talk without shouting.

I got down to the core of what was on my mind: What was he doing to get me out? I told the interpreter I didn't need any bullshit. I told Talavera he had to petition the prison warden to have me transferred out of Two Baja immediately and placed in a better environment, citing the robbery that had occurred earlier that day as an example of just how dangerous my situation was. Be patient, Talavera said; he would get things done. Yes, he knew I was in the worst part of the prison. He was working to get me moved to Two Alto. I was furious; my lawyer was now working to make my environment safer rather than concentrating on getting me out. I needed to phone Canada and talk to Grant, I insisted, but it was impossible to get to a phone in Two Baja.

He was doing everything to get me out, Talavera replied. He was in contact with Grant on a daily basis. He knew Commandant Molina and he would get permission from him for me to phone Canada. When I said my personal effects had been taken from me and reading was difficult without my eyeglasses, he told me he would go to the courthouse and get the document necessary for the police to release my personal effects to him. And then he told me January twenty-second was the day he was working on for my release.

"You will be home on that day!" Talavera said.

He and the interpreter left to bring Ivonne in to see me. When she walked through the door I rose to greet her, and she walked toward me beaming, her smile radiant with love. What a beautiful sight to behold! I took her in my arms and we held each other for several minutes. Perhaps each of us was afraid of losing this special moment. We spent the time that remained talking earnestly. There was so much information to exchange. She had brought a letter she'd written detailing what was going on and I gave her the list that I had compiled. I found out from her that Orietta Benivides had made a request to Interpol for the extradition of the company principals from Canada, along with Nicaraguan expatriate Danilo Blandon. The newspapers were becoming more supportive, she said. She'd talked with Grant and Danilo yesterday and Grant had told her he'd be sending money for her today.

The guard came in and told us the time was up. We kissed and she said she would be back on the regular visit day for my gallery. When the guard turned his back, she slipped some money into my hand. I tried to get her to take it back but, as was typical of her, she would have no part of that. Standing in front of the barbershop waiting to be taken back to my cell, I thought, what if they search me and find the money? Going to Gallery Ten didn't excite me. When the guard came, I asked to be taken to the Bar. He led me across the courtyard and along a well-worn trail flanked by mango trees that ran beside Commandant Molina's office. One hundred meters ahead of me was the south wall. Our path intersected a concrete sidewalk that led to the Bar and a huge visitation hall. At the Bar, I ordered two Coca-Colas and gave the guard one before I opened an account with the commissary. Inmates ran the commissary, or Bar, under the direction of the military guards. The guy behind the counter made fun of the Canadian who couldn't understand Spanish but I didn't mind; it was a lot better being made fun of out here than being back in the dungeon.

We finished our sodas and I was given my receipt for the deposit I had made. We retraced our path to Molina's office, walking past the classrooms where the English classes were held. With any luck, I would be teaching there soon. When we went by the telephone, I asked my guard if I could use it. His answer was a curt "no"; I guess going for a Coke and making a telephone call were too much to ask for in one day. I returned to my cell just in time for supper - if I was lucky, another meal of rice and beans. If not, I would be having Soya. Denis had made a deal with the guys next door. They had a hot plate so he supplied them with a dozen eggs that he had managed to keep safe during the robbery. They would cook our meals, incorporating the eggs, in an effort to make the meals more appetising. It turned out to be a good idea. Whatever those guys did to the food transformed it from glutinous slop into palatable food.

After the daily ritual of standing at the cell door to be counted and then waiting for the guards to come by to lock us down, I watched the activity in the cells across from us. Some men were preparing food while others were engaged in its delivery. Plates of food were passed from cell to cell to recipients up and down the gallery. I called Denis to the door to witness this. He told me to watch how things were passed across the corridor. Inmates made string by unravelling feed sacks. One guy would throw the ball of string across to another cell and the occupant of that cell would tie something onto the string to be pulled across to the other side. When I saw this, I laughed at the jailhouse ingenuity. My laughter was infectious - Denis started to laugh with me. It was good for him to laugh; it would get him out of the depression he was feeling. I couldn't imagine what he felt like - knowing that the food they were passing from cell to cell was his!

I washed our plates before the water was turned off for the night, using my shirt for a dishrag. For the next two days we would be locked down, so I had time to wash and dry my one shirt and only pair of underwear. As we lay on our makeshift beds, the talk drifted to our loved ones. I had Ivonne's letter to read, but I needed a quiet moment. It was with that comforting thought that I fell asleep.

In the morning, while washing myself, I noticed a rash appearing in my groin. It was sore to the touch and burned continually, so that I felt persistent discomfort. I tried to make myself comfortable to read the letter that Ivonne had written. She said that Don Wirtshafter had tried his best to persuade the courts to release me, but to no avail. They discredited the one hundred pages of journal articles that Don had provided on industrial hemp, translated into Spanish, claiming that the documents were inadmissible because they were not originals! Public sentiment was starting to swing in our favour though, she said. I knew that sooner or later - hopefully sooner - the public would see through this injustice and realise the truth of what we were claiming.

It was such a positive letter - a real morale booster. Ivonne felt I would be coming home soon and I believed that too. Talavera had said the magic words: January 22nd for my release!

The weekend went by slowly. I managed my time by reading. I could see why English language books were like gold. In here, if you couldn't speak or read Spanish, you had to have something for your mind to focus on or you would be crazy in no time.

After La Cuenta and breakfast, I, like the rest of the inmates, was ready to explode from my cell to release some pent-up energy. Someone started banging on his cell door and soon more joined in. The noise climbed to a deafening roar that went on and on. Finally the guards came with their tools to open the doors, and the gallery quietened down.

I expected Lieutenant Freddy to show up today, since this was the beginning of the week. I waited again for the phantom lieutenant, but once again I was let down. Later in the day, I heard my name being called. I went up to the front of the gallery, and the guards took me out to see Commandant Molina and another guard who spoke English. They asked me if I would object to being interviewed by a reporter from a Canadian newspaper. I granted my permission for the interview, of course. I couldn't help wondering how the reporter got in here when I couldn't even get to a telephone. That was the first question I asked the reporter when I met her in Molina's office. She said that the prison officials were only too happy to grant her permission. She and the photographer brought with them some North American articles from the Star Mart: a carton of Lucky Strike cigarettes, Gatorade, and an apple and some cookies. I really appreciated this kindness because such things were considered gold in prison, but at the same time, I knew that I could very well be killed for them. I described the place to the reporter and revealed that when I returned to my cell with these articles, they could get me killed.

They didn't believe a word I said. Perhaps if I'd been sobbing, they might have thought me credible. The story I told them was unbelievable to Western ears. I think that they thought this was a 'good story', and that was all. My innocence was immaterial as far as they were concerned; selling copy was their only concern – fucking parasites, I thought. The photographer took parting shots as I walked back to my cellblock with the bag of goodies tucked under my arm.

It didn't take long. I'd just gotten into my cell when they came at me - five of them. The first one through the door had a knife in his hand; the guy behind him had a pipe. The other three dashed toward me and grabbed anything they could lay their hands on. I managed to rip a plastic bag away from one of them before they retreated to the door. When I tried to follow, the guy with the knife barred my way. It was all over in a couple of minutes, but I had lost the cigarettes and worse, I now had to explain to Damien that his book had been stolen. Bummed out from the robbery, I spent the remainder of the day in my cell, reading. At least they hadn't stuck me or beat me with that pipe. That was a small consolation for the way I felt though. I walked over to Damien's cell to apologise for losing his book. He saw me coming and rose to meet me.

"I heard all about it", he said. "Let's go for a walk and you can tell me what happened".

I told him how it all went down while he listened.

I finished with, "I'm sorry Damien, but I lost your book. It was in one of the bags that they took".

"Don't worry about the book. I'll get it back from them. I doubt that they can read Spanish, let alone English - that book won't do them a bit of good", Damien assured me. "What I hear is, the only reason they took that stuff from you was because your cellmate went to the bulls and told them about getting robbed by those punks. Since you guys are together, you're getting fucked around too".

"That's just what I wanted to hear", I replied wryly. "I think I need to change cells. I don't need any trouble right now - my lawyer thinks that on the twenty-second, I'll be cut loose. I don't want any bad reports that could jeopardise my chances of getting out".

We hung out, and Damien pointed out some of the guys who were in here for doing some terrible crimes. Looking at just about all of the worst offenders in here, you'd never be able to tell that they'd committed such horrendous acts of violence.

Just before dinnertime we parted company. I got to my cell in time to pick up my bowl and go for dinner. After lockdown, I received a note that had been passed down to me cell by cell. The note was from Angel. I read it and passed it to Denis to read. It seemed Angel was sorry to hear what had been happening to us and wanted to meet with us in the morning.

"What do you make of this?" asked Denis.

"There's only one way to find out", I said. "We go and see him".

Denis and I discussed our situation and formulated a plan for when the thieves came back. The best place for a confrontation was at the cell door. Only one person at a time could enter, no matter how many of them there were - we would use that bottleneck to our advantage. Sleep was difficult. I could not get comfortable; being on a concrete floor probably had something to do with it.

In the morning Angel called down that Freddy was here; we should go up to the lieutenant's office immediately. The guys next door watched our belongings - those we had left - while Denis and I went to see Freddy. Angel said he had already talked with him. "Hang tight", he told us, "till our names were called". We were summoned into the lieutenant's cramped office. Denis and I sat down in front of the desk facing the lieutenant, and behind me stood Angel. I could tell Angel got along well with Freddy, or at least knew how to push the right buttons, because Freddy seemed genuinely concerned and eager to help. I explained that I had to call my family in Canada because they had not heard from me since before Christmas and would be concerned about my safety. Angel translated this to Freddy, who immediately responded with an affirmative. Denis, who'd been listening up to this point, started asking questions. When he was finished, Denis turned and told me that immediately after this interview, Freddy would take us to the phone.

Denis had also asked about visitation days. Because Two Baja had a disciplinary problem, there was only one visit day per month. Only a couple of weeks before we arrived, Denis relayed that this gallery had been completely locked down. The occupants had only been allowed out of their cells to 'test their behaviour.' Freddy had heard about the assault and robbery and wanted to know who the perpetrators were.

"Don't tell him anything", I snapped. "If you say one word to him, I'll fuckin' kill you!"

I knew that if he told the lieutenant who was responsible

for the robberies, we would not make it through the day alive. The lieutenant asked a few more questions pertaining to the daily rigors of life in prison, I guess to see if we were adjusting or if we were going nuts, and then our interview ended. I was not taken to the telephone. Besides staying alive, I needed to get to that phone.

We met in Angel's cell afterward. Angel suggested that I move in with him and Denis would move in with a friend of Angel's. It was a great idea all the way around; not only was the living situation better, but Angel offered me mobility. I'd be able to get out of there for at least part of the day, and it would be closer to that telephone. We decided that we would switch cells in the next couple of days, but first we had to get permission - that was Angel's job.

Just before lunch the guards came for me. I was to have a visit with the representatives from the Canadian Consul. I was taken to Commandant Molina's office, a spacious room with all the fittings: air-conditioning and luxurious furnishing. Marion Chamorrow sat on the comfortable sofa and across from her sat Jack Adams in a barrel chair. Molina came over to me like he was my long-lost friend - putting on a show for the visitors, the phoney prick.

"How are you holding up, Mr. Wylie?" Marion asked.

"If I told you the truth, I'm afraid you wouldn't believe me", I said.

We waited for Molina to excuse himself before continuing our conversation.

"I am very thankful that you've come", I told them. "They have me in the worst part of the prison, where the worst offenders in Nicaragua are housed. I've been robbed at knifepoint of everything I own. Please understand me - I'm not making any of this up! I need to be moved to a better environment immediately! You have to make a formal request to Molina that I be moved. I've asked Talavera to do the same; the more pressure we put on Molina, the faster he will act".

Marion agreed, adding to Jack, "This is a life-threatening situation".

"Has Talavera been to see you?" asked Adams.

"Yes, he came to see me last Friday. I asked him to get my reading glasses and personal effects from the police. It is a strain on my eyes to read without my glasses. I also asked him to apply to have me moved to Two Alta; that's the best gallery in the prison. Since Friday, the violence has escalated".

"Tomorrow Lloyd Axworthy, our Minister of Foreign Affairs, arrives here in Managua to talk with the Nicaraguan government about a foreign aid package, but your situation is also on the agenda", Jack Adams told me. "The Canadian Ambassador to Central America will also be flying in from Costa Rica tomorrow. He will be here to see you in the afternoon. I was talking to your nephew, Grant Sanders, and he told me to tell you everything that can be done is being done to get you released. He wants you to call him in Canada immediately".

"Jack, there is one telephone for three thousand prisoners", I said. "Today was the first time since I got here that I was able to talk to anybody in authority".

"We will address that with Molina", Adams assured me. "I am having a problem with this lawyer, Talavera. He doesn't answer or return any calls. That makes our job difficult. Canada wants to be updated on what is going on here and Talavera seems reluctant to give us any information. I tend to think that he's stalling because nothing is going on. Is he telling you anything?" I told him that José Talavera had said I could be set free on the twenty-second. We called Molina back in to discuss getting me moved to Two Alta. He agreed that Two Baja was a very dangerous place for me and said he would have me moved at the first available opportunity. He also said I would be allowed access to the telephone that day! He was agreeable to everything that I had wanted; I guess it was hard for him to say no with the Canadian Consuls present.

Our time was up but I was happy with what we had accomplished. I was left with a good feeling, knowing that back in Canada, Grant was doing what was required. Whenever things needed to be done, Grant was the best man for the job.

"Do you need anything, Mr. Wylie?" Marion asked as we

stood in the doorway shaking hands.

"Yes, books - lots of books".

"What kind of books do you like?" she asked.

"In here, beggars can't be choosers. Anything at all", I replied.

We said our farewells and they promised me they would return with the Ambassador the following day.

Back at the cell, I was in good spirits and feeling very positive. I felt that it wouldn't be long now. I was getting support from our government in Canada - with pressure from them, I would surely be released. Probably on the twenty-second, I told myself. That was the day Talavera was so sure of. That would be the day I would be released. I walked down to the end of the gallery to feel the breeze that always blew in the big window in the activity room. Out in the yard there was a 'soccer' game going on. I moved closer to the window for a better look. The goalkeeper looked over at me and shouted in passable English, "Hey you, the Canadian. We got a cell made up for you. Don't worry, in one or two days more, you're coming upstairs. Everybody follows your case. We have been watching it on TV every day".

"What is your name?" I asked.

"Alex Quintero. I am one of the 'Narco Jet' guys. There are five of us in here. We were in Two Baja for thirty days, so I know you are going to like it upstairs. It's quiet; a lot better people".

He was a likeable guy, this Alex Quintero. He seemed content just to try to make his time easier. I had only met him, but his grin was infectious. I decided to go and find Damien and learn more about the 'Narco Jet' guys. I found Damien, as always, reading. I wanted to tell him about my day, about how positive I felt, but I didn't know him well enough to chance downloading on him. I had to be guarded about my case and trust no one, I reminded myself.

"What's up, Canada?" Damien asked.

"I was talking to a guy in the exercise yard named Quintero", I said. "What do you know of him?"

"He is one of the Narco Jet guys - a helicopter pilot. Those guys were in here with me. They got busted about the same time I did. We were all at Fifty House together before coming over here".

"What was that Narco Jet case all about?"

"Until you came along, that was the biggest case in here", Damien said. "They were accused of using the President's Lear-jet to smuggle cocaine from Columbia. Then they found out the jet was stolen. In the United States, there were a lot of political questions. Those guys have a lot of power in here; whatever they want, they get!"

This was indeed an interesting day, I thought, making my way back to my cell for some much needed downtime. After La Cuenta and once we had finished our dinner, I told Denis about the Consuls' visit and said I expected to be moved within the next day or so. He seemed preoccupied. When I asked him what the problem was, he told me that his lawyer hadn't been in touch with his wife in the last couple of days and he was concerned that the lawyer had taken the money and ran, a common complaint here. He'd told his wife not to bring the hot plate that she had bought. When she asked why, he told her that he'd been robbed. She took it hard. I guess that was what was bothering him. I decided not to press for details and left him alone.

During the night, when the gallery was quiet, I heard a cat scream. I jumped up and went to the door just in time to see a cat being dragged across the floor. While hunting for rats someone had made a lasso and thrown the noose around the cat's head. Now someone had fresh protein for tomorrow's stew pot.

In the morning, I waited by the gallery entrance. I was hoping I could get someone to take me out to use the phone. I waited all morning. Various functionaries came by, but they all said to wait, or asked for my authorisation. When I told them I had permission from Molina, they laughed. I was frustrated, to say the least, but equally determined. I was not going to leave until I got my phone call. The guards finally came to take me out. I assumed that I was going to make my phone call, but they had come to take me to Molina's office to meet with the Canadian Ambassador.

As I walked into the office Marion rose to greet me and introduce the Ambassador, his assistant and of course, Jack Adams. The Ambassador reiterated the fact that the government of Canada had no jurisdiction in the judicial system of a foreign country, but what the government could do was ensure that I would receive a fair trial and that my rights would be protected. He went on to say that the Napoleonic system of law was slow and, at best, confusing. He said that Lloyd Axworthy was here and that he would be addressing my situation with a clear understanding that I would receive a fair and just trial. Basically, he was just giving me political rhetoric. None of these diplomats knew anything of Nicaraguan law, but I wasn't going to let him go without getting Molina to not only grant me a telephone call, but also have him put it in writing.

Molina was called in and asked why I hadn't been allowed to make my phone call. The directive hadn't been passed on, he said, but he would ensure that I could place a call immediately.

I said my farewells when I saw the guard being called to escort me back. Marion said that she would return next week with the books I'd requested. The guard took me to the telephone to place a call. It was a frustrating time. The call would go through to Canada, but when Grant answered, I heard a click and the line went dead. I tried over and over – even the guard tried, but with the same result. I would have to buy a phone card at the Bar. That raised another problem: how was I going to get there to buy one? The guard said I had exceeded the fifteen minutes that they allotted for using the phone.

Back in my cell, I told Dennis what had happened at the phone. He said he would go with me next time, and I would get the call through. I spent the rest of the day reading until lockdown and hoped that tomorrow I would get my call to Canada.

In the morning, after the usual La Cuenta, the guard told me to pack up - I was being moved. I didn't take long; I only had one plastic bag to grab. I said good-bye to Denis and told him that I hoped he would be moved soon. If he doesn't get out of here, I thought, I wouldn't be seeing him again. Then I hurried after the guard. I didn't want to spend another minute in that disease-infested hole.

Chapter Six

"DOS ALTA"

I WAS RELIEVED BUT at the same time, apprehensive about going into a new situation. I knew, though, that it could not possibly be as terrible as the place I'd just left. As usual, people stood at the door to Two Alto talking and shouting at one another but when the door was finally unlocked for us and we proceeded inside, no one tried to grab at my pockets or hit on me for cigarettes.

We climbed an L-shaped flight of stairs with a landing about halfway up. At the top of the stairs, to my right, a window looked out over the yard. From this vantage point on the second floor, the yard took on a different perspective. The walkway on the left took us through a metal door into the gallery and I was introduced to the Consejo, or inmate in charge of the gallery. His name was José Castillo. He was about my age - mid forties - and a large man, standing just over six feet tall. His complexion was pasty from being indoors for too long. I was left in his care.

When he spoke to me, he spoke in English. "You can call me Chepe", he told me. "It's what everybody calls me. We have been expecting you for the last couple of days. I have moved you into cell twenty-seven, with a guy by the name of

Caseres Kerr. He doesn't speak English, but he is a great guy - easy to get along with. I'll need some information from you and then I will try to explain to you the rules and procedures of this place".

As he asked his questions and explained the daily routines, I couldn't help noticing that this area was quiet compared to the animal bin downstairs. You didn't have to yell when conversing. If it weren't for the bars and the cells, you wouldn't have guessed that this was the same prison.

Where we were sitting, I could look down the gallery through the barred window. About ten meters from me, a television was set up in the middle of the gallery and inmates watched from the two benches in front of it. The walls appeared freshly painted - no graffiti adorned them. It was brighter in here and the air didn't have the musty smell caused by poor ventilation. At the opposite end of the gallery, huge letters above the church doorway proclaimed Dios es Libertad - God is Freedom.

"How about a haircut", Chepe said. "We've got a good barber here. It's nice to feel better after coming up from down there".

"Just what I need, a haircut!" I said, laughing.

Chepe called for the barber. While we waited, Chepe asked me what I had to sleep on. I told him I'd been robbed twice in three days, and that they had taken everything, including my underwear. Chepe told me I could use a heavy blanket to lie on for now, but tomorrow he would arrange a telephone call and a special visit for Ivonne to bring me clothes, bedding and a hot plate to cook my food on. There were food items that were prohibited, such as chillies and lemons, Chepe said. He would give me a list to pass on to Ivonne.

The barber was short, fat and happy. He and Chepe laughed and joked with each other while he cut my hair. He did a fine job, using only a pair of scissors and a disposable razor. They even had a mirror in here, and for the first time I had a good look at myself. Chepe was right - it did feel good. I thanked the barber and followed Chepe down the gallery to my new home – at least for a little while, I wished. There was a freezer just outside my cell. My thoughts drifted to ice; it seemed like forever since I'd had a cold drink.

My thoughts were reined in when I heard Chepe introducing my new cellmate. I am not a big man, and fortunately, neither was he. When he rose to shake my hand, I realised this cell was smaller than those downstairs. I wondered where I was going to sleep. Besides his bed, he had a bookcase crammed full of what looked like medical preparations. His belongings hung from the walls in plastic bags. Beside me, a piece of plywood covered the sink and supported a two-burner hotplate. There were no electrical outlets, so instead, the hotplate's plug had been removed and the power cord hot-wired to a cable that ran into the light socket dangling from the ceiling.

Caseres saw me marvelling at his electrical handy-work and smiled, probably thinking what a rube I was. He tried to explain how it worked but his English was so broken, I understood less than if he'd spoken in Spanish. I finally caught the drift when he demonstrated. The hotwire was run through the bottom of a syringe while the negative was passed through the plunger end. When the plunger was pushed down, it made a connection and you had light. Pulling the plunger back broke the contact and turned off the light.

Under the sink was the kitchen storage centre for pots, pans and containers of various dry goods. Next to the sink was a concrete retaining wall that jutted out from the main wall at a thirty-degree angle. It acted as a privacy screen for the concrete toilet. The wall had a dual purpose; the four-inch-wide top held spices for cooking and was a handy place to put plates and glasses.

The toilet also served two purposes. Besides the obvious one, the toilet tank was also the principal means of water collection. A solitary tap was left open to run whenever water was made available to the cell - usually in the morning and late afternoon. When the toilet tank was full, instead of turning off the precious water, Caseres put a hose in the tank and siphoned the water into two five-gallon buckets that he had stored in the shower. If no one was available to siphon the water, he had rigged up an overflow that would direct the water into the toilet bowl. Beside the toilet ran the three-foot wall for the shower stall. There was no working plumbing in the stall. When you bathed, the water came from the bucket, so you could never forget about siphoning the water. In the end wall, a window looked out over the exercise yard - or garbage dump, whatever you prefer. The most disgusting aspect of the view was that all the homosexuals lived in the gallery directly across from ours. I don't have a problem with homosexuality, but such open sexuality becomes too much to look at, day in and day out. Caseres made me feel welcome right from the start. That was a good thing since we were going to be living elbow to elbow for a while.

Alex, the soccer player who had talked with me downstairs, came to formally introduce himself. A genuinely friendly guy, he acted like the welcome wagon and toured me around the gallery, introducing me to people that he considered 'okay'. Alex spoke passable English, which was a Godsend for me. It is difficult being in a strange environment when you don't fully understand what is going on around you. It was good to have someone there to translate for me. After the tour, Alex took me back to his cell to meet his roommate, Gordo. The man was fat. He liked to eat, and that was a good thing for Alex - he would never go hungry as long as Gordo was his cellmate.

I discovered that Talavera represented both of them, as well. Their animated discussion on the topic of Talavera left me worried about my choice of legal representation!

The conversations in Alex's cell turned from heated debates one moment to light-hearted backslapping the next – distinctly Latin American. Gordo was preparing what looked to me like a huge meal. I thought I had better return to my cell before my tongue fell onto the floor. The cooking odours were a sensory delight, but reminded me of how long it had been since I'd had a prepared meal. I promised Alex I would return later to talk, but for now there was enough for my mind to digest.

When I returned to my cell I was greeted by Caseres; who was busy cooking dinner. He asked me what I liked to eat. I told him I could eat anything right about now. He thought that was funny. Everyone knew how bad the food was in here. After dinner, Caseres put the leftovers onto a plate. He walked out into the gallery and called out a name. A moment later, a guy appeared who didn't look like he had all his wits about him. Caseres introduced him as Primo. For table scraps, he would wash the dishes or perform any chore that Caseres needed done. Primo looked at me and said with a smile, "Hola Cañamo". It was hard not to like him, for he was truly at one with himself in these harsh surroundings. You could tell he was happy being here, resigned to his fate. Totally insane? You bet!

We were joined by one of Caseres' friends, a career criminal who had been in La Modela several times. He was from the Atlantic coast, so he understood some English. I asked him if there were any English books on the gallery. He took me to the Church office and asked them if I could borrow some books to read. I selected a couple of books I liked and promised to return them when finished reading. Caseres said he had to deliver medicine to the inmates who required medication, a task that he performed once in the morning and once at night. I showed him the rash I had in my groin. It had gotten worse; there was a visible circular sore, about the size of a fifty-cent piece. One look from Caseres confirmed my suspicions - it was ringworm. He promptly tossed over a tube of ointment and said that would fix the problem. I was grateful for the salve; the burning sensation the ringworm caused had been making walking increasingly uncomfortable.

I settled in for a night of reading. The cells in this gallery didn't get locked down till ten o'clock, so the inmates were free to walk around visiting or to sit and watch television. This was a different atmosphere than where I'd been, but I wasn't kidding myself - this was still prison and I would have to fight like hell to get out. Caseres returned from his rounds before lockdown. He carried notes from other inmates throughout the prison. My cellmate was a one-man mail service. In the morning when he was doing his rounds, he told me, he would distribute the notes gathered during his previous rounds. Before turning off the light, I read the letter from Ivonne one more time. And with her in my mind I fell asleep.

I woke in the morning to the sound of running water, a signal to rise and shine. The guards came by around the same time to unbolt the cell door. Since my new cellmate still slept, I ventured out into the gallery. I noted that some guys were loosening up in preparation for a run; others were sipping coffee and smoking cigarettes, warming up to a new day on the tier. The call echoed up and down the gallery: La Cuenta. It was a good thing I was up to fold my blanket and put it away, because where I slept was where we had to stand to be counted. Everyone returned to their cells to be reviewed by the officials. My cellmate stood at the cell door with his blanket draped around him, barely awake. He couldn't wait for the guards to walk by so he could return to the warmth and security of his bed.

The clock read 5:45, still too early for most of the inmates. At six o'clock, a group went to the church for a prayer meeting. At the same time, the television was being turned on for the first news broadcast of the day on CNN en Español. I joined the guys on the bench to watch the news. It was a real treat to see what was going on in the outside world. The news broadcast was interrupted when breakfast was delivered. The Consejo shut the television off and took one of the benches for the food servers to sit on. I thought I had better go and see if Caseres wanted breakfast.

Caseres was just getting up when I entered the cell.

"Good morning, Caseres. The breakfast has arrived", I announced.

Caseres motioned for me to wait; he would cook breakfast in a moment. He explained that he and I would never eat the food that was served in here. To do so would make us sick. Same fare as that downstairs.

I went back out into the gallery to give Caseres time to shower and get ready for his workday. The prison breakfast didn't take too long to serve up; there weren't many eating it. They put the bench back in front of the television and we resumed watching the news programming. Caseres came down to tell me to join him back at the cell - my breakfast was ready. After eating, I told him that I would clean the dishes while he was at work.

The call came for Docencia. Almost every man in the gallery moved toward the door. They were dressed in blue jeans, clean pressed shirts and shined shoes, and there I stood, wearing the same swimsuit I'd worn for the last two weeks. I was told that the men were either attending school or teaching at the school here. Perhaps I would be going to teach soon, if the Cuban wasn't lying. I lay on Caseres' bed, revelling in comfort. I read to pass the time until I could talk to Alex about getting a telephone call. Later in the day, when I was tired of reading, I went in search of Alex in the hope that he'd have answers to some of my questions.

I found Alex just getting up, even though it was almost eleven o'clock. His cellmate Gordo was cooking. It seemed to me that cooking was his fulltime occupation, or maybe I always happened to be along at the right time. They immediately made me feel at home, giving me a drink of pinol, which is a drink made from cacao and corn meal - quite tasty. Gordo, Alex, a man named Layton and I sat around the cell, wherever we could find a spot to get comfortable. I explained the trouble I was having trying to call Canada and asked Alex how I could make a phone call. After a brief discussion, Alex said that the best time to phone was in the evening after La Cuenta. He said he would take me that evening.

I told him that I didn't have a phone card. Would I be able to buy one? Alex told me not to worry; I could borrow his. The Bar came to the gallery on Mondays and Wednesdays; I could buy my own card on Monday.

All of us had Talavera as legal counsel and none of us were impressed with his conduct or his expertise as a lawyer. Gordo was going to change counsel; he'd had enough of Talavera and was already negotiating with another lawyer. Alex said that Talavera was very good at the beginning. He'd almost been set free but then, after staying in the military hospital on a medical waiver to avoid being taken to prison, his finances were depleted. He was taken to prison and since then he'd not heard from or seen Talavera. Layton explained that in Nicaragua, the lawyers are very bad; once they have your money, they forget about you and leave you to rot in prison. They painted a very grim picture especially regarding Talavera's competence. It seemed to me he was allowing me to sink deeper and deeper into this cauldron of hot water. I said my good-byes and went back to my cell and with my book to ponder what I'd been told.

Later in the day, Caseres returned from work with his box of medicines and the mail that needed to be delivered that evening. Caseres taught me my first cooking lesson: preparing rice and beans. It was a good distraction, better than lying around thinking about my problems. The meal was great. I didn't think rice and beans could be so appetising, but after what I'd been eating, this tasted like prime rib! After La Cuenta, Alex, true to his word, took me downstairs to the phone. We had to wait at the door for a particular guard to come by. Alex had a pack of cigarettes for him - the standard pay off to use the phone.

"I will introduce you to him, then he will know you're okay", Alex said.

The minutes turned into hours and I was getting anxious, thinking that this was just a waste of time. The guard finally appeared. Alex explained to him that I didn't speak the language and I didn't understand the phone system - it would be necessary that Alex accompany me to help with the call.

With a nod of his head, the guard swung the door open to allow Alex and me out. Alex passed him the cigarettes and told him what a great guy I was all the way to the telephone. I think the guard was so sick of Alex's non-stop talking that he left us by ourselves at the phone. We tried every way possible to call Canada, but the call could not go through. I could hear the party on the line but they could not hear me. I telephoned Ivonne and told her of my transfer - it was safe now to bring barco for me. She was glad that visit day for the gallery was on the nineteenth - next Tuesday - it had been almost two weeks since we'd last seen each other. I could tell she was having a hard time of it. My five minutes were up but I didn't want to hang the phone up. I felt doing so would sever my ties to the outside world, possibly forever. This was truly a tragic time for us. The worst part was that I could do nothing about it; everything was out of my control.

Back in my cell, I stared out into the blackness of the night. Despair gripped me like a vice. I was alone in a violent world here; I couldn't take anything for granted. Nothing was what it appeared to be. Friends were foes, foes were friends, answers became questions, and questions were seldom answered. My world was topsy-turvy. I needed to hold onto something solid to weather out this storm, but that solidity would have to come from me. As far as I could see, next to Ivonne, I was the only thing that was rock solid! The next day was the start of the weekend, which signalled the start of activities: volleyball, basketball, Ping-Pong, and for the not so athletically inclined, there were chess and dominoes. It all kicked off at one o'clock, following the family visits.

If you worked during the week you had a four-hour family visit on Saturday, and these guys were pumped up! All wore their best clothes, freshly laundered and pressed. All were happy with the expectation of seeing their family and receiving barco. Caseres was one of those; his smile ran from ear to ear. He told me not to worry about lunch - he would be coming back with lots of food. When he left for his visit I settled down with my book to pass the time. True to his word, Caseres arrived back from his visit with a feed sack full of food from his family. After we had eaten and Primo had finished the dishes, I asked Primo how long he had been in prison. Eight years of a thirty-year sentence, he told me, for a triple homicide. In here that was the death sentence. Nobody does thirty years - disease would kill you sooner!

In the afternoon Alex visited and said he had somebody for me to meet. He took me to the cell of Mario Rivas Montenegro and Danilo Almendarez. After a brief introduction, Chepe, Alvarro Miranda and Layton joined us. They were the principals of the famous Narco Jet case that had dominated the media for a year before my case came along. Mario Rivas came from a well-connected family. His uncle was the police chief Franco Montenegro. He was also related to President Aleman, who had appointed him head of Aeronautics for the Republic of Nicaragua. His cellmate Danilo Almendarez had been the co-pilot on the ill-fated trip. José "Chepe" Castillo was a pilot for La Costena, the only Nicaraguan airline company. He had piloted the aircraft on that day. Alvarro Miranda, a lawyer whose speciality was aeronautics, had, unfortunately, been implicated. Layton also was implicated, by being the chauffeur for Mario. Alex wasn't involved at all, but had nonetheless found himself implicated.

Everyone present spoke English with the exception of Alvarro and Layton, who listened to what they had to say. They were a proverbial gold mine of information for me. I could glean all the ins and outs that would make my life easier during my stay here. They considered themselves political prisoners, incarcerated for no other reason than to implicate those in high levels of the government in cocaine trafficking. It was certainly possible; after all, look at me. Could I be part of a multinational conspiracy? The thought had often crossed my mind. There are some people in the US government who do not want Cannabis to be cultivated for legitimate reasons, the history of which goes back to the 1930's and those same people have been fighting a phoney 'war on drugs' to increase militarisation all over the World. I suspected my incarceration was as a direct result of DEA policy – not that of Nicaragua.

Chepe assured me he would do his best to help concerning prison issues. I decided that this was a good time to leave. Walking out into the gallery, I had to duck thrown balls and dodge to avoid colliding with people who stopped in front of me or suddenly changed direction. Back in my cell I could shut out the noise and have some peace to read. On Sunday it was the same routine, except only the Narco Jet guys went for visits. Caseres said that they got a lot of visits. Their wives even came up here into the gallery with a priest from the church. That day, I made a resolution that I would write to Ivonne in Spanish every day. I would learn Spanish and it would fill my idle time with something constructive.

One of the guys had a dictionary that I borrowed for a few hours each day to learn new words to be used in my letters to Ivonne. On that first Sunday I completed my first letter, with the aid of the dictionary.

On Monday the gallery returned to normal. It was quiet again; I could read without too much interruption and I had time to study the dictionary to compose another letter to Ivonne. Tomorrow was visit day and I wanted to write a love letter for her. It would be such a beautiful day; even though our four-hour visit would be within the confines of a prison, I would still be close to her.

When I awoke to my first visit day I understood the excitement everyone experienced. This was a time to get connected to the real world and to disconnect with prison life, even if only for a few hours. I had no new clothes to wear but I had washed my shirt and the swimsuit I'd been wearing for the last three weeks. At any rate, I was clean. After today I would have the new clothes that Ivonne brings me, not to mention barco. Caseres has been providing me with my meals since I arrived in the gallery. I would feel a lot better when I had my own food to share with him.

When the call came, those of us who had a visit went down to the end of the gallery, where an official called out our names. We were expected to respond before passing through. We were held at the door downstairs until everyone's name had been called, then taken to the visit hall and lined up at the door where the officials counted us off. When satisfied that all were present, we were marched single file into the visit hall. The place was cavernous, a little smaller than a football field and filled with rows of picnic tables. Everyone scurried to his favourite table to await his family's arrival. Standing back, watching the scene, I was reminded of the ants at Fifty House during feeding time.

At the south end of the hall were the washrooms. I was warned to avoid these unless absolutely necessary, and even then I'd better hold my breath. At the opposite end there was a stage for the prison band to perform on. The walls of the stage were painted with revolutionary slogans from the Civil

War that had engulfed the country for over a decade. In the middle of the hall, there was a Bar against the wall. People were already lining up for sodas and sundries; the Bar would do a brisk business today. The gate that would let in the families, after they checked in their barco, was also beside the bar.

At eight o'clock the first visitors were let in. They were of all ages - children seeing their fathers, mothers and fathers seeing their sons, all bearing gifts of food. I walked around the hall, stopping frequently at the gate to look out, hoping to see Ivonne. After a couple of hours, I thought I should sit for a while. I wondered where Ivonne was. Maybe she'd had a problem with the buses - she had to take three buses to get here and they weren't the most reliable. It's possible she had difficulty carrying the barco; I knew she would be bringing a lot of things for me. The next two hours passed with no sign of Ivonne. I was devastated as the siren blew, signifying the visit was over and the guests were to leave. We watched the visitors leave from beside the stage. When the last one filed out, we were searched.

They lined us up and told us to undress. When we were buck-ass naked, we were told to walk to the other side of the hall while the guards went through our belongings, checking for contraband. After they had searched our clothes, we each had to squat in front of a guard to have both mouth and anus checked for contraband - a thoroughly degrading experience. In my time at Tipitapa Prison, nothing was ever found in a body search, proving how pointless the ritual was. We were finally allowed to dress, and waited at the door for the guard to let us back up to our gallery.

I was determined to find out why Ivonne had not shown up. I could not believe her absence was any fault of hers, although 'Dear John' letters were common in here. I decided to go and see Chepe for help. I found him in the Consejo's office, talking to others about their problems. Chepe ran the gallery and he was expected to resolve everyone's problems. It was a huge task; I don't think he had a moment to himself. When he finally managed to turn his attention to me, he could tell that I was agitated.

"What's up?" he asked as he leaned back in his chair. He threw his hands up in the air. "You see what I go through, every single day?"

"Well, I got a problem and I was hoping that you could help me with it. As you know, I don't speak Spanish, so it's difficult to explain things to the lieutenant. Today I was expecting a visit, and that visit was important to me. I need clothing and food, not to mention that I haven't seen my girlfriend since I got here!"

"I know you didn't get a visit today", Chepe said. "I personally made up the visitors list that went to the gatehouse. As soon as the Captain is free we will talk to him. He is only next door, talking with Freddy".

While we waited, Chepe took me over to the bulletin board and showed me the visit days for the month. The next visit was a conjugal; it was only two days away. He promised that he would make the Captain personally guarantee that visit to me. He explained that sometimes the visits were close together while other times, they were further apart - it just depended upon who made up the visit list.

We could see Freddy emerging from the Captain's office so Chepe signalled me to follow and told me to wait while he knocked on the Captain's door.

"Come in", shouted the Captain.

Chepe entered and he and the Captain were, I presumed, discussing my dilemma. After five minutes or so, I was invited in. Chepe introduced me to Captain Roche, a slight man in what appeared to be his middle fifties. He was curt but amiable in manner. Chepe acted as interpreter as the Captain spoke. Apparently the guards at the outside gate had refused Ivonne admission because, as far as they were concerned, I was in Two Baja. I could feel my blood boil - those bastards! The Captain sat behind his desk smiling at my noticeable discomfort, knowing that I could do nothing; after all, he was king of the hill. If I could have reached across the desk and grabbed him, I would have. Chepe argued that he had submitted the roster to the gatehouse and then asked the Captain to sign a personal authorisation for Ivonne to be admitted for the next conjugal visit. He considered this request and then, in a twist of character that surprised me, he said, "Does he need to make a phone call to let his girlfriend know of the visit time?"

"Chepe, ask him if I can phone to Canada as well". I knew I was pushing my luck, but I had nothing to lose in trying.

"I don't see why not. Tell him to come with me after I finish here and I will take him to the phone", the Captain said.

We didn't leave the office until the Captain wrote a requisition for Ivonne to be permitted entry. With that paper in my hand, I felt reassured that my request would be fulfilled. Chepe and I talked while waiting for Captain Roche to finish with gallery business.

"You see how important it is to have a requisition; without one, you have shit", Chepe stated. "Their word means nothing. They will tell you 'yes' to everything, but you end up with nothing!"

True to his word, Captain Roche took me out to the phone. I prayed that Ivonne was at home. This would be my only chance to call before the visit. On the second ring, she answered. It was a great relief to hear her voice.

She told me how disappointed she'd been at being refused entry. She had to bring the barco back home - no easy feat, since the barco probably weighed more than she did. I assured her that next time there would be no problem with admission, since I had authorisation from the Captain.

The Captain was standing next to me and asked to talk to her, so I gave him the phone. They talked for a few moments, then he handed the receiver back and Ivonne relayed what he had said: if there were any future problems, to tell the guards at the gate to phone Captain Roche. After declaring our love we said good-bye.

That had been a great phone call. I just hoped the call to Canada would be just as good. I tried several times - even Captain Roche tried - but to no avail. We experienced the same problem as before. I had to figure out how to get in touch with Canada, and fast! I couldn't help wondering if outgoing calls to Canada were barred, I was the only Canadian here. The days were going by and it was crucial that I talk with Grant.

On the day of the conjugal visit, I was showered and ready. Conjugal visits were conducted differently from the family visits. Since there were a limited number of rooms, they could only take so many inmates at a time. This was done on a first come, first serve basis. Every two hours there was a turnaround; if you missed the first visit, you had a two-hour wait till the next one. On the second round, my name was called. They had difficulty saying my name, so I was now being referred to as "Cañamo" which is Spanish for Cannabis, but distinguished from "marijuana". My group was taken out by the barbershop to await our visits. It was the longest wait of my life. Finally Ivonne appeared. She looked so beautiful; her smile seemed to radiate through every pore in my skin, reaching the very depths of my soul!

We stood together, holding hands and talking in low tones, waiting for them to grant us a room number. Ivonne had brought a large, heavy-gauge plastic bag containing a new bed set, including a pillow and a new towel. She also had a picnic basket filled with fried chicken, coleslaw and Coca-Colas. My name was called out, and we followed the female guard to our designated room, where we were left to our own devices. We wasted no time. Our arms and bodies entwined and we kissed each other passionately. We held onto each other, not wanting to let go for fear that the moment would dissolve. I couldn't believe that the smell of a woman would cause such a sensory reaction. It was like the smell of a spring day after being cooped up for the entire winter.

Ivonne set about putting the fresh sheets on a mattress stained by countless sweat-soaked encounters. Looking around the room with its concrete block walls and furniture that had seen better days, it struck me as the kind of motel seen in the seedy part of the city – probably worse. The bathroom toilet had overflowed onto the floor, so it was impossible to enter without getting your feet wet. The surroundings weren't going to deter us, I thought; our lovemaking would create all the beauty necessary to transform this ugliness! Our lovemaking was deliberately slow at first; gathering in intensity until it drove us to an ecstasy I'd thought unobtainable.

We paused just long enough to exchange our letters and eat, but we didn't even read the letters or finish the food - the only hunger we felt was for each other. We made love again, then held each other, mutually spent and sexually satisfied, until the buzzer sounded announcing the end of our conjugal visit. It was too soon. We hadn't really talked; those two hours went by so fast, they seemed like mere minutes! Ivonne was folding the bedding when a knock at the door prompted us to hurry. I told Ivonne to relax; what were they going to do, put me in prison? That lightened the heaviness that had settled in the air with the knowledge that we would have to say good-bye. As we walked arm in arm, she told me to check the barco; she'd written an inventory of all the goods that she'd brought. She'd paid the guards money to make sure I received the barco, she told me, and that inventory was in with the letter she wrote. At the door, she pressed money into my hand and said she would be back with more barco and, if possible, a special visit.

Standing in line waiting to go back to the gallery, I noticed Angel over by the classrooms. He was calling out something to me, but I couldn't make out what he said. When the guards come to take us back, I told them I had money to deposit at the Bar. The guard told me he would take me over to deposit the money after the search – which he did. On the way over, Angel intercepted us.

"I did it, man - I got you out to teach with me!" he said.

"When?"

"This afternoon", he replied. "The lieutenant is coming to get you out of your gallery".

He saw where I was headed and knew I had money, so he put the squeeze on me for a Coca-Cola. I couldn't say 'no' to that; after he'd told me I was going to teach, I would have bought him Coca-Colas for life. I felt good, returning to the gallery with a bounce in my step for the first time since I'd arrived in this hellhole. I took the stairs two at a time, full of renewed energy. I was on a roll now! Chepe stood at the top of the stairs, watching me bound up them. "Look at you!" Chepe laughed. "Two hours with a woman and you're a changed man. What a difference!"

I told Chepe that I was to be called out to teach in the afternoon, but I was expecting a large barco. Could he receive the barco for me?

"Teaching what?" he asked.

"I got a job teaching English", I said. "The pay is crummy, but the fringe benefits are great".

"You just got moved here, and you're already going out. Shit, that's early. Usually they keep you upstairs here for a couple of months before they let you go to work. Just remember you don't have to work while you're waiting for appeal", Chepe added. "You get two days off your prison time for every one day served, whether or not you work. So anytime you feel like you don't like it, tell them to go to hell and stay up here. I can get you a class to teach right here in the gallery".

"I'll keep that in mind, Chepe".

It would take a lot to keep me here, I thought. At least outside, the air was fresh. But my prime motivation for taking this teaching job was close proximity to that solitary telephone - my as yet unconnected lifeline to Canada.

As I lay on the bed reading the letters from Ivonne, I began to realise how much support I had out there. Grant and Danilo were working day and night to gain my release. They'd hired a new hotshot lawyer to handle the case; Talavera was to assist. I would have to find out about this new lawyer, Mario Sequiera who hopefully he had a better reputation than Talavera - from what I had heard he couldn't be worse. I had requested the transcripts of the court proceedings from Talavera to which he'd told Ivonne they were being translated; when that was completed, he would bring them to me. Ivonne had also talked with Yuri's brother about my passport. She'd asked him where the money I'd given him was; since he'd failed to supply the updated passport, the money should be returned. Like the common thief he was, he came up with a lame excuse for what had happened to the money.

Another interesting piece of information was that Ivonne's sister Johanna and Jorge Vega had gone to Interpol to talk to a relative of Jorge's who worked there. Jorge was trying to exchange information about me for an American visa! That turncoat son of a bitch! I'd shared the last of my money with him, defended him with my associates when they wanted to have him expelled from the company, and now he was stabbing me in the back. I sensed the tension this must be causing in Ivonne's family. It must hurt to have a sister as an enemy who, before this, was quite close.

Included in the letter was the barco inventory. I marvelled at the length of the list. She had not left out anything I had wanted. For her to take three buses while carting this stuff was an incredible feat! I heard my name being called and put my letters away in my new pillow, then I stepped out into the gallery, taking care to make sure the cell door was locked before going in search of the caller. A well-groomed officer sporting lieutenant's bars met me. He spoke no English so our conversation was limited - or should I say, non-existent - until Angel met us at the classroom.

Angel said that I would be shown around today, and be given a chance to look over the curriculum for the four levels of English classes. The lieutenant inquired whether I wanted copies of the course, so I could familiarise myself with it. They didn't have a photocopy machine so the lieutenant volunteered to copy the material after work, if I would supply the money to have the copies made. I agreed, but said I would have to go to the Bar to get some money out of my account.

Over Coca-Colas, the three of us discussed the problems they were having with the English classes and called it a day after about an hour. I gave the lieutenant more than enough money to get the photocopying done, hoping my generosity would cement a trusting relationship.

Prisoners were required to have an escort whenever they walked anywhere within the prison and as the lieutenant was taking us back to our respective galleries we passed the telephone. I asked if I could make a call to Canada. The lieutenant, feeling magnanimous, granted the call without the usual "wait till later" speech that was usually a cue to pay him.

I prayed I would get an operator that would put me through to Canada. Again I was stymied - the call could go through but when it was answered the line went dead. The lieutenant tried and the same thing happened - the line was cut off. The lieutenant did provide an explanation for what was happening, though. He said that the police monitored all the calls on this phone; when the phone tap kicked in, the operator assumed the party had come on the line and so the operator hung up, cutting off the call. The only place where I could get a call through, he said, was at the prison administration office for which I would need special permission from Captain Roche. This was not great news, but at least now I had a more or less logical explanation for what was happening during my attempts to call Canada.

Returning to the gallery, my spirits soared again - Chepe had my barco! Caseres helped me haul it down to the cell. I felt like a kid opening his Christmas presents! Tonight, I would sleep on a new mattress with clean sheets and a real pillow to rest my head on. Between us, we had a good supply of provisions and it felt good to finally repay Caseres for all the kindness he'd shown since I'd been dumped in his cell. After a dinner of fried chicken that Ivonne had brought, Caseres assisted me with my letter to Ivonne. I was extremely fortunate to have a good cellmate.

I arose early to prepare for my first full day of teaching. For the first time since my arrival, I had clean new clothes to wear. No shoes yet, but I was thankful just to have clothes on my back and food in my belly. This was the twenty-second, the day that Talavera had said was so important. I thought I would go and have a coffee with the Narco Jet guys and hear the news. Mario and José were in the Consejo's office drinking their morning coffee. When I approached, Mario looked up and said with a smile, "What's up, Paulie? Brand new clothes, a new job, and I hear you got something soft to sleep on".

"It feels good too", I said. "Mario, I almost feel human again".

"We were just talking about the Supreme Court ruling to enact the new 'Organic Law' today", Chepe said.

"What is this new law?" I asked.

"It says that all prisoners awaiting trial have a right to bail. We were wondering if that pertains to drug cases", Mario said.

I decided to tell them what Talavera had said to me about the twenty-second, that I might be released today.

They looked at one another and then Mario said, "Paulie, we've been through all the false hopes, only to be let down. Don't get your hopes up too high. This is not an easy place to get out of once you're here". The call came for Docencia so I said my good-byes and made my way down the stairs.

The morning went by like lightning. I spent my time getting acquainted with the students in all four classrooms, introducing myself and making notes. In the afternoon Angel, the lieutenant, and I discussed the course curriculum. I referred to the observations I had made that morning and shared my ideas for how we, as teachers, could make the learning process easier for the students. The lieutenant had photocopied the curriculum for me and presented this and my change from the money I had given him. Angel suggested that the lieutenant hold onto the money - if I needed a soda I could get the money from him to go across to the Bar near the barbershop to buy some. The lieutenant agreed to this, so I suggested that we all go over now for a soda and cookies to celebrate our new-found trust.

I asked Angel to pass along a request to the lieutenant: since the lieutenant was working that weekend, would he mind granting me a special visit on Sunday? Angel translated this to him and when he started to make some excuse, Angel said something to him that made him agree to the request. Then the lieutenant excused himself and left us alone at the Bar.

"What did you say to him that made him say yes to the visit?" I asked.

"I told him that you were going to quit the program if you didn't get the visit".

When we were heading back to the gallery, I once again asked the lieutenant for permission to use the telephone, this time for a local call. I tried to call Ivonne but there was no answer. I hoped to get a chance later to get out to phone.

The next day was the start of the weekend and the thirtieth day of my incarceration. It felt like it had been a lot longer. I thought this would be a good time to stay in my cell and study the course curriculum to get a feel for what I was going to teach. It also offered the opportunity for me to increase my Spanish vocabulary, so I could include more in the letters I was writing. After La Cuenta I went downstairs to see if I could get out to phone Ivonne. It was a terrible wait - four hours of hanging off the cell door! What made matters worse were the constant excuses. The guard would say "wait till the guards come back from taking count", then after they returned there was another excuse. Finally, when I was just about to give up and go back to my cell, the guard let me out, but before I could use the phone I had to pay him the required pack of cigarettes. I only had five minutes for my call, so I would have to talk fast. I wanted to let Ivonne know that she should come tomorrow and see the lieutenant so he could escort her in. The phone rang and rang. I couldn't believe it - no answer! I tried again, thinking she might be outside and trying to get to the phone. No answer again. Wouldn't you know it? No one was at home. My heart sank. I would have no visit tomorrow. I returned to the gallery, my spirits deflated. I wanted only to go to sleep and wake up when this whole ordeal was over!

In the morning, I awoke feeling edgy. I wanted to go home! I hated this place! I thought that being cooped up like this would drive me mad. Perhaps that's what is happening to me, I thought; I'm slowly going crazy. I went and had a coffee with Mario and Danilo Almendarez. They always provided good conversation and on this particular morning I needed something inspirational. The topic of the day was how to get special visits and telephone calls, both of which were major causes of frustration for everyone. Mario said that the only reason special requests were granted was so they would have something to take away from you; it was their way of exerting control. They liked to keep you frustrated. This was especially true in the treatment of foreigners. I'd been living a kaleidoscope of numbing pain and raw fear; the tactics Mario described were clearly working on me. I would need to call upon my intestinal fortitude for the patience to overcome such psychological terror. It was futile to let emotions show; to do so would give the adversary the edge. It was best to remain calm and aloof to the goings-on around me.

I spent the rest of the day studying and reading in preparation for my class the next day. It felt good to be able to shut out everyone for a day and keep my mind focused on something besides what was going on in here, or what I didn't know was going on outside. The first morning I spent teaching was a welcome change. The students were eager to learn and I really enjoyed it. Except for the constant interruptions by Angel, it went smoothly. After lunch I was called into Molina's office to meet with the Canadian Consul. Marion Chamorrow and her driver were there but Jack Adams was absent. Marion said that from now on, only she would be visiting, and the visits would be less frequent, probably only once a month. I decided to push the Consul; after all, they were supposedly there on my behalf.

"I still have not been able to call Canada", I told her. "I can get my call through to Canada, but as soon as the call is answered the line is cut off. I've been told it's because all calls are monitored by the police, and as soon as the bugging device is activated the line to Canada is cut".

"I will talk to Molina about that", Marion replied. "We have been receiving calls from Grant Sanders, wondering why you haven't called yet. Can you write out a letter for him and I'll fax it off today? While you do that, I will talk with Molina about your call".

I began to write, telling Grant all of what had happened. I made sure he was aware of the distrust I felt toward my legal counsel. I told him that Talavera had avoided me and when I did talk to him, he'd told me he would have me out soon, only to see the days go by while I was pulled deeper into the system. I read over what I had written, hoping I'd given Grant a clear understanding of what was going on. There was just so much to tell him, I couldn't possibly get it all down on paper. It seemed so long ago that I had last talked with Grant. I wondered when the next time would be. Marion returned after talking with Molina. She'd been given yet another promise that I would get a call to Canada. I handed her the hand-written papers for her to fax for me.

"Has Talavera been here to see you?" inquired Marion.

"No, he hasn't. He avoids this place like the plague", I said.

"He is a hard person to track down. Even when he talks with us, he's evasive and skirts all the issues. I've given up trying to talk with him. Instead, I direct all questioning to his associate Sequiera, who is more co-operative. I understand that tomorrow you will be taken to the courthouse to sign release papers so they'll give your personal effects to Talavera".

"At last, I get my glasses", I said. "It has been extremely difficult reading without them. I've had daily headaches".

"I brought you some books. I didn't know what you liked so I got a mixture".

I thanked her. "I appreciate the books", I told her, "it's all I do to pass the time".

They stood to go. Our visit was over and it was time to say our good-byes. I walked with them to the door and watched them as they passed the gates before I returned to the classroom. I asked the lieutenant if I could return to the gallery, anxious to look over the books Marion had brought me. I found sitting around after class boring, and Angel's company was beginning to wear at me. I think Angel felt that he had done me a favour and I owed him. I didn't owe him anything. He was a transparent conman; he might be able to fool the other inmates but he wasn't fooling me, and that afternoon I told him what I thought. He didn't like it, but tough luck; I had my own problems and could ill afford more.

The second guard I asked to take me back to the gallery was going my way; he agreed. Moving around was often like hitchhiking: sometimes you stood waiting awhile and other times you got a ride straight away. I told Mario and Danilo Almendarez about my meeting with the Consul and about going to the courthouse to sign the release papers for my eyeglasses. Mario suggested I phone my lawyer and ask him to pick me up and take me there personally because the bus ride and the wait at the courthouse were terrible. I knew better than to call Talavera; he wouldn't come here. For a start there were too many people that knew him here.

In the morning I got myself ready early. They came first thing to take out the inmates who were going to court. There were two of us from Two Alto going this morning; Gordo 'the diner' was going to change lawyers. He had no kind words to describe Talavera. He urged me to sign up with this new lawyer of his, but I declined his offer. This could be a good thing for me. Perhaps since Talavera had dump-trucked Gordo and Alex, he could devote his excess free time to my case. We were paired up and handcuffed to await the bus that would take us to the courthouse. The sun beat down upon us as we stood in the gravel courtyard. At first there was a lot of talking and laughing among the inmates, but then the sun took control, subduing everyone with its intensity.

When the bus finally arrived, we were loaded onto it like sedated cattle riding to the slaughterhouse. We filled the seats from back to front. I noticed that the windows were closed and barred and could not be opened from the inside. The heat was stifling. We were stuck in there with no ventilation. I was sure cattle would at least be given fresh air to breathe. I looked out the window at the sights of the city. We passed roadside vendors hawking their cheap trinkets for an even cheaper existence. It seemed such a long time ago that I had witnessed these sights, but it had only been a month. We were off-loaded and taken into a concrete block holding pen where they took off our handcuffs and left us to find what available comfort there was. There was none. I had to breathe through my shirt. The stench was deplorable; there were pools of piss along the far wall from the day before. The only place to sit was on the bare concrete floor amongst the filth. I stood by the door. At least there, I could get a breath of fresh air every time the door was opened.

It seemed like an eternity passed before my name was called. At first the light blinded me; it took a few moments to acclimate my eyes. During this time I greedily gulped air to clean the foul stench of the pen from my lungs. I was pushed and prodded toward the courthouse. This time there were no cameras waiting to snap my picture, just a court secretary waiting only for my signature. It took all of a minute before being returned to the holding pen. My spot by the door was taken, so I made my way through the group till I saw a familiar face. Gordo sat on the floor with his back to the wall, dining. He motioned me to sit down beside him and offered me some of his food. His wife had come down to the courthouse with food for him, because she knew Gordo couldn't go an hour without food. How the hell he could eat in this hole, I'll never know, but he wasn't alone - others were eating in there too.

The hours wore on. Gordo explained to me how he'd been busted. In his shrimp processing plant, all boxes containing shrimp were to be thirty-five pounds. But in this instance, the workers putting cocaine in the boxes failed to weigh each box to make sure it was thirty-five pounds. At the port the cargo was weighed and the weight discrepancy was noted. Gordo was sentenced to ten years in prison, which he was appealing. Today he was changing his lawyer, Talavera, for another hotshot, an "international mouthpiece with deep pockets". I took his card and promised I would call. I think that made Gordo happy. I was never happier to have the handcuffs put back on my wrists for the ride back to prison. We were loaded back onto the bus in the same order that we'd been taken off, so I had the same window seat on the way back. I thought I would never go through this again. Talavera would have to come and pick me up and take me to court. I closed my eyes and thought about a shower, hoping there would be enough water.

When I got back to the gallery, Caseres had his usual companions in the cell. I was used to seeing the one who spoke a little English; he had a girlfriend over in the women's dormitory, probably some fat old murderess because he was no oil painting to look at. They were reading letters the women had given them, having a good old time of it, laughing and chortling. I didn't understand a word of what they were saying so I opened my book and read, giving up any ideas of having a shower. Caseres not only delivered mail but, since some could not read or write, he often read them their letters and then composed replies. I could not imagine someone composing a love letter to my wife for me. Being illiterate must be very difficult to bear.

When Caseres had finished with the mail he introduced me to a man named Guido, who had been in the gallery for the past eight years. Guido told me he had an iron stashed. If I wanted clothes ironed, I could bring them to his cell, as long as it was after La Cuenta, when the guards were gone. I thanked him for offering me his services. My ironing had consisted of laying my clothes out on the floor and sleeping on them.

Caseres reached under his bed and produced a small bundle of letters, which he passed over to me. They were all addressed to me, mostly written in English. They were from inmates situated in every gallery in the prison. All the letters told of some problem they were having and requested that I help. It was overwhelming to think that these people put their hope in me to resolve their problems. Some of the letters were desperate, from people needing medical supplies that would make the difference between life and death! Little did they know that the only difference between them and I was that I had Grant and Ivonne on the outside looking after my welfare. This posed a serious problem. How could I help? If I helped one, then I would be expected to help them all. How would I decide what claim was legitimate and which one wasn't? There would be no way of knowing! I needed to sleep on this.

In the morning I walked down to the Consejo's office for my morning coffee with Mario and Chepe.

"Good morning, Paul. How was your trip to court yesterday?" inquired Mario.

"Mario, I do not want to do that again - it was disgusting! I thought I'd go crazy in that holding tank. If you suffered from claustrophobia and had an attack in there, you'd never be the same again!" I paused to reach into my pocket and pull out a letter requesting medical supplies. "I know you guys have been here longer and have seen just about everything in here, but how would you respond to this?" Passing them the letter.

Mario and Chepe both took a turn at reading the request.

"Things in here are harder for you because you're alone", Mario said. "You don't speak the language, and you are visible. With us, there were six of us. When we first arrived, we stayed close together. None of us had been in this kind of a situation before, so we didn't know what to expect. We thought if we supplied some meals for the gallery, some paint for the walls, put some medical supplies here in the gallery, it would help their situation and in turn help our situation".

"Do nothing", Chepe interjected. "Most of those who want help are only trying to take advantage of you. They think, 'rich Gringo, give me money!' "

"Paul, I was surprised that you were allowed out so soon", said Mario. "You are big news in the prison. Everybody wants to be your friend; they will hit on you for everything. Remember, cigarettes are money in here and people can get killed over a cigarette. Be very careful who you give them out to, or who sees you. Chepe is right - do nothing for now. All of us involved in the Narco Jet case stay right here in this gallery. We don't leave here except for phone calls and visits".

"Remember, trust no one in here, either", Chepe added. "There are Sapos, or rats, in this gallery. They will go and talk to the officials in exchange for a phone call. There are a lot of Sandinistas in here; be careful what you say. Some are military, like that crazy Captain Hernandez, or police, like Flores - walk softly. If for any reason you don't want to be outside, just don't go. They can't do anything if you refuse".

The call for Docencia came. I excused myself and, with the rest of the teachers, proceeded down the stairs to the door to await the guard who would take us to school.

Angel was just as irritating as he'd been on the previous day. He wanted to know why I hadn't come to classes the day before. I thought it was none of his business and told him that. He interrupted me countless times and displayed condescending behaviour that aggravated me to the point where I thought I would choke him. I had too much on my plate to deal with the likes of him! Just before lunch one of the guys popped his head in the door and told me to look across the courtyard. Standing in the sunlight, her hair shining brightly and reflecting a soft glow, stood my Ivonne. She was a sight to behold. I excused myself from the class and walked across the courtyard. When she turned to greet me, her happy, smiling face made my heart beat a little faster. It also made me walk a little faster. I could see out of the corner of my eye that the guards were converging in on us. We hugged each other and I gave her a kiss before the guards ordered me back. Before retreating, she told me that she'd been granted a special visit. That made my day; perhaps she brought some good news. I told her that I would wait for the visit and not allow the guard to lead me back to the classroom. My students thought it was hilarious, me leaving the classroom to go see a woman, both of which were prohibited. The only one who didn't find any humour in it was Angel.

Around one o'clock, two hours after I had first seen Ivonne, they called me to go to the visit room. Ivonne had waited two hours for a fifteen-minute visit. She brought me a small photo album containing pictures of a life from what seemed like a distant past. It was beautiful and allowed me to connect with what I'd had. I told Ivonne that I needed ointment for a fungal infection. In this place, fungal infections were always a constant threat; skin diseases were rampant. Your health became all-important when any infection could kill you! I could tell Ivonne was upset over something. She was having a hard time deciding whether or not to tell me.

"Paul, I heard from Grant this morning. He sent me some money through Western Union. I wrote down the exact amount I received and how much I spent on groceries. There is an itemised account of precisely what I have spent. I think

Grant thinks I'm lying to him", she stated.

"Why would you say that?"

"The General wants me to pay an extra six hundred dollars rent in three days time, or leave. I don't know what to do. I thought we were paid up to February fifteenth. Now Grant thinks I'm lying. You know me, Paul - I am a not a liar! The General says that we owe two hundred dollars in phone bills; that is a lie! Someone is lying and it's not me, why are they doing this to us? I hate that place. Every day, I want to leave. I can't go on like this. I wish I didn't need Grant to send me money. I feel like I'm begging, and then to be humiliated like this . . ". Ivonne took a handkerchief out of her pocket to stop the tears before they fell from her eyes. I was trying to comprehend what she had just told me. I was shocked to realise that Ivonne was going through very real difficulties. I had been too preoccupied with my own problems.

The matron came in to tell us that our visit was over. We held each other tightly and kissed good-bye. We promised that we would see each other February second, during a gallery family visit. Then she pressed her letters into my hand. I watched as she walked out the door. The sadness I felt was heavy. Later that night my sadness turned to a quiet rage as I read her letters. That son of a bitch, I thought; treating Ivonne like this! You can't say everything you want to in fifteen minutes. There are always things you forget to say. I had to phone Ivonne right away and so I went down to the gallery entrance to try and get out to call, but after two hours of waiting I finally gave up. Now I was on the verge of snapping, my problems at home compounded by the added frustration of not being able to call.

I was not well rested when I awoke in the morning. I could tell this would be a long day. If Angel even asked me for a cigarette, I'd bite his head off. My only concern was the telephone. I'd reasoned it out during the night: Ivonne had to phone Danilo Blandon. He was a good friend of the General; he could straighten this mess out with a phone call. I also wanted to tell Ivonne to find another place to live, possibly move in with her brother until I could get out of here. She needed to be with family, those who could give her the support that she needed.

Angel continued to irritate me. I knew what he was up to and I didn't want to be part of any scheme of his that involved the prison officials; it could be a dangerous game. Sapos were killed in here all the time and Angel was talking to Molina constantly. I decided it was time to distance myself before it was too late - I had more concerns than to be taken out of here in a body bag for being stupid! Besides, I thought being close to the phone was all-important and it was frustrating me right now. I had to be tranquilo. I spent the rest of the day trying to call Ivonne, but there was always a queue for the phone or nobody at home when I called. In the afternoon, Angel lectured me about my conduct, saying I couldn't walk around on my own; it was against prison policy. "Whose policy?" I replied, "the officials' or yours?" He didn't have an answer for that, but his silence told me it was over between us.

On the way back to the gallery I asked permission to make a call, hoping Ivonne would be home, but there was no answer. Later that night I waited at the door for four hours; I was promised a call but never let out. I returned to my cell feeling uneasy, like a burning coal smouldered in the pit of my stomach. I felt a deep-seated hatred toward every slime-ball prison official, the judicial system that put me here, the blood-sucking judge Orietta Benavides, and mostly toward the person(s) or organisation that was responsible for this whole situation. The more I thought about it, the DEA had to have had some direct involvement in this – their presence could not possibly be coincidental.

I lay on my mattress. I heard nothing but silence. I stared into the darkness, searching my inner self, holding dearly to the hatred I felt. I had to make positive use of this strong emotion. If I used it to wreak havoc it would destroy me, but if I harnessed its energy, it would build such strength inside me! I vowed I would push myself physically, channel the emotion positively to build both strength of mind and body, ready for the day when I would be called upon to use it!

I spent the day in class talking with the students, trying to develop the conversational English skills they could use every day on the outside. We acted out situations such as going into a store to buy groceries, and each one would take a turn being clerk, then the customer. I even lightened up the situation by staging a bank robbery. To these career criminals, it was a knee-slapping good time. Angel didn't like it, of course, but he knew enough to keep quiet. I had made up my mind that today was my last day outside the gallery. I would be free of Angel and the telephone once and for all.

In the afternoon I received a visit from Talavera. He brought an interpreter with him. I wasted no time with small talk. Through the interpreter, I said, "José, I hope you brought my glasses with you".

"No. I'm sorry, but I have been to the DIC and they say that it will be one or two days more. As soon as I get them I will bring them to you. I brought very good news, though". Talavera beamed. "As you know, I'm working with Mario Sequiera on your appeal. The defence, in essence, is that if no crime was committed, then there can be no trial. Therefore, you should be released immediately!"

"I want transcripts of all the legal work that has been conducted on my behalf, since the start", I told him. "I don't care if they're in Spanish, I want those transcripts immediately so I can begin to review my case".

After the translator finished, Talavera said he would comply immediately, but if everything went as planned, I would be free the first part of the week. My hopes soared once again. Freedom - that magical word seemed to transform my very soul. I left the visit room with a bounce in my step. I felt closer to the door and the freedom that lay beyond.

I returned to the classroom where Angel was talking his usual bullshit. He saw me happy and thought he could hit on me - fresh from a visit. I would have money.

"Hey bro, why don't you buy us a couple of tickets for the Valentine dance?" Angel asked. "It's only five pesos, man".

"Listen, I'm not your brother and who the fuck do you think I am, Santa Claus?" I countered. Then I gave him a short little rabbit punch that knocked him out of his chair. I left him sitting on the floor, holding his jaw and wondering what had hit him.

I told the lieutenant I wanted to go back to the gallery. On the way there, he asked me what had happened. I told him Angel had gotten dizzy and fallen out of his chair. Then I asked if I could use the phone to call Ivonne. The lieutenant offered to dial the number. I was surprised; Ivonne answered the phone on the second ring. I wanted to rip the phone out of the lieutenant's hand, but my inner control kicked in, keeping my elation at bay.

"Hola, amor", she said.

I couldn't believe it; she sounded so positive compared to the last conversation we'd had. It seemed the General had been better, but I still told her to phone Danilo to have the mess straightened out. I suggested she find another place to live until my release, which, according to Talavera, could be as early as next week. Ivonne was happy, laughing and as excited as I was at the prospect of my imminent release.

I told her I would bring a fax for her to send to Grant next time she came to visit, on February second, and asked her to somehow track down my passport. It might be necessary to escape the country immediately after my release. There was so much to say, I didn't want to hang up. I could have talked forever but the lieutenant was urging me to conclude the call. I said my good-byes and promised we would see each other in only four more days, during the gallery visit.

Returning to the gallery with new prospects for freedom, I felt great. I'd put Angel in his place and, more importantly, I knew that Ivonne was all right. I could now settle in for a weekend of studying, writing and reading - just putting in time until visit day. I told the Narco Jet guys that I was not going to continue teaching because working with Angel was difficult. I added that I didn't need any more frustration than I already had, and that included standing at the door for four hours waiting to pay some guard a pack of cigarettes to use the telephone for five minutes. They all agreed that removing myself from the forefront would keep me away from the troublemakers. I wouldn't be a target for prison welfare bums who relentlessly asked for everything, including toilet paper. There was no way I was going to have Ivonne bring extra toilet paper for everyone! I didn't care how itchy their assholes got.

The next morning was Saturday - recreation time for the people who didn't have visits. I felt a little bit of sun would be good for me. Our recreation yard was the large space between Gallery Five and the children's Gallery Seven; it was also where the infamous Gallery Ten was situated. This being my first time there, I didn't know what to expect. I soon wished I had my running shoes. A group was running around the perimeter; the loop was roughly a kilometre round. Off to one side, several inmates stood around warming up on a basketball court. Others hung out along the sidelines, greeting old friends from different galleries. At the far end was a baseball diamond where a team from each gallery played on alternating Saturdays. Today there was a soccer game. I didn't know where to walk or where to sit; it seemed I was always on somebody's playing field. It was typically Nicaraguan: disorganised mayhem. Balls were flying around, seemingly at random; players, possibly from different games, collided with each other. It was hard to be tranquilo surrounded by chaos.

I looked out of place, standing in the midst of this confusion armed with a book. Another inmate came over and introduced himself and took me to a less active corner to talk. His English was not very good, but I could tell he was trying to learn, so I tried to accommodate him by correcting his mistakes and helping him with a few problems he was having with grammar. He was in his late fifties and I could tell he was once an educated professional. When I asked him what he had done, he answered that he had fallen on hard times and had turned to crime to feed his family, until he found himself in here. He introduced me to the prison artist who was responsible for the murals on the prison walls. He was no Diego, but he was talented in his portrayals of the revolutionaries. I commissioned him to paint and agreed that I would provide him with a photograph the following week.

It was better here than the other gallery exercise yards, which were nothing more than garbage dumps, but it was still dusty and dirty and I could not wait for the buzzer to ring so

I could go back and have a shower. The time seemed to drag. Four hours out here were too long for me.

I had the cell to myself when I got back; Caseres was still at visit. I summoned Primo to fetch up two buckets of water for me for the princely sum of three cigarettes, and I took a two-bucket bath. Then I laid out my mattress and read; when I got tired of that I studied Spanish and wrote Ivonne a letter that included the new words that I learned. That night I went down and watched a movie with some of the guys before being locked down at ten o'clock. I filled another night with dreams of freedom.

The next day was the last day of the month - only two days to visit day! I was glad of the books the Consul had brought, putting in the hours by reading. With Caseres cooking and Primo coming to clean the dishes and running any errands, there wasn't much for me to do but put in time.

Chapter Seven

"YOU ARE JUST A CASH COW"

IN THE MORNING, as was becoming customary; I walked down to the Consejo's office to talk with Mario and Chepe. This morning I wanted to ask about getting an authorisation for running shoes. I needed to start working out immediately. I remembered vividly the promise I'd made to myself. I would call it my quiet resolve; no one would know what burned deep within.

"Good morning, guys! What's new in paradise this morning?" I said in a voice that got their attention.

"Why are you so happy, don't you realise where you are?" exclaimed Chepe. "This is a loonie bin; go away and come back miserable, will you, or we'll think you've gone fuckin' nuts!"

"Now that I've got your attention, Chepe, I need an authorisation for a pair of running shoes and blue jeans. I don't want any fuck-ups with the guards not allowing me shoes".

"You type it out and I'll have Roche sign it", Chepe told me.

"I'm out of here; I think Danilo is finished with the bathroom", Mario said as he got out of his chair. Turning to me, he said, "Paulie, I asked the Padre if your wife could be included in the gallery visits with our wives. He said it would be necessary for her to phone him to set up the visit".

"Thanks, Mario. I'll tell Ivonne tomorrow".

"Don't put too much faith in those visits", Chepe warned. "You haven't been here long so they may turn you down".

While we were sitting talking, an older man - probably in his sixties - walked in and rudely interrupted our conversation. Nicaraguan people in general appear ill mannered to outsiders. It often irritated me, but they didn't see anything wrong with their behaviour. This man was one of the old guys in the gallery. There were about ten or eleven of them, mostly in for charges of sexual violation, which I knew must have been impossible for most of them. I doubted that they'd had an erection in the last ten years! This could happen if someone's siblings wanted the property or the accumulated wealth of another, but didn't want to wait for the owner to go on to the next World. They cried rape, and because there was no testing, the rightful owner ended up in prison, stripped of everything and conveniently out of the way for life.

Chepe introduced this man as Concho and told me he was totally insane. I could not understand a word Concho said, but he was talking directly to me, waving his arms, laughing and carrying on, telling me some fantastic story. He was having such a good time that he had me laughing along with him. It meant nothing to him that I could not understand a word; he was truly enjoying himself as he told his tale. Chepe interrupted him to send him on an errand.

"Do you know what he was saying to you do you?" Chepe asked between his own chuckles.

"No, I don't have a clue. All I know is, he had a great time telling me his story", I said.

"He was telling you that he worked in the mountains at the coffee plantations. He takes young girls into the bushes where he holds a machete to their throats while raping them. The ones that resist he kills and disposes of the bodies in the jungle".

I was floored. I sat there too dumbstruck to speak, thinking, what the fuck, could this be true?

"I told you he was crazy", exclaimed Chepe.

"Yeah, but that's not crazy. That son of bitch needs to be put down like the rabid animal he is! Jesus Christ, Chepe, that's too much! He was actually enjoying talking about it. I hope society never has to deal with the likes of him again!" I was nearly shouting. I had to leave the office. I told Chepe I would prepare the authorisation for the shoes and be back.

I wrote out a rough draft of the authorisation, and then I had to borrow a typewriter. The guy across the gallery from me, Carmona, had one; for a cigarette, I could use it. Carmona was an artist of sorts. He made cards with hand-drawn decorations wrapped around flowery text. I bought one for Ivonne and promised him I would buy another for Valentine's Day.

I dropped off the authorisation with Chepe and made sure it was satisfactory before leaving. I reiterated my concern for the request.

"Paul, how would you like to teach a class here in the gallery?" inquired Chepe. "You could have a space in the church for a couple of hours in the afternoon".

"Let me think about it, okay, Chepe?"

"Yeah, but don't think too long. I need a reply".

Back in the solitude of my cell, I immersed myself in the novel I was reading. Later in the day, when Caseres returned, he handed me more prison notes. I was accumulating a stack of them now. Since I wasn't answering any of them, I didn't bother reading any. Gathering up our laundry, Caseres explained how many cigarettes we would have to pay for each item laundered. Then he introduced me to Silvia, who ran the laundry service.

Caseres told me he'd been notified that he would be going home soon. If I needed to know who to go to for services, I'd better ask him now. In the Nicaraguan prison system, you are not told your release date when you're sentenced, just the number of years received. Since there is no parole, release dates are always a mystery and serving your time doesn't mean that you will get out either. If there is nobody on the outside working for your release, you stay until someone brings the release papers to the prison. Caseres had a caring family that would go to any lengths to gain his freedom, so I knew they would be calling him out any day now. I was truly happy for him. Two years in this shit hole was a lifetime!

That night I took my clothes to Guido for pressing. I wanted to look good in the new clothes Ivonne had bought for me. Guido said he would bring them down to my cell when he was finished.

In the morning, I was ready to go, showered, shaved and looking fine in my new pressed clothes. I was anxious to see Ivonne. There was so much to talk over. I was glad we would have a full four hours in which to talk. After the routine of waiting to be taken to the visit hall, we were finally let in. This time I knew where I was going: the concrete table by the visitors' door. From this vantage point, I could see the walkway leading to the hall. I didn't have to wait long - Ivonne was one of the first visitors to arrive. I met her at the door. She looked ravishing in a chocolate brown dress with a cream floral print.

We smiled and laughed. It was a truly a great moment. I steered her over to a table where nobody was sitting, but in close proximity to the bar. When I had finished wiping the seat and tabletop off, we sat facing each other, holding hands. At that moment she was like a shining star to me, so bright and beautiful. She pulled her hands from mine to present me with a file folder. "Here, I brought you these newspaper clippings", she said. "I collected every one that pertained to your case. I thought that you would want them".

"Thank you", I said, holding my hand out for the folder.

"Has Talavera been here to see you?" asked Ivonne.

"No, he hasn't been around. I went to the courthouse to sign some papers to release my personal effects to Talavera. That was last week and I'm still waiting for him to bring my glasses". I changed the subject. "I have a fax that I want you to send to Grant for me, okay? Also I need a pair of running shoes; here is an authorisation for the shoes and pants, can you bring me a pair of blue jeans from home?" I handed her the signed authorisation form that Chepe had provided.

She looked up after putting the authorisation in her purse and said, "That Talavera lies; any man that lies cannot be trusted! He told me he was coming here with your glasses last Friday. I told him you couldn't teach without your glasses, that it is giving you headaches. I think he only cares about the money he receives from Grant! Grant doesn't know what is going on here with these lawyers; he only believes what they tell him!"

"Here is the fax for Grant and my letters that I wrote to you; put them away in your purse before you lose them. That fax will explain to Grant just what is going on down here. See, the problem is, I can't phone him to let him know what is what. You can't tell him anything because of the language barrier, and Grant can't call Talavera for the same reason. It's a communication mess. Everyone has to rely on Blandon and that's shaky - he's not even here! Let's go for a walk", I added, "I'm getting stiff sitting here".

I rose and looked around for someone to watch our table. I spotted a kid named William and asked him to keep an eye on our table, while Ivonne and I strolled arm-in-arm around the perimeter of the visit hall, talking in subdued tones. Only occasionally would one of us say something funny to make the other laugh. We were lost in each other, impervious to the stares or the comments being made about us.

We stopped on one of our rounds to look at a table that was set up to sell artwork that the prisoners made. The handiwork was the typical jailhouse variety: plastic fishnet hammocks, greeting cards, beaded jewellery and other small trinkets that could be manufactured here. I promised Ivonne I would buy her something for Valentine's Day and then directed her over to the bar. I wanted to get something to drink. It was becoming hot in this enclosed cavern.

After buying Coca-Colas, we returned to our table where I introduced William to Ivonne and gave William a Coke for watching the table and sent him on his way.

"Has the Consul been here to see you?" Ivonne asked.

"Yes, last week. They're having problems with Talavera; he's not returning their calls. They were the ones who told me I would be going to court to sign the papers".

The buzzer sounded, announcing the visit was officially over, and none too soon - it was becoming a sauna in there!

We walked together to the end of the hall and shared a last good-bye kiss. Then Ivonne was gone and I was left with only the lingering scent of her perfume.

After the degrading strip search, I lined up to receive my barco. I was amazed once again by how Ivonne had managed to carry so much for such a distance - it was truly incredible!

Back in my cell, I made myself busy putting away the food supplies before I sat down to read the letters Ivonne had given me. When you have nothing left, when you've been stripped of your freedom, it's the small things that count, like a moment to be by yourself to read a letter - this is a big thing! I was fortunate. With Caseres working, I had the cell to myself. All I had to do was put my towel up on the door to signal that I was not to be disturbed. A visit from Ivonne, some letters to read, and food in the larder. I felt great, my spirits were lifted. I was happy that everything with Ivonne was good; she too, had been in high spirits today. Perhaps that was a good sign!

I spent the rest of the day cooking my first meal for Caseres and myself. It was a beef stew that I knew he wouldn't have tried before. I would make rice though - every meal had to contain rice, or Caseres would surely bitch!

I walked down to see Chepe and Mario to catch up on the latest news the next morning. They had received news that they had won their appeal - at least two magistrates had signed in their favour; all they were waiting for now was the third magistrate's signature. It didn't matter whether the vote was in their favour or not; they had the required two of three signatures in favour of acquittal.

"Here we are, fuckin' innocent, and we are still here", shouted Chepe.

Mario seemed to be more in control. He said, "We will have a meeting tonight to see what course of action to take - possibly a hunger strike. Something has to be done to get the magistrate to sign off". He then turned to me and said, "You see Paulie; this is what is going to happen to you. Remember this: you are at the beginning. I'm afraid you have a long way to go. We are fortunate to have family on the outside who are pushing the appeals court every day, but still they are taking their time!"

I listened a little while longer. I didn't believe Mario because I still held the belief that I would be exonerated soon - anything he told me was empty rhetoric.

"Chepe", I said, "I've decided, if you can get enough people for a class, I will teach. Just tell me where and when".

"Beautiful, I'll have the list today for you", Chepe replied. "This really helps out. There are some guys that need the two for one benefit. I'll see you later on today".

With that over with, I stopped to see what was on the television. As usual, the men were watching soap operas from Mexico. Every day, it seemed, the soaps were on. I went back to my cell to read and kill some time. Chepe showed up with the list of inmates who'd signed on for English class. I left the list on Caseres' bed and joined Chepe for a walk down the hall. I could see Carillo Hernandez motioning me over to his cell.

Chepe leaned over to me and said, "He's crazy. Wait till you hear what he has to say to you".

I looked at Chepes' back as I slowed down to see what this guy wanted. I was thinking about the last conversation I'd had with a crazy person.

I tried my best to explain to him that I didn't understand what the hell he was saying. He was persistent, beckoning me into his cell; I must say I was a little intrigued. Crazy this guy might be, but he had the attention and the respect of the Sandinistas in here. I knew that he was a captain in the military; he had a no-nonsense look about him despite a playful demeanour. You could tell by his scarred face that he'd had his share of scraps and his nose appeared not just broken, but one nostril had been cut. His one deformed hand was missing a few digits; it gave him a battle-worn look.

He motioned me to sit down on a board that covered the toilet seat. I could see he was clean - the cell was spotless.

His cellmate was lying on his bed. I only knew this man as Carillo's uncle. It was certainly plausible; they shared the same last name. Carillo, I noticed, slept on the floor, as I did. A chalkboard measuring a full three feet leaned against the wall. It was this he wanted me to see. He began to write the Spanish alphabet on the board and so I began to write and pronounce the same, only in English. He had heard I was going to have English class in the church starting tomorrow, so naturally I should be trying to learn Spanish with him! The Hernandez' got a good laugh at having the gringo learning Spanish in their cell. I stayed for an hour or so, enjoying the Captain's playful banter. I promised I would come back to continue my Spanish the next day.

My daily ritual of having coffee with Mario and Chepe continued. There was no one else around at that time of the morning to have coffee with or to speak English with, but I was beginning to converse in Spanish. On the first day of classes, Chepe helped me get started and set up but the inmates wouldn't come on their own; we had to go up and down the gallery rousting the students, even though they were aware of the time the class started. Out of the eleven enrolled, eight showed up, which was pretty good, I thought! I started teaching them the alphabet the first day. The students had different language skills so I decided to start with the basics. Some could not read or write in their native language; others, like Chavarria, the man I borrowed the dictionary from, had good language skills already. The two hours went by quickly and I was happy with the first day.

Caseres was watching the classes from the door. I asked him if he wanted to come out the next afternoon. He told me that when I'd arrived, he'd known no English, but now he was beginning to understand a few words and it had interested him enough to learn more. It made me feel good to hear him say that. I would surely miss him when he went home. There was no telling who I'd get stuck with next! The next afternoon, just before the lesson started, I heard my name being called: "Cañamo!" Whenever anyone is called for a visit, their name is shouted up and down the gallery until they acknowledge that they are coming. I hurriedly turned the class over to Chavarria, my best pupil, explaining to him the lesson for the day and giving him the outline I had prepared. He had not expected anything like this, becoming the teacher on the second day. I reassured him, saying I would be back in a half hour or so. Just follow the outline I had prepared, I told him. I left Chavarria scratching his head wondering where to start and ran to the other end of the gallery.

I was taken to Molina's office to meet with the Canadian Consul. Marion and her driver were there to give me books and to tell me it was necessary for Ivonne to phone Talavera for my glasses because he wasn't returning any of their calls. It was a short visit. Marion explained that they had to get back but she would be out next week to see if the issue of my glasses had been resolved. I thanked her for the books and for coming by and told her I would see her next week.

Back in the gallery, Chavarria was doing a great job so I stayed at the back of the class, observing. I decided, since I didn't have the Spanish skills necessary to communicate with the class, I would use Chavarria as a teacher's helper. That way it would keep him from getting bored and quitting the class and it would give the students someone they could direct questions to. I noticed that today four people were missing from the class; one of those was the Captain. After dismissing the class I went down to the Captain's cell to see why he hadn't come to class. He invited me in and offered me a cold drink and a cigarette, which I accepted. He was standing at his stove cooking what appeared to be some kind of meat but I didn't recognise the smell and I didn't want to ask what it was.

"I missed you at the English class today", I said.

"You weren't there either", he countered.

I decided to let that go and asked him what had happened to his hand. I expected a war story, but he told me a story about him and a buddy getting plastered on bottles of Ron Plata at a mountain cantina. After four bottles of rum, the girls started to look good. They went to the house of one of the girls for a late night party and, finding him too drunk to get it up, the girl threw him out of the house. With nowhere to go and nowhere to sleep, he fell down beside the pigpen. The big boar decided he would make a good meal and attacked him, biting and crushing his hand.

He was smiling as he told me this tall tale, so when I called the story bullshit, he broke out laughing, thinking that he'd had me going for a while. He grew serious. It was like a dark cloud had arrived, bringing with it ominous memories of a time best forgotten. His brows drew together and he looked down at his hand and let out a long sigh. Then he turned his head toward me and said, "Twenty years ago, at the start of the revolution, I was fourteen years old. I killed my first man! It was at first difficult for me, the killing. Then, with the training I received in Bulgaria, it became easier. We were all idealists, all thought there was glory in war, but in the end we all lost a bit of ourselves. Some physically, others mentally. With me . . . I was leading a supply convoy when we came under mortar attack. The armoured transport carrier took a direct hit and I was thrown out. When I came to, I crawled to the nearest farmhouse. After six months in the hospital, I was left with this". He took down his pants to show me where the shrapnel had embedded in his leg, thigh and buttock.

The call came for La Cuenta, so I told Carrillo I would talk later and returned to my cell for count. After a supper of bean soup, I started a letter to Ivonne. Alex came to my cell door. "I got permission for us to use the phone right now. I told them that you needed to call home, but because you don't understand Spanish, you need me to translate for you. You have cigarettes? We have to pay the lieutenant a pack of cigarettes". I knew I was getting hustled for a pack, but what the hell; I needed to call Ivonne anyway. I followed Alex down the stairs to the door, where we were told to wait. The lieutenant came down to get us for our call and I paid him the pack and he left us at the phone. Alex called his wife first so I thought of what to say when Ivonne answered the phone while I waited for my turn. When Alex said good-bye to his wife and hung up, I dialled Ivonne's number, hoping that she was home. On the third ring a strange woman's voice answered. I told her who I was and asked her to get Ivonne. The woman didn't even know who I was.

Ivonne's voice came on the line.

"What the hell is going on?" I asked.

"I have to move out of here right now!" Her voice sounded harried and desperate. I heard the receiver click and the line went dead.

"Ivonne! Ivonne! Hello - Ivonne!" I shouted into the phone. It was no use; she wasn't there.

Alex watched me while I dialled the number again. I didn't want him to know what was going on or it would be all over the gallery in a snap of your fingers.

The phone rang busy. This was not right!

"What's the matter?" Alex asked.

"This fuckin' telephone cut off my call!"

"How much time you got left on your card? Maybe the card ran out. I got a new card, use it if you want", offered Alex.

"No, it's okay. I was finished talking anyway", I said, but I wondered what the hell was going on now!

I knew I wouldn't be sleeping that night. My mind was reeling, trying to sort out what was happening. I tried to write, but the words that came out sounded desperate. I tore the paper up and decided to walk. Maybe some exercise would help me sort out this new dilemma. At the very least, it might make me tired enough to sleep. Anger seethed inside me; the exercise would help to contain it. I spent the night working out different scenarios, followed by sordid dreams that left me exhausted in the morning. I jumped at the chance to go outside for fresh air. I would bring a photo of Ivonne for Alex to do a painting from.

The day was hot. The sun shone down with such intensity that it felt like my skull had become a pressure cooker slowly boiling my brain, nevertheless it felt great to be sitting in the sun letting nature charge my internal batteries. It felt good to relax after the tormented night I'd had!

I found Alex in the same corner of the exercise yard he'd been in the week before. When I showed him a picture of Ivonne, he said that she was a very beautiful woman. It would take one month to complete, maybe a little longer, because he wanted to capture the beauty of her face. I agreed, but secretly I thought I wouldn't be here to see its completion. After talking with Alex I couldn't wait to get back to the gallery to compose a letter to Ivonne. She must have been going through a terrible time and it was all because I was stuck in this place. Someone has to be held responsible for what they've done to my life, I thought.

I was happy to hear the buzzer sound, signalling a return to the gallery. I went directly to my cell and began to compose the letter. At first I tried to write in Spanish, but I found I couldn't express myself in the way I needed to. I needed to convey my thoughts in English. I felt a whole hodgepodge of conflicting emotions in my head. Ivonne had told me everything was all right with General Montealegre; the rent was paid, or so I was led to believe. Why, then, were people I didn't know answering my telephone? Why had the phone been cut off? I was suspicious; I needed to talk with Ivonne immediately. For now, though, I would have to be satisfied with writing her letters and trying not to think on matters I had no control over. I would have to wait patiently for visit day in four days' time in order to find the answers to these disturbing questions.

The weekends were always boring for me but with this added problem, I was having a difficult case of "commando cable", or burning wire. This was what the inmates called it when you became lost in your thoughts with worry or concern. By Monday I felt sick and feverish, with a sore throat - classic symptoms of the flu. Luckily my cellmate had medication to control it before it got any worse. Illness like this is dangerous here. Starting with flu-like symptoms, the infection would spread like wildfire. There were bacterial infections everywhere; you could never be too careful. After contracting ringworm, I'd become very cautious when going to the bathroom. I always placed toilet paper on the toilet seat and sprayed the toilet with disinfectant as a precautionary measure. I washed my hands several times a day just to try and control the passage of bacteria. Death by communicable disease was a real threat that had to be dealt with every day.

The Canadian Consul came to see me on Tuesday. Marion told me that Ivonne had moved to her parents' home in Granada. I sat there impassively listening. I knew that I would be talking with Ivonne the next day and then I would understand what was going on. They left me books, as usual, and I asked them to ask Talavera to bring my glasses to me. Again, the meeting was short but I was glad, as I didn't feel like talking to anyone.

The next day was the one I'd been waiting for - conjugal visit! I hoped Ivonne would be here early, but, since she had to come from Granada, I knew the likelihood of that was slim. At best, she could make the second round at ten o'clock. After the call came for the third round, I went to check the roster for Ivonne's name. I could not believe that Ivonne would miss coming! I had to keep my mind from conjuring worse case scenarios. The fourth and final call came. I stood at my cell door waiting to hear my name called. At last my name was called. My nervous energy exploded into such happiness! Relief poured out of me like a dam spilling water; I sprinted down the gallery toward the door.

I saw Ivonne approaching and I couldn't help but smile. She looked so beautiful. That smiling face of hers was enough to melt butter. Moments like this would be etched in my mind forever. We were given our room and Ivonne set about making the bed up while I read her letters to me. I felt selfish that I was only thinking about myself, when she was having a difficult time with Alberto Montealegre. We sat on the bed, facing each other and looking into each other's eyes, searching for signs of pain. Our lovemaking was slow and sensual; each drinking of each other's caresses like they were fine wine.

When we were finished, lying in each other's arms, she began to recount events of the past days. I became very sick, Paul. I thought it would be best to go to my mother's for a couple of days, until I could feel better. When I came home, I found strangers in our house - I couldn't believe this! I confronted Don Alberto. He said, 'I have no contract with you. I want you off the property immediately.' I didn't know what to do; he only allowed me to take our clothing from the house, and said he was keeping the furniture! I was there packing our clothing when you called. I am sorry Paul, but their stupid child pulled the telephone cable from the wall and cut off our conversation. I had no choice but to return to mothers. I phoned Marion at the Consul, hoping they would be in touch with you, to let you know that I had moved from that awful place. I'm happier now, to be away from that evil man!"

I pressed Ivonne closer to me and gave her a consoling pat on the back. Everything would be all right in the end, I told her; we would win! But all the while I stared at the wall, seeing nothing, feeling only the hate igniting somewhere in the bottom of my soul. That feeling of hatred was becoming all too familiar to me.

After our exchange of letters and her vow to phone Talavera and tell him to get his ass in here with my glasses, she also promised to bring a pair of jeans and running shoes on the next visit day. She had tried today, but for some reason they were refused.

"I think they don't like me, Paul. I came here today at ten o'clock but they made me wait till this afternoon to see you. When I protested that this wasn't fair, the woman said that she wasn't going to allow the clothes today! I thought I had better say nothing because I wanted to see you - they could easily have said no visit".

"My brother sent you this", she added, holding out a small bag that contained medical preparations for fungal infections and capsules of antibiotic.

"Thank Norman for me. This is really appreciated", I said.

The buzzer sounded announcing the end of the visit. These conjugal visits seemed to go too fast. Hurriedly we dressed. I was finished first so I put the linen into the plastic bag along with my medication and Ivonne's letters. When Ivonne had straightened her hair we stepped out into the hall and walked down the corridor that led to the waiting room. We hugged and kissed; I reassured her that everything would get straightened out.

"I will try to get a special visit when I find out from Talavera about your glasses and the trial transcripts", Ivonne said.

The matrons came in to usher the visitors out. I watched till I could no longer see her and then I turned to follow the rest of the inmates out to the line-up to be counted and strip-searched. On my way back to the gallery, my feelings were bittersweet. Seeing Ivonne left me, as always, in a good mood. Only this time, I also felt intense hatred toward Alberto Montealegre. How could that man do what he'd done to Ivonne?! If he thought that this would be taken lightly, he had made a mistake - I would never forget this!

In the afternoon I was called to collect the barco that Ivonne had brought. I put away the groceries and spent the rest of the day talking with Caseres and preparing my English class for the following day. Later when the lights were off and the gallery was silent, I went over in my mind the new events that were unfolding. Why was the General taking action against me; what could his motive be? Whatever motivated him did not matter; his actions were what mattered. He was no more than a common thief - nothing more, nothing less. I would seek my revenge, but until then I would take pleasure in the hatred I felt.

I decided to ask Captain Hernandez questions about making and detonating bombs. He was a professional soldier, schooled in the art of guerrilla warfare - he could teach me. I started spending the mornings with the Captain, learning how to construct letter bombs, car bombs and how different combinations of household chemicals could be fashioned into lethal exploding devices. We also covered killing technique, such as how to properly garrotte and where to place a knife to kill instantaneously.

It was all very bizarre. It's true what people say about prison, incarceration breeds criminality. I had gone from creator of plants to creator of bombs! However, I took comfort that in the afternoons at least my English classes were constructive, while the evenings were spent studying new Spanish vocabulary to incorporate into the daily letters I wrote to Ivonne.

Caseres came back to the gallery after the next visit with his family with confirmation that he was going home the following day. Caseres, as was customary when leaving the gallery, went to say his farewells and to give away the articles that he had collected during his time here. He gave me his bed, pots and pans, all the food, and his bookcase. The only things he gave away to others were his clothes and his hot plate. True to his lawyer's word, Caseres was given his freedom. I was sad, yet happy for him - he was a good cellmate! I had a cell to myself now. It was a great feeling to have my own bed and privacy, but I knew it would be short-lived - nobody had their own cell for very long.

Over morning coffee with Chepe and Mario, Chepe asked me whom I would like for a cellmate. My heart sank.

"Chepe, I don't want anybody right now. I've just had privacy for one night; can't I stay by myself for a little while longer?"

"I know what it feels like to have a cell to yourself", Chepe conceded. "Okay, but the fact is they won't allow it. They want to put three in a cell, but so far I've been able to argue around it. In the other galleries the cells are a little bigger, but they have five to eight people living in each cell. The poor bastards have to take turns sleeping! I'll leave you alone for now, but don't expect it for long. They're moving Damien up here from down below today or tomorrow. Do you want him for a cellmate?"

"If I have to have a cellmate, then I want Damien. But see what you can do to leave me by myself for a little while longer", I said.

The next morning, everyone was getting ready for their visits. It felt good to be able to use as much water as I wanted for a shower. I didn't have to roll up my sleeping mattress or be careful not to wake up Caseres. The call came, and dressed in their best, everyone made their way to the front of the gallery to begin the process of roll call, taking a position in line, and calling out a position number before being allowed into the visit hall.

I didn't wait long. Ivonne was prompt to enter the hall.

Ivonne was by far the most beautiful woman in the visit hall, and everyone knew it. I was proud as a peacock, parading around the visit hall with her on my arm!

She'd brought me my pants. She'd had to pay money to get them in here. The officials would not allow the shoes. I was furious. I had permission; I needed those shoes to start running. I needed to start an exercise program right away. I located Chepe, who in turn talked to Freddy. He said there should be no problem with a pair of running shoes; he would find out what the problem was. That didn't help me today - this meant yet another week of waiting. Ivonne was feeling much better, now that she was staying with her family. At least there, she didn't have to put up with the added aggravation of Montealegre, and her family's support was helpful. By noon, the place was sweltering hot. When the buzzer sounded signalling the end of visit, it was none too soon. We traded letters and Ivonne promised to be back next week on visit day with better news, she hoped.

After hauling my groceries up to the gallery and putting them away, I went over to the cell that Damien had been transferred into to invite him over for a North American-style supper. After all, we were the only two North Americans in the prison; it was only fitting that we should share a meal of meat and potatoes! His eyes lit up at the prospect of that. I knew that where he'd been it simply wasn't possible to eat well. After count, Damien came over to my cell as we had planned. I had the meal prepared: a stew consisting of steak, potatoes, carrots, onions and a Central American vegetable called chayote. I'd seasoned it with lots of garlic, salt and pepper and served it up with fresh bread. It was a celebratory meal to welcome Damien to this gallery. He had spent nine months in that hellhole, Two Baja - he was due for a good, home-cooked meal!

"Smells good in here", Damien said as he entered and breathed deeply of the cooking odours.

"Come on in and sit down. We are styling tonight - we have the best of everything. Help yourself to the cigarettes, they're over there", I said, pointing to the bookcase.

"Shit, man, you've got furniture in here. A bookcase, at that!" He whistled appreciatively, then asked, "You don't mind me looking at the books, do you?"

"Not at all, Damien. If you see anything you like, take it with you to read - that's what they're for. Make yourself comfortable while I dish up the stew". I set about dishing up two bowls of steaming-hot stew while Damien made himself comfortable, sitting on the toilet to thumb through a mystery book. When he saw me bringing the bowls of food over, he put the book back in the exact place he had taken it from. We ate in silence, savouring every bite. When we had finished I asked him if he would like a Coca-Cola with ice. Damien nodded, still looking over the cell.

"This is a nice cell. Fresh paint on the walls, and clean". He stood and shook his legs to get the circulation going, then walked over to the window.

"The view sucks, and I mean that literally - across the way is where the homosexuals are", I told him.

"They used to have them downstairs, with the tuberculosis patients. They had to take them out – many of them have AIDS and the diseases were spreading. The TB cases were the worst. You know at the back, where the guys used to play chess? That's where they were housed. The ventilation was so poor down there they were getting sicker, so they moved them too. You see that sickly kid up here? His name is William".

"Yeah".

"Well, he is one of the TB patients and he is crazy, and I mean crazy", Damien said. "You know he has only one eye - that's why he wears those sunglasses all the time. I was there when he yanked his eye out; he was as cool as a cucumber. He thought God told him to take out his eyes so he could get rid of the demons. He stuck his finger into his eye socket and popped out the eyeball. They got to him just before he popped out the other one".

"You got to be kidding", I said in total disbelief, even though, coming from Damien, I knew it was the truth.

"Don't get too close to him, close enough for him to breathe on you. The last thing you need is tuberculosis", said Damien.

"How is Denis doing?" I inquired.

"You mean the guy you came in with?" When I nodded,

he said, "He moved in with Angel for awhile, until one day Angel stole his bar receipt. Denis couldn't prove it but he was the only person in the cell at the time. That fucker Angel is going to be a dead man soon; the talk is, he's a rat. He is going to be moved real soon. In fact, I was surprised that I was moved before him. The word is, you had a little altercation with the asshole", Damien added. "You know what kind of a guy he is; I would watch him when he's around".

"I don't care about him, he's just a low life. Since I stay in the gallery now, I don't have to deal with any problems out there. Take a look at all the requests for things I get". I had a shoebox full of them, which I passed to Damien.

"Damien, between me and you, I don't trust anybody in here. They're going to move somebody in here with me. I told Chepe that I wanted to be alone for as long as I could, but when they move somebody in here with me I want that somebody to be you".

"That's good for me - we both like to read and between us we have more books than anybody in the prison! If you like, I'll bring over my books tonight. They're kind of crowding the cell, over where I am".

Damien went to get the books and I went to find Primo to do my dishes.

The bookcase was filling up now - what a beautiful sight! I told Damien to help himself to the books anytime.

When the call for lockdown came, Damien had a hard time believing it was ten o'clock. For a long time, he'd been used to seven o'clock lockdown; that three hours made a big difference when you weren't used to it. We said good night and he left for his cell. I took out my pen and paper and began a letter to Ivonne in the quiet solitude of my personal cell.

In the morning I had my usual coffee with Mario and Chepe. They were discussing the action Chepe, Alex and Layton should take. They were tired of sitting in prison waiting for the last magistrate to sign off on their appeal. Drastic measures were being discussed. Mario's wife and Chepe's wife were organising pickets in front of the courthouse, while Chepe, Alex, and Layton were going on a hunger strike to protest. The Narco Jet guys had had a visit from Captain Marcia, who was next in line to Molina in the chain of command. Captain Marcia was concerned because their actions would draw a lot of Press coverage and she was concerned for the prison image.

During the talks, my name had been brought up. Captain Marcia told Mario and Danilo that I had told the students in the class I was teaching that they were all stupid, and that I had complete disregard for the prison authorities! Danilo, speaking in my defence, had told her that she was mistaken. He knew me and could verify the remarks were totally out of character. I knew instantly who was behind this smear campaign - none other than that rat, bastard Angel!

"This explains a lot of things, like why I'm having problems getting a pair of running shoes in here, and why they're treating Ivonne terribly and making her wait to visit me", I said.

"You didn't say anything like that, did you?" asked Mario.

"No, of course not! It's that Cuban son of a bitch, telling her all that bullshit".

I left them to their problems and with my new found ones, went back to my cell. I added a little more hate to my soul.

Later that afternoon I developed a stomach ache. At first it was a hollow feeling accompanied by gas. I tried having a bowel movement, thinking it was possible I was constipated, but the pain continued to intensify - the more I burped, the worse it got. I could not lie down; the pain was just too intense. I decided to walk. Up and down the gallery I walked, but the throbbing pain remained intense and unrelenting. The pressure was forcing my belly to protrude. The upper quadrant of my belly was as hard as a rock!

I went in search of the gallery medic, who, after looking at me, knew I was in considerable pain. He gave me an injection of Diclothinac to relieve the pain. Tomorrow I would have to go to the prison hospital to see the doctor, he told me. Finally the pain subsided enough that I could sleep. I only hoped that when I awoke, I would feel fine. I didn't need to be sick in here!

Every other day, the sick were taken down to the infirmary.

The next morning I was groggy from the medication, but I went to the hospital despite my reservations. The stories I'd heard about the place were enough to make anybody steer clear. We were taken into the hospital and seated outside the examination room. From where I sat, I could see the door leading into what looked like a laboratory. I heard screaming outside. It got louder as the footsteps accompanying the screaming drew closer. The door swung open so forcefully, I thought it would be ripped from its hinges. Two officers held a man by the arms. They half dragged, half guided him, heedless of his wails. When I looked closer, I could see that his stomach was cut open and the blood was seeping through his dirty t-shirt. They took him into the laboratory, where they laid him on the table and proceeded to stitch him up - no sedative, nothing.

I was glad when they called my name, just to get away from the man's screams. The doctor was a young woman who, after introducing herself, took samples of my blood, checked vital signs and questioned me as to the severity of the pain. She suggested that I make an appointment with an outside facility for a CAT scan then wrote a prescription for pain medication that needed to be injected. She asked me if I had anyone on the outside to pick up the medication for me. After she finished writing her report, I asked her about what I had seen out in the lobby - was that commonplace here? Yes, she told me. Some cut themselves for sympathy, others cut themselves trying to commit suicide, and others cut each other fighting.

"No, I mean for the hospital to stitch a man up without freezing or sedating him", I said. I could still hear the guy sobbing.

"You are lucky; you can afford to buy medication and to have quality care administered. Most here cannot, and we cannot provide medication and care because we simply don't have the money. We rely on donations - perhaps you would like to donate", she said, smiling.

"I want to see you if you have another attack", she continued. "And I need to know when and where your CAT scan appointment is, so I can make the necessary arrangements for transport".

I thanked her and walked back out to the waiting room. I had to wait until everyone had seen the doctor, then we were escorted back upstairs to the gallery.

Chepe stopped me outside the office to tell me that he had to move Damien into my cell the next day. He asked me if I had seen the newspaper. In the El Nuevo Diario there was a full page explaining Hemp-Agro's defence appeal.

"Do you have a copy of the paper, Chepe?" I asked, feeling that familiar feeling of hope building.

"Yes, I have it here. It is very good, Paul - well prepared". Chepe went back inside to fetch the newspaper. I followed him over to the desk, where the paper lay open. At first glance I could tell it was professionally done, complete with a banner headline reading "Hemp-Agro believes in the power of justice".

"You should have Alvarro Miranda look it over so he can explain to you the context and, most importantly, how this can benefit your situation. I'm no lawyer - he is - but from what I read, it was presented very well, at a great cost. It is not cheap, taking out a whole page in the newspaper", Chepe said.

"Mind if I take this with me? I'll return it after I'm finished", I said absently. I was already lost in its contents while walking toward the door. It was in small print, which made it difficult to read.

Later in the day, when Alvarro had time to read the article, he came over to my cell to discuss its legal aspects. He said that it was a well-written and well thought through defence strategy. Things were proceeding fast in my case, he said, at least faster than in their case. I thanked Alvarro for his legal interpretation and his personal thoughts on the newspaper piece, but my opinion differed and so I said to Damien.

"This is too much too late".

"What do you mean by that?" Damien asked.

"Well, I've been in here for nearly two months and not one word was said in my defence. There was only negative publicity in which I was referred to as 'narcotrafficker' and 'mafia', and never once were the goals and aims of Hemp-Agro ever revealed. This is the first time my defence is being made public. Now, it shows quite correctly our innocence in all matters, but it's nothing but legalese jargon that maybe two percent of the population can understand, much less bother to read!"

I stood to put some water on to boil. While I fidgeted with the hotplate control, Damien said something interesting that touched a nerve.

"Face it, you are just a cash cow! Those lawyers you have, they're going to keep you here as long as they can, to milk you dry. You don't have to be Perry Mason to understand that one. It says right here". Damien picked up the article and pointed to the pertinent section, then read it aloud:

"In the absence of Corpus Delicti there can be no continuance of a judicial trial. Why didn't they argue that at the start! You have to break a law before you can have criminal proceedings!" Damien stated. "No, man, I don't want to rain on your parade, but you are going to be here a long time - until they're tired of milking you".

I took the boiling water off the burner and produced two cups. "You want a cup of coffee, Damien?" I asked. "Why don't we talk about something a little lighter, like gang violence back in San Bernardino?"

We spent the rest of the evening talking about Damien's past life in the gangs, The Crypts and The Bloods. Before we shut it down for the evening we made plans to move him over in the morning.

It didn't take long as his books were already there. My few days of privacy were over but at least I had someone to relate to who spoke English.

Later in the day I received barco from Ivonne. Along with the food supplies came her letters. They expressed her undying love and a renewed faith that now my freedom was imminent. I too felt that I would soon be set free. Any idiot could see that Hemp-Agro hadn't committed an offence. They had to set me free now!

Damien introduced me to dominoes, and we spent the weekend playing. At least, he was playing - I was being beaten so badly, you couldn't call it playing. I noticed that my eyes were getting very bad. I couldn't hold a book far enough away to see the print without squinting. I found that if I stared at the pages for a little while my eyes would focus enough to read, but after a couple of hours the headache would start. It was maddening to think that Talavera hadn't been to see me in three weeks! He knew I needed my glasses and yet he obviously didn't care!

We got through the weekend noise and boredom okay. All I could think about was the conjugal visit coming up. It was the only thing there was to look forward to; besides the visit itself that was the only time I got any news from the outside world.

On Monday, Chepe and a lieutenant I had not seen before came to our cell just before lunch.

"May we come in?" Chepe asked.

"What's up, Chepe?"

"The lieutenant is here to collect your bookcase".

"No way!" I jumped up to confront them. "That belongs to me! When Caseres left, he gave the bookcase to me. Come on, Chepe, I need that for my books!"

"The lieutenant says it is needed down in the hospital", said Chepe.

"Tell him to go get his own. This is mine", I protested.

The lieutenant turned and motioned to Chepe to follow. When they were gone, I said to Damien, "What do you make of that?"

"He will be back with more of them", Damien said.

Sure enough, the lieutenant returned with a platoon of guards, all carrying clubs. He pointed at the bookcase and said, "That is prohibited. It is made of wood and cannot be in your possession".

There was no sense in protesting. Getting a beating for a bookcase wasn't worth it. I reluctantly cleared my books from the shelves. Watching our bookcase being carried out was gut wrenching, but even more maddening were the smirks on the faces of the goons that had come to intimidate me.

Finally visit day arrived and on the second round I was

called. As always, it was a time when I could recharge my batteries and feel normal, get in touch with the real world. With her visits and in her letters, Ivonne gave me the love that I needed to counterbalance the hate that I felt. With these two very powerful emotions, I was able to generate a great strength that enabled me to overcome anything they could throw at me.

Chapter Eight

"THEN THERE WAS HOPE"

THE PAIN IN my belly hit as it had before, starting as a dull ache in the pit of my stomach and gradually building in intensity. As before, the pain became relentless and the pressure constant. I had just given Ivonne the prescription issued to me by the prison Doctor on visit day, but she'd had no time in which to return with the pain killers. The next visit day wasn't for another four days.

It must have been exasperating for Damien to hear me in that much pain. I spent much of the night pacing back and forth; counting out loud how many paces I took in each direction. One, two, three, four - turn around - one, two, three, four. I don't know how long this went on, but the counting kept the pain from driving me crazy. I was afraid to eat, thinking that something in my diet was causing the attacks, but the following day I felt fine, as if nothing had happened.

On the first day of March the church notified Chepe that they needed the space where I taught in the afternoons, so would I mind conducting my lessons somewhere else? Just like that, I was railroaded out of my classes. I told Chepe that

I did mind, and I would not be conducting any more lessons anywhere. From now on, I vowed, I wasn't going to be frustrated by anything. They can't take anything from you if you don't have anything to take! I had a visit from the Canadian Consul that afternoon. It was about time; I needed fresh reading material and, hopefully, some good news! Marion met with me in Molina's office, and we discussed the same things we'd discussed on her last visit.

"Marion, I still have not seen Talavera", I told her, "and quite frankly, I don't care if I ever see him, but I do need my glasses! I've had enough of this, begging for my own glasses. I will make other arrangements to buy a new pair if my request is being denied!"

"We have sent letters to the court as well as to Talavera, requesting your eyeglasses be given to you immediately", Marion replied. "Our hands are tied on this issue. It's Talavera who has to get to work on this matter".

"As you know, I've had difficulties with the telephone", I told her. "I still haven't made the call that was promised me weeks ago. I've been here for two months and I've had no opportunity to phone my family in Canada. I believe that is a direct violation of human rights!" I paused to sit down on an overstuffed sofa. I thought I'd gone to heaven, the comfort felt so wickedly decadent.

"We can surely do something to make sure that you have calls to Canada on a regular basis", she said.

"Marion, Commandant Molina does not like me", I stated. "He'll always tell you there is no problem with me phoning, but when you leave here the call is forgotten. It's necessary for him to give me written authorisation for a prescribed time to phone from the administration office".

"I will make sure you get that call!" Marion said, nodding her head in agreement. "When I return to the Consulate I'll talk to Jack Adams to see if he'll get authorisation from the Ministry in charge of the penal system". Marion knew what these military men could be like.

"I brought you more books", she added. "I hope you like them".

"In here, beggars can't be choosers. I like all books", I told her. "Marion, could you please send a fax to Canada for me?" I handed her a letter to Grant. As she accepted it, I thanked her and rose. "Until the next time".

"I'll be here next week with Mr. Adams to take care of this phone calling business", she assured me.

The only good thing I got were the books, I thought as I watched her go. With the books held tight under my arm, I went in search of a guard to escort me back to the gallery.

The next morning was visit day and I was ready. I sat at the table by the door that afforded me a view of the walkway. As the hours passed, I became more morose; there would be no visit for me today. I wanted to go back to the gallery before I had to subject myself to the degrading strip-search. I found the officer that had brought us to the visit hall. He told me I would have to wait till eleven o'clock. That was fine by me; I'd only have to wait thirty more minutes. When I returned, Damien tried to lighten the dark cloud that hung over me. We played dominoes for several hours to pass the time. I think he even let me win to keep me playing.

Alex had moved out of Gordo's cell and moved in with Layton. Since they both were on a hunger strike, he didn't want to be around Gordo – wise move. Damien and I went down to ask them over for dinner, hoping to catch them cheating. They were steadfast in their resolve to stay on the hunger strike. Alex was giving interviews to La Prenza and I swear all that negative talk was wearing him down - he looked old. There was a sickly look to him; I hoped he got his resolution soon, before he became bedridden.

The next afternoon I received a visit from Talavera. He and the interpreter were waiting in the hallway for me. As usual, he was smiling and saying he had good news for me. The only news I wanted to hear was that I was going home! When I asked about my glasses he said that he'd given them to Commandant Molina, who would deliver them to the gallery. Talavera had the trial transcripts as well as the appeal declaration printed out for me. Not all of it was in English, but that didn't matter; at least I had something pertaining to my case in my possession.

He also brought a fax from Grant explaining to me what they were trying to do to get me out. Talavera said it was possible that I could be released for medical reasons, but I would have to get permission from Ivonne's family to stay in their care. A doctor would also have to provide the necessary documentation. I was once again feeling pangs of hope. Talavera's excitement was catching. My mind was scrambling through possibilities; everything seemed to be falling into place. I really did have a medical problem, and the prison authorities were aware of it. I would apply for Carcel por Casa, or home arrest.

For the rest of the day, I was elated. I was sure this would work because I knew many people had done it in the past. I talked with Alvarro about the possibility and he assured me that after the doctors diagnosed that surgery was necessary, I would have a good case for convalescing at home. I wrote to Ivonne and told her what had transpired and what I needed her to do. My only hope was that I would see Ivonne, somehow, this week. Perhaps she could come on a special visit pass, but how was I to get in touch with her? They make everything so damn difficult!

This was everything I'd hoped for; I think I was finally getting a celestial push. I received a visit from Ivonne and she apologised for missing the last visit day as she'd only received funds from Grant on the previous afternoon. I wasn't concerned about the last visit day now; I was brimming with good news - I could feel the freedom! Taking a deep breath to contain my excitement I told her about the plan and what she must do.

"I wrote everything down here that I need you to do", I said, giving her the letters that I had composed. Dropping my voice so we could not be overheard, I added, "Your brother Norman can supply me with a doctor's letter saying that I'll be in his care while convalescing at your parents' home in Granada".

"Oh yes, Paul, Norman will help any way that he can. My family will help. Oh Paulie, can it be true - to have you home?"

Ivonne clasped my hand tighter. "We will do everything that is required", she said, looking into my eyes. Her sincerity burned deep.

"With all my heart I know that, Ivonne. I will be home soon". I replied. "Ivonne, phone Marion Chamorrow today. I need to talk to her. She said she would be here with Jack Adams this week, but I need to make sure that they are coming". Now is the time to get them involved, I thought.

"What's in the bag?" I asked. "What did you bring me?"

"Guess. What have you needed?" she asked.

"Not a pair of running shoes. I gave up on them; you must have paid double to get them in here", I said. We both got a good laugh at that, after all the grief that pair of shoes had caused! The matron came in to let us know our time was up. It was a great visit; even though it had been only fifteen minutes long, it had been most gratifying. We said our good-byes, kissed, and hugged before being led away.

In the afternoon the barco that Ivonne had brought was delivered, and Molina paid an unexpected visit to the gallery. He came to my cell to look around and give me my glasses. At last, I could see. Perhaps I wouldn't get daily headaches anymore. All in one day's visit, everything seemed to be coming together: barco, shoes and my glasses. I was definitely on a roll now, if I could just roll on out of here...

Damien and I had a good meal of meat and potatoes, then settled in for a night of television. Every once in a while, they showed a good movie. It was in Spanish, but entertaining nonetheless. Just as the movie was about to start, the lights went out. There we were, sitting in the dark. I managed to locate Mario and borrowed a candle so we could at least have a little light. Since it was the weekend, we had to endure the next two days without any lights or water. The pumps that move water from the ground to the holding tank and from the holding tank to the galleries were powered by electricity. Damien told me that the last time this had happened, it took a week to repair. The guys downstairs had resorted to collecting the rainwater dripping from the roof.

Monday morning came and there still wasn't any water,

but the electricity was turned back on. A good thing, as I had to cook up the meat before it went bad. Later in the day I was called out for a visit. When the guards took me out, instead of going to Molina's office, I was taken to the front gates to be signed out. I had no idea where they were taking me. They escorted me outside the prison walls to one of the administration buildings. I was taken into a reception area and told to sit down. Someone would be with me in a few minutes. A lady who had been a neighbour of mine when I'd lived in Granada came out to greet me. She told me that she was Dr. Frech's personal assistant and directed me to follow her to Dr. Frech's office. When I entered the office I saw Jack Adams and Marion Chamorrow seated in front of a large mahogany desk. A man in his mid-fifties, with slightly greying hair that gave him a distinguished look, rose behind the desk.

"Hello, my name is William Frech. I am the Director of Penal Institutions. Please sit down", he said, gesturing toward the empty chair beside Jack.

"Your name is Wylie", he said, looking over his reading glasses. "I am familiar with your case and hope that it gets resolved soon. It's been a terrible ordeal for you. Now, what can I do for you?" he asked.

"I need to phone my family in Canada", I said. "The telephone that services the prison is unable to place international calls. Dr. Frech, I need signed authorisation for a designated time to call from an accessible telephone. Secondly, sir, could I please have visits with my girlfriend on Sundays, as it is easier for her to come here on Sundays. Also, my cellmate and I are the only two North Americans in the prison. Because we don't speak Spanish, we are disadvantaged. Can we take Spanish lessons in the prison?" I asked him all of this in a no-nonsense way, but I left him room to bargain. He was either going to help, or not. I didn't expect to have all my requests granted.

"I have just been assigned this post as Director and I believe there has to be prison reform", he told me. "I am moving my office here permanently, where I think I can do the most good. During the next month I want to interview as many prisoners as possible to evaluate the conditions here.

"When do you want to call Canada?" he asked.

"On Sundays; in the evening would be a good time", I stated.

"Okay".

"Excuse me, but could he phone his family immediately?" Adams interjected. "They are quite worried, and justly so. It's been almost three months since they've heard from him".

"When would be a good time?" Dr Frech looked toward me for an answer.

"This Thursday, either in the morning or the evening", I said.

"Fine". He called his assistant in and told her to make the necessary authorisations for him to sign. Then he looked over at me and said, "As far as the visits with your girlfriend on Sundays, I don't see why not. Tell her to come in and see me and I will give her the proper authorisation.

"I believe that educating yourself is time well spent - it can only benefit everyone concerned. I will have Catrina make out the necessary paperwork. If you have any more problems, I want you to come directly here to see me. I want to be accessible to everyone. Now, if you could kindly wait for Catrina to finish with the authorisations in her office?" he said as he rose. He showed us to the door and directed us to Catrina's office.

Waiting in the hallway just outside the assistant's door, I explained to Adams the problem I was having with my stomach and the immediate need for me to have a CAT scan performed at a good medical clinic. Marion said she knew of a clinic that had state-of-the-art equipment available. She told me to have Ivonne phone her to set up an appointment. Catrina called us into her office and handed me an authorisation. I read every word to make sure that it was correct. It stated that, on Thursday, March eleventh at nine a.m. and at six p.m., I was to be allowed to use the phone at the prison administration office to call Canada. It looked fine to me; all it needed was Dr. Frech's signature. Catrina took the authorisation to get it signed. I said to the Consul representatives that it was fortunate that we had Dr. Frech here; maybe he could invoke some changes, since he wasn't military. Adams said there would be a formal announcement of his appointment that week.

Catrina returned and handed me the paper, saying that I should have Ivonne come in to pick up the visit authorisation, and she would come and deliver the telephone authorisation for this following Sunday. I thanked her and said good-bye to the Consul representatives before being taken back to my gallery. I told Damien of my visit with Frech and he was amazed that I could even get over there - quite frankly, so was I. Frech hadn't bargained with me, he'd given me everything that I'd requested. I wondered how the military officials were going to react to his open-door policy. It could get ugly, especially when he tried to take control from the military. I have to get out of here, now! I told myself.

In the morning there was still no running water. Everyone had to wait in line at the bottom of the stairs to fill whatever container they had with water. The water came on for a certain period of time during the day, and getting some was on a first-come, first-serve basis. I waited for an hour for two buckets of water. People pushed and shoved, all trying to be in the front of the line. This was a potential trouble spot - like a volcano, sooner or later it would erupt.

After carrying water up to my cell, I sought out Mario and Danilo for coffee and gossip. Today there was much bitching going on - I think the Narco Jet guys were getting very anxious and stressed. The strain was taking a toll on them. They knew they were getting out, but the question was, when? I listened for a while and then decided to run. After all, I had waited a long time for the shoes; it was time to break them in. Danilo, seeing me heading for the door, asked what I was up to.

"I'm going running", I said. "I got to do something. I can't sit around here all day".

"Wait up, I'll go running with you". Danilo said, and added, "It's exactly ninety meters from the television to the church. I know - I've paced it off".

"Feels good to have a pair of shoes on my feet", I said as we started off at a slow, comfortable talking pace.

"You had a hard time getting those shoes. I think somebody doesn't like you they're making things difficult for you", Danilo said.

"Hot tip, Danilo. I think I have an ally now - at least, he seemed very receptive to my requests",

"Who is that?"

"The new director, Dr. Frech. I was in his office yesterday with the Canadian Consul. He gave me authorisation to phone Canada every Sunday and have visits with Ivonne on Sundays. He seems to be a genuine guy. I think he really wants to make some changes around here", I said.

"Well, don't get your hopes up. The military have the power here and they won't give it up to some Liberal civilian, especially one that is appointed by Aleman. How did you get over to see him?" he asked. "Very few people know of his appointment".

"The Consulate. I needed to call Canada and Molina was making that difficult, so it was necessary to go beyond these walls".

"Mario has got a job now", Danilo told me. "He is working at the shoe factory taking inventory and, I guess, getting it ready to start up again",

"When?"

"Today, tomorrow, any day soon, you know how it is. Did you hear that today they are going to announce a government amnesty and let six hundred prisoners go free! That means over half the gallery will go out. The military and police prisoners and the old prisoners will be set free first, and that's a good percentage of this gallery", Danilo said.

"I've had enough running for now; let's slow down and walk for a bit", I said, feeling the effects of my heartbeat's acceleration. I could see Damien waving from the end of the gallery, so I excused myself and headed towards him.

"I thought you might be hungry and cooked up breakfast", Damien said, scooping a heaped pile of scrambled eggs onto a plate and then passing it to me with some pieces of the charred bread we call toast.

"You were inside my mind! How did you know I was hungry?" I gladly accepted the plate.

As we ate, I relayed to Damien what I'd heard from Danilo about the amnesty.

"All that's going to do is put the thieves back on the street", Damien said. "Why don't they send me home? I'll promise I never come back here".

"Not a chance in hell of that occurring, my friend. Your best hope is that they lessen your sentence on appeal". I could trust Damien, so I told him that I expected to go home on a medical release - at least that was what I was working toward.

"Good luck. I guess if you grease some palms, you might pull it off", Damien said.

"I have a legitimate beef", I stated. "I know they're going to operate on me. I want to make sure that I convalesce outside of here. That's a reasonable request, why would they turn that down?"

"It's Nicaragua", Damien countered. "They don't need reason here".

"Okay, smart ass, rain on my parade. Do we have any gallon water jugs around?" I asked.

"Sure. There's a couple of empty ones behind the toilet". Damien pointed.

I pulled them out from behind the toilet.

"What are you going to do with them?" asked Damien.

"Fill them up with water and use them to do some flies. I know it's not much weight, but it's all I've got. I will just do more sets and reps. I'm going to spend some time working out every day. I have got too much pent-up energy - I have to do something with it. I'm going downstairs to fill these up. Talk to you later".

On my way down to the water tap, the medic stopped me to tell me that he had some medication from the hospital for me. We went into his cell, where all the medications were stored. He presented me three vials of Diclothenac, the syringes to go with it and said to come and see him when I needed an injection - he would administer the drug. He also had some multivitamins, which I took with me to keep in my cell.

Getting the water for the two-gallon jugs proved to be a hassle, so I left them with Primo to fill and bring to the cell. The next day was conjugal visit day and I would need Guido to iron my clothes for the occasion, despite the fact they wouldn't be on my back too long!

I awoke early and as soon as the cell door was opened, I went to haul water, thinking this would be the best time. Since this was visit day, I thought I would postpone exercising till the following day. I had my conjugal kit prepared and sat waiting for my name to be called. After lunch was served, I knew that Ivonne wasn't coming so I reluctantly took my pillow and sheets out of the kit that I had prepared. I took off my blue jeans and stowed them under my mattress for the next visit. I put on my shorts and tried reading, but that didn't work. There were all these worse case scenarios going through my mind. I had to shake these commando cable thoughts. Maybe playing dominoes would allay my disappointment. Playing with Damien was an act of self-abuse. He could win at will, which frustrated me. One day, I vowed, I would win!

The next morning I set about configuring a routine for myself. First, before daylight I would start my day with one set of crunches - one hundred of them. Then I would go down to the tap to haul water back to the cell before count. After count was taken, I would have my morning coffee with Mario and Chepe.

At seven-thirty they cleaned the gallery floors. All prisoners in the gallery were required to wait in their cells till the cleaning detail was finished. I began my floor exercises in the church, since it wasn't occupied at that time. I alternated push-ups with chair dips till the cleaning was done. Then back to my cell to do flies with the water jugs. In between sets of flies, I walked a lap around the gallery to recuperate. Then, while breakfast was cooking, I started composing a letter to Ivonne. After breakfast I ran until fatigue set in. It felt great. If I could keep this pace up, in no time I would feel much stronger mentally as well as physically - ready to take on any obstacle!

Sunday morning, at the prescribed time, I made my way to the door downstairs to show the guard my authorisation. I was allowed to phone to Canada. It was incredible to hear Grant's voice. We were actually communicating with each other! I had almost given up hope of having any calls to Canada. It seemed so long ago that I'd talked to Grant; it was like I was in another world and I had just bridged a communication gap, allowing me access to my home planet. I didn't realise how starved I'd been for information concerning life back home. Every scrap of information concerning family was important, I felt reconnected. Grant and I used every minute allotted for the call. We formulated a game plan to follow in an attempt to gain a medical release. I had a good excuse; I was often in severe pain and surgery was necessary.

I told Grant that I would call back in the evening for another thirty-minute call. Grant and I were able to talk again during the second call. This time I was able to discuss all the things that I'd forgotten to mention in the first call, which had been too emotional. This time I was more settled down. I explained to Grant the importance of having all paperwork ready for Ivonne and me to leave the country. We both believed that when my release became public, whoever was behind this conspiracy might take retribution.

We compared notes, trying to sort out what had happened, who was behind this, who was pulling the strings. I knew it could not be Jorge Vega. He might have started the ball rolling with his lying, but he was too inconsequential. Was it a Sandinista political plot directed toward embarrassing the Liberal government, or was it an American DEA sting operation, or was it both, one hand ironically - in this case - feeding the other?

Since 1961, the US federal government had been (and still is) in direct contravention of the United Nations Single Convention On Narcotics. This piece of legislation was designed to co-ordinate the international 'war on drugs', which is a separate topic from hemp. This Treaty clearly recognises the industrial significance of hemp, thus the legislation does not apply to Cannabis when grown for industrial purposes such as fibre and seed: a fact reflected in the sheer number of countries cultivating Cannabis for industrial use today. However, the United States government has never made a distinction between marijuana and hemp – some believe because Cannabis could challenge the global hegemony of the petrochemical, timber and some print media industries that US politicians have always been so close to.

In addition, the situation in Nicaragua, whereby a government is in power at the expense of another, under highly ideological and brutal circumstances involving the US government funding one side, necessarily means there are some people who would like to see the end of both governments and their ideology and/or business agendas. Since this is unlikely, they may have to make do with embarrassing government ministers. I felt like a pawn in a political game that had no clearly defined rules or ethics. I was an innocent man. The lawyers said it would take two weeks to get a medical release, provided I had the necessary doctor's documentation. I assured Grant I would be ready.

My thirty minutes were up; the officials were making signs for me to end the call. I told Grant that from now on, every Sunday at six in the evening I would be allowed to phone Canada. I returned to the gallery in high sprits. Maybe this ordeal was finally going to be over. With everyone leaving the prison this month, I was confident I would be included. I settled into my routine of exercise, studying and writing, feeling positive about my situation. At long last, things were changing in my favour!

True to Dr. Frech's word, his assistant Catrina came to the gallery to deliver my authorisation for Sunday telephone calls. All I needed was to have Ivonne pick up the Sunday visit authorisation.

On visit day Ivonne was there right on time, as beautiful as ever. We had lots to talk about on this visit. A lot had transpired since I had seen her last. She told me that she had been talking with Danilo Blandon and Grant and everything was ready for me to stay at her family's home in Granada. I told her I had received the medication and the vitamins intact, thanked her and described my meeting with the director, Dr. Frech, and told her that I believed in him. She listened intently, neither agreeing nor disagreeing, until I was finished.

"Paul, I have been praying all week long that your freedom be granted. Perhaps this is God's answer to my prayers". Ivonne said. Her face looked angelic as she gazed longingly into my eyes, searching for acknowledgement.

"Perhaps, amor, perhaps. God works in mysterious ways. After this visit, you will need to go to the office of Dr. Frech to pick up an authorisation for Sunday visits", I told her, and gave directions to his office.

"Paul, you won't be here for me to come and visit on Sundays".

"I'm not taking any chances - we have been let down before! You need to phone the Consulate to have them prepare a visa for you to enter Canada. You need a passport, so go apply for one now and tell them you want it granted immediately. Remember, we've only got two weeks, so we must be prepared!" I hoped I was driving home the urgency. We exchanged letters and held each other, knowing that in a little more time, we would be together again. I watched her as she departed. I drew in a deep breath and exhaled slowly, trying to keep control. I felt an urge to run after her. I turned away to follow the matron out of the waiting room.

On the evening news there was an interview with Dr Frech, confirming his appointment as the new director. The appointment received mixed reviews in the gallery, for obvious reasons - half the people were Sandinista and Dr. Frech was a Liberal. But all that really mattered to them was the amnesty that was to be granted before Semana Santa, or Holy Week. Cardinal Obando was on the newscast along with government officials, confirming the amnesty. Cheers went up in the gallery, and for good reason. About two-thirds of them would be going home.

The next day the representative from the amnesty committee came to have a meeting in the gallery. He called out the names of those who had been selected for freedom. Of the ninety-four prisoners, sixty were to go free. I knew I wasn't on the list, but it really was something to see these people so happy at the prospect of getting out!

On Sunday, as was planned, I was called out for a visit with Ivonne. Our first Sunday visit! Mario and his family were also in the waiting room, but they were allowed to go outside to have a family gathering under the shade of the mango trees. That left Ivonne and I alone in the waiting room. I asked the official in charge if we too could go outside, but he turned us down, saying we needed special permission for that. I didn't press the point. Just seeing Ivonne here on a Sunday was accomplishment enough! Ivonne brought with her all the makings for a picnic. She had been in contact with the Consulate. Her passport papers were all filled out; all that was left to do was wait.

She explained that she'd been told that this Sunday was a special visit and that the authorisation for permanent Sunday visits would follow Semana Santa. There would be no visits granted during the Holy Week, and that included deliveries of barco. We had a great visit for four hours. In the evening, my call to Canada would make this Sunday the best day so far this year! Saying good-bye to Ivonne wasn't as difficult this time. We knew we would be seeing each other in three days' time!

In the afternoon a group of us congregated in Mario's cell. It was confirmed: the Narco Jet guys were going home - all three magistrates had signed off. There was much jubilation. Their ordeal was now over; they would be going out either Friday night or Saturday morning, conveniently, when all the media would be focused on the release of the amnesty people. Amidst the celebration, Mario said to me, "Paulie, I'm afraid after we're gone, things are going to get bad in here. I hope you get out of here soon!"

"I'll be right behind you guys", I replied. They didn't realise I was sincere.

"I don't want to leave you behind. I wish that you were coming too", said Danilo.

"I wish I was too!" I said.

It was time to go, to let them make their own plans. I

excused myself and made my way back to my cell. In the evening I went to make my call but it wasn't as easy as the first time. The guard made me wait for his superior to okay the authorisation. Finally I was allowed out - an hour late for my call, but at least I'd been let out. On the second ring, Grant answered. Thank God, he was home. I told Grant what was going on here with the amnesty thing, and that the Narco Jet guys were going home. This would be a good time for me to be released, amongst the confusion. Grant said he was just waiting for confirmation from the lawyers as to when I'd go for the medical. We talked for the full half-hour and parted with a promise to chat next Sunday.

I felt very positive that my time here was counting down. I settled into my routine and tried not to think about things too much. My next visit with Ivonne was, as always, great. This time, though, we really felt that all our prayers were being answered and I would be free soon. We talked of our future, how this horrible, negative and utterly dark time would be transformed into something positive. Ivonne brought with her as much food supplies as she could carry, since there would be no visits till after the Holy Week. In Nicaragua, like all Latin Countries, this is a time for celebration with family and friends. It is a time when everything shuts down. There is an exodus from the cities as people flock to the beaches to party.

The two-hour bell sounded, announcing another end to another conjugal visit. We parted knowing that the coming week was important. I needed to be taken to a clinic for the ultrasound and have an appointment set with a surgeon before Semana Santa. The bombshell fell on Friday. Succumbing to media pressure, the government reneged on the amnesty. The stance they took was that all these hardened criminals being set free endangered the populace. The release date of the amnesty was put off until the following October. This was catastrophic for the inmates who'd been prepared to go home. Some had given away all their jailhouse possessions; the smarter ones had just promised their things to others. Damien was the recipient of Alvarro Miranda's television.

I think he was secretly praying that the Narco Jet guys would be released. He really wanted to keep that television!

The next morning the Narco Jet guys were released. All except Alex Quintero, who was held back. It seemed his lawyer, Talavera, hadn't submitted the necessary documents to the courts. The poor man was devastated. Here was a man who, during his hunger strike, had aged right before my eyes. Then news came that he was to be released after all, and this decrepit, sickly looking man was transformed into a bouncing ball of vitality.

Damien was happy; he inherited the television, so now we had our own TV in the cell. We could watch what we wanted when we wanted - not that I watched much but it was a nice luxury. There were only three days remaining before the start of the Holy Week. I had a feeling of impending gloom; doubt came to hang on my shoulders like a dark cloud. I stepped up my exercise routines in order to ward off the depression, trying in vain to remain positive but once again my hopes of freedom dissolved.

It might be a holiday on the outside, but it was no holiday in here. They were short staffed so we were confined to the gallery for the duration of the Holy Week, with no visits or barco. The news report had declared that the food in the prison was going to be upgraded; more money was going to be spent on prisoners' welfare. What a bunch of shit! During the Holy Week, the food sometimes didn't get delivered to our gallery at all, and when it was delivered, it was never on time. This made food supplies the number one commodity until the supply of cigarettes grew short, and then the nicotine addicts would sell their soul for a fix. I just hoped that our supplies lasted till visit day. Our drinking water was getting precariously low and the commissary wasn't making any deliveries.

I felt achy in my joints, a sure sign of malaria. I took some medication, but for the next few days I was bedridden. I hoped to God I could kick whatever it was making me so ill! On the third day I started exercising, thinking I could sweat it out. The following day the fever broke and I was able to eat a little. I felt drained but at least I was mobile. Thank God visiting day came along, ending the worst week I'd had to endure. Ivonne brought fresh supplies and a special treat: Snickers bars. I devoured two of them in short order and washed them down with Coca-Cola.

There was no news. Everybody was just getting back to work, so we didn't expect anything to happen until later in the week. We were both tired of waiting, only to be let down time after time. I'd composed letters for Ivonne to read whenever she felt alone and ready to throw the towel in. We are strong, I told her. We have endured a difficult time, but it will soon be over. For every bad moment we've had, we will be rewarded several times over with many good moments. It's God's way, our balance with life, I said. Our love for each other was exceptional; we'd become one, both in spirit and in our hearts. There could be no others to replace what we had, for we were united in love before man and in God's eyes. It was becoming more difficult to watch her leave. Our lives seemed filled with false hopes and promises.

Later that evening, just after the conclusion of the evening news, I could feel the familiar rumblings in my stomach that signalled another attack. I knew I had to get the problem looked at soon. I was becoming afraid of the impending pain. I knew enough to immediately take an injection and start walking. I hoped the pain would subside in time for lockdown. It was a terrible thing to deal with in the confines of a five by ten jail cell. As luck would have it, the pain did subside into a dull ache and I was able to sleep.

On Monday the Consul came to visit - just in time, I needed fresh books to read. They expressed concern that my medical condition was not being addressed. I explained that it was impossible to get permission during Semana Santa to leave the prison. Since the holiday was now over, I would most definitely get the CAT scan done. I asked Marion about a visa for Ivonne and told them in no uncertain terms that, when I was freed, Ivonne would be coming with me to Canada.

Marion said that they were receiving faxes daily from Canada from people wanting to know the status of the case. My brother had been in Ottawa lobbying the government for my release. They had received a transmission from Foreign Affairs on his behalf, saying that it was necessary for me to call him in Canada at a specified time. She said that they were sending a fax to Dr. Frech later that day, requesting that I be allowed to make that call. This was great news - just maybe, with pressure from the Canadian government, they would resolve my case fast! I thanked Marion for coming out with the news and, of course, the reading material.

Back in the cell, I found Damien had good news as well. He'd been asked to take a teaching position. That was indeed good news. Since the Narco Jet guys were gone, the Bar did not do any more deliveries to the gallery. One of us had to get access to the Bar to buy our drinking water.

"Damien, you sure you want to work with that Cuban rat?" I asked as I crashed onto my bed.

"I can put up with Angel if it means I get my two for one. It is important for me to work. I don't want to be here for the next ten fuckin' years. Freddy always gave me the two for one when I was downstairs; he would just mark me down as working. But since I'm up here, I don't know about that", Damien said. He looked at the books I'd brought and smiled. "Right on time. Your embassy at least gives you books - mine gives me shit. They don't even come here anymore, the fuckin' assholes".

"When do you start downstairs?" I asked.

"This week sometime; probably Wednesday".

"Good, that solves our problem with the Bar. I'll give you my bar receipt to go and get us water", I said.

"Sure thing. And I will be able to call home. I haven't talked to my wife and children in a long time. Have you seen the pictures of my family? I got a picture in a letter - the first letter I received since I've been here!" He pulled the family picture from an envelope.

"That's real nice, Damien. You have a nice family here". I said, looking at the smiling faces of the young children, all dressed up nice. His wife wore a big smile, as if to say, see daddy, they're all getting bigger and looking fine. I passed the picture back. Damien looked longingly at his family. After Damien beat me thoroughly at dominoes, we settled in to watch the evening movie. Tomorrow was another day; I would see what it would bring.

The next morning, after my daily workout, I was summoned over to Dr. Frech's office. Catrina met me in the reception area and led me to his office. I accepted his invitation to sit down, selecting a chair opposite him.

" I have received a fax from the Canadian Consul for you", he said, passing me a manila folder. "They have requested that you call Canada tonight at six o'clock. The information is enclosed in the folder". He gestured at the folder. I made no move to open the folder to display the contents. I was sure he had already examined the document prior to giving it to me. "Do I have your authorisation for that call, Dr. Frech?"

"Yes, of course. I had the girl make the authorisation out this afternoon". He hesitated; then changed the subject. "Have you noticed any difference in the food?" he asked.

"I haven't noticed. I try not to eat the food".

"I think from now on, the food will be significantly better. There will be a better variety of meals. Meat is to be included at least three times per week", he said.

"Would you care for my candid opinion, Dr. Frech?" I asked.

"Yes, please; your input is necessary if significant changes are to happen".

I sat forward in my chair and said in a conspiratorial tone, "I have heard a lot of grumbling going on that since you started, we haven't had running water. The men are getting a little testy. They're demanding the pump be fixed so they don't have to carry their water. A simple thing like fixing the water problem would go a long way for prison morale, Dr. Frech".

"The pump was brand new, under warranty when it malfunctioned. It had to be sent back to the manufacturer, but as soon as we receive the replacement, it will be installed. I don't even have water here!" he said, gesturing toward his en-suite bathroom. "I have to bring bottled water to drink. The water problem will be fixed", he added.

"One more thing, Dr. Frech. Do you think you could get the food servers to wash their hands before serving the food? A little hygiene goes a long way and it doesn't cost any money".

"Rome wasn't built in a day", he replied, rising. "We will do what we can with the resources at hand".

I took that to mean that the interview was over and stood up and shook his hand, thanking him for his help. He showed me to the door and delivered me into Catrina's care. She gave me the authorisation for my call and said to get a message over to her if I needed to send a fax, and she would make sure it was sent. I thanked her and met the guard at the front door to be escorted back to the gallery.

That evening, I got my call. It was the first time I had heard my mother's voice in a long time. I thought perhaps I wouldn't be talking to her or seeing her again. She was eighty-five years old and in failing health. I knew that my situation was extremely hard on her. I assured her that everything was fine and that my release was imminent, possibly only a matter of days. My brother, Provan, had been in Ottawa the past week, trying to push the government into pressuring the Nicaraguan government to speed up the judicial process. He'd enlisted the help of Gerry Byrne, MP for Corner Brook, to aid in lobbying the government. Mr. Byrne had been demanding action from various governmental department chiefs. A letter had been delivered to the office of the Prime Minister, asking that the Minister of Foreign Affairs, Lloyd Axworthy, and his Nicaraguan counterpart negotiate my immediate release. Failing any fast resolution in this intolerable abuse of human rights and justice, immediate diplomatic action and/or sanctions by Canada would proceed. Provan also said that Mr. Byrne would continue to talk with the Prime Minister, Finance Minister and the Foreign Affairs Minister to gain my release.

It was a great call, a real spirit builder to know that everyone was standing behind me, working to get me out. I was confident that, with this kind of pressure, the Nicaraguan justice system would expedite my case faster. I went to sleep that night feeling a little more at ease.

The next day Damien was called out to start his first day teaching English. That left me with the cell to myself. My exercise routine helped me to relax; between my writing, reading and exercise, I kept busy. In the evening, Damien and I played dominoes and watched television. On Saturday I thought I had better go out to the yard to get some sun - I was getting a little pasty looking from spending too much time inside. Ivonne was coming the next day and I thought I would see if Alex had the painting of Ivonne done. When I stepped out into the yard, I looked for Alex; sure enough, there he was, standing in the same spot where I'd left him a month ago.

"Alex, how are you doing?" I inquired as I approached.

"I thought maybe you were released", Alex said. "I haven't seen you out here for quite a while".

"Yeah, well, you know how it is, Alex - easy to come here, tough to get out", I said. I looked around, taking in the people around us. You could never be sure that someone wouldn't come at you and shove a knife in your back. The rule of thumb was, always be alert.

"You got the painting completed yet?" I asked.

"Sure, I've had it done for two weeks now; been taking it out with me to the yard in the hope I'd see you". He reached down to pick up a sketchbook and opened it to extract the painting. It was crude, but the likeness to Ivonne was good. Alex had what I would call a developing talent; it was neither good nor bad, but somewhere in between.

"How much do I owe you?" I asked.

"Nothing. Consider this my gift to you", he said as he presented the canvas to me. Reaching in his pants pocket, he produced the photo of Ivonne. "Here, I almost forgot this".

"Thank you, Alex. I think she will be very excited to have this. Who knows, maybe one day this will be worth some money", I said. We had a good laugh at that. I rolled up the masterpiece and tucked it down my shirt for safekeeping.

I walked over to the wall of Ten Gallery and sat down. The sun shone directly overhead. It felt good. I closed my eyes and let my thoughts drift away to another place and time.

The buzzer sounded, snapping me back to reality. Shit! This place would be great if I was in a coma, I thought; just wake me up when it's time to go home!

I had much to look forward to the next day - a visit with Ivonne and my phone call to Grant in the evening. It seemed like quite a while since I had talked to Grant. This call would fill me in on what was going on.

I was able to persuade the official to allow Ivonne and myself to leave the visit area and sit outside in the courtyard. It was very private; we chose a beautiful spot under a lemon tree, and I went and got a wooden bench for us to sit on. The sunlight filtering through the tree created a dappled effect that danced all around us.

Marvin, the inmate who was in charge of the Bar, lived here and they allowed him to have a few animals. He had a dog and kept chickens - not many, because he had to keep them leashed to keep them from running loose and, I suppose, to keep them from somebody's stew pot. It almost felt like we were in a farmyard instead of in a prison, and it was a pleasant feeling to be left alone in peace. I was sorry when they came and told us the visit was over, but we knew that our next visit was only in a couple more days. I said good-bye to Ivonne and went with the guard back to the gallery. The best thing about the Sunday visits was the lack of a degrading strip-search.

At six o'clock I went downstairs for my phone call to Grant. The bastards knew I had a signed authorisation from the director, but they played games with me - not flat-out refusing, but one would look at the paper, then pass it to someone else, who in turn would pass it to someone else while I waited. It was a good exercise in patience, trying to remain calm through this stupidity. Over an hour later, I was finally granted permission to be let out, only to go through the same procedure at the administration office.

When Grant answered the phone, it was like someone opened a floodgate as my relief came pouring forth. Grant was excited to talk to me. The last time we had spoken was before Easter, when we were expecting my release for medical reasons. I told him to expect calls regularly on Sundays from now on, thanks to the new civilian director. Grant described what had gone wrong with the medical release idea. The court had ruled that, since I was a foreigner, it would be too easy for me to leave the country, fleeing the charges. The request for medical home detention was denied. There was more going on, though. The Canadian government was stepping up the pressure to have the case against us dealt with and Danilo Blandon had been working night and day with the lawyers, keeping after them to ensure that they were working. The last consensus was that there would be a ruling early next month. By Nicaraguan justice standards, that was fast.

"Early next month" was music to my ears. I could do that time with my eyes closed, now. I told Grant that I had to go and get a CAT scan done immediately. The frequency of the attacks was increasing along with their severity; even with opiates, the pain was excruciating.

The signal came to end the call. The time had passed by quickly but, as always, I'd deeply enjoyed the call. I was left with a positive feeling that everything that could be done was being done. I promised Grant I would phone on the following Sunday and hung up. I was taken back to my gallery for yet another week. I told Damien of the support I was getting back home and how the Canadian government was applying pressure to the Nicaraguans to resolve this issue. The Nicaraguan government was sending the wrong signals to the business community when Canadian business people were abducted and charged for crimes that were not committed! Just how democratic is a country whose justice system allows human rights abuse? I suppose they were just following the lead of their wealthiest neighbours.

Early in the week there was trouble in the prison. A couple of prisoners from Two Baja escaped by breaking through the gallery doors and had climbed up onto the roof. It was ridiculous, because they had nowhere to go - they were stranded on the roof. Prisoners in the galleries below were rioting in support of their comrades on the roof. The police showed up wearing riot gear, armed with AK47s, mortars and equipped with tear gas canisters. Shots rang out with some severity as the police tried to dislodge the prisoners on the roof. Since they were firing in my direction, I thought it wise not to stand in front of the window. I could hear bullets ricocheting off the metal bars. Someone shouted out that we were being gassed. Sure enough, they began firing tear gas into the gallery. I, like everyone else, grabbed the closest shirt and soaked it in water to cover my face, especially my eyes, to try to stop the burning.

It took three hours to get the situation under control but it took us three days to get the smell of the gas out of our clothes and we had to throw out any food that had been exposed during the gas attack. Damien missed the action, being in the classroom, but he was able to get the play-by-play report. The prisoners had been told they weren't being allowed out to the exercise yard because weapons were found during the monthly search. That provoked two inmates to force their way out. One major question that no one seemed to consider: Where were the guards? Damien suspected that the guards had either turned a blind eye or they had actively helped. Another Sandinista versus Liberal play – the Civil War was alive and well, at least in this hellhole.

That night on the television there were interviews with prison officials, including Dr. Frech, concerning the trouble. The military was saying that before Frech there was no trouble; now, with this new liberal civilian in charge, there was unrest among the prisoners. Frech said that he'd ensured that prisoners had nutritional meals, and more prisoner benefits were being planned. I had to agree with Frech - since his arrival, the meals had improved. He had also put his foot down and not allowed the military guards to steal the food. The military personal were robbing this institution of everything they could get their hands on. They resented Frech because he was cutting this off, the battle lines were being drawn and we, the prisoners, were merely pawns.

They brought up new prisoners to fill the vacancy left by the departure of the Narco Jet guys. One of these was a guy by the name of Norman Cuadra. He was in his mid-fifties, a professional. He had a law degree and owned a private practice in Managua at one time, before his incarceration. Carmona, our resident artist, told me Cuadra was an accomplished artist. If I liked, Carmona said he would introduce me to him. After all, he spoke English, and anybody who could speak more than two words of English was somebody that I should meet. I gave Carmona a couple of cigarettes for this information and told him to set up a meeting with Cuadra and tell him that I'd be interested in commissioning him to do some artwork for me.

After he had gone, Damien looked over at me and laughed. "You've got things happening in here, man. Anybody coming up here that's worth anything, they got to see you. You have more visits than anybody else in the whole prison. You also have the largest case in the prison. There isn't a person in here that doesn't know who you are. Hell, even the guards talk about you! Man, they think you're cool".

"Well, since you think I'm the man, go get some water, will you?" I said.

Carmona returned and I followed him over to meet Cuadra. Carmona took off after our introductions, leaving us alone.

"You are interested in some of my artwork?" Cuadra asked in English.

"Yes, if it's not an inconvenience to you. I like to buy art from time to time. The work in here is poor; there isn't much to choose from and I'm afraid I've bought most of Carmona's cards, so I'm looking for something new". I noticed that he had not yet put away his possessions, mostly art supplies. "I could come back another time, when you are more settled in".

"You've come to the right place for art, but as you can see, I haven't got anything unpacked", he said. "I usually don't have people breaking down my door to buy art around here. This gallery is not only quiet but, if everyone has money to buy my art like you, it will be profitable".

"What gallery did you come from?" I asked.

"Number five. I was there for two years, two long years". He replied, pausing to reflect. Then he added, "You would never imagine what it is like over there, with those kids yelling and screaming day and night. Nothing is safe; they steal everything. Crowded conditions - five people to a cell, almost lying on top of each other. This is much better, Paul".

"There is no stealing here, and lockdown isn't until ten o'clock. I'll tell you what: I'll let you get settled in and then come back in the morning", I said, extending my hand. "Welcome to Two Alta, Norman. I'll see you in the morning", I added. As I left his cell, I thought that there was more to the man than met the eye. Besides the obvious - the man was intelligent. No, there was something lurking behind that self-confident smile of his; perhaps he was a little crazy.

In the morning, after my exercise routine, I dropped in to see Norman and his artwork. Norman was an early riser and, as I found out, a coffee addict. I invited him over to my cell for a coffee fix, since he didn't have any. He readily accepted and gathered up his art portfolio. We made our way over to my cell.

I gave him the most comfortable seat in the house - the toilet - while I put water on to boil.

"Have you had a jailhouse cappuccino?" he inquired.

"No, can't say that I've had the pleasure".

"All I need is some sugar and coffee with a drop of water", he said.

"The sugar is in that one-litre coffee container over on the ledge". I pointed at the container.

Norman got up and took the two cups over to the ledge. I watched him open the sugar container and then dump three heaped tablespoons in each cup. I was about to protest when Norman put his hand up and said, "Wait until you taste. The coffee becomes something else".

Well, if I didn't like it, I could always dump it down the toilet, I thought. He added a teaspoon of water to the mixture and stirred it into a caramel froth before adding the boiling water. This produced a creamy drink without the milk. The taste was sweet, but it was a pleasant change from plain coffee.

We sat down, sipping our coffees and looking through his art. It was very impressive, the best by far that I'd seen in the prison. I commissioned him to make up two cards, complete with poetry. I even gave him three packets of cigarettes up front, something I never did around here - they take the up-front money and that's the last you see of them. I knew Norman wasn't going anywhere too fast; it was a safe bet I would get my cards. He talked of his art career. It turned out he'd been an accomplished artist before he got into trouble. He and his law partner had an argument over the law practice. His partner was trying to screw him over, so Norman shot him. He didn't kill him, but it was enough to sentence him to four years in Tipitapa Prison.

Our talk shifted over to my situation. I explained to him the importance of hemp agriculture in Nicaragua. I became impassioned when I talked of hemp and its benefits, of what we were trying to do in this country. I had proven that the plant could grow in this climate; our introduction of the variety was successful, despite the low germination (5%) rate of the Chinese hemp seeds. The next step was to begin putting the infrastructure for industrialisation in place. The hemp industry would supply countless jobs, both directly and indirectly, and a long-term sustainability to a fledgling agricultural marketplace. This country would benefit as a World leader in finished hemp products, much sought after commodities in the global marketplace!

I told Norman I wanted to find out who was responsible for my situation. Since he was a lawyer, could he go over the transcripts I had? Perhaps there were clues in the papers that would suggest who was behind this conspiracy. Norman listened intently to what I had told him, then said, "Paul, in my country there have always been injustices; whether they are political or caused by outside nations flexing their political will, they have always existed here. It is terrible that you, someone here only to help my people, have been caught in this political tug-of-war. I will help in any way I can to get you out of here. Let me see those transcripts. It will take me the better part of today to read them. I will return them as soon as I'm done. The only person I know who could help you find out who is behind this conspiracy is Norvyn Meneses. He comes to this gallery with the church every few days. Have you been introduced to him?"

"No, but I have heard a lot about him", I said. "He and my partner, Danilo Blandon, were involved in funding the Contras during the Civil War. I know he is a very respected man around here, second only to the Pope".

"Norvyn and I go back a long time", said Norman. "When we were growing up, Managua was a small town; everyone knew one another then. That was before the politics changed things. The next time Norvyn comes up here, I will ask him to talk with you. He may choose to help, he may not - that will be between you and him".

I pulled the transcripts from under my bed and gave them to him to read. We stood and shook hands and promised to be in touch later.

I lay on my bed and went over what I knew of Norvyn Meneses, also known as El Rey de la Drogas (literally, "King of the Drugs") around the prison. He was known as a man who could get things done. He built the church and donated it to the prison, and continued to donate his time to helping both prisoners and church. He was like a liaison officer. The rumour was that the cell I was in used to be his - he served six years here for a thirty-year drug conviction that had implicated Danilo Blandon. He'd also been written of in the book Dark Alliance as the cocaine supplier in collusion between LA's biggest crack operation and the CIA-directed rebels fighting the Sandinista regime throughout the 1980s. He was a very powerful man even today; with his close government ties he heard and saw a lot. If anyone could get me some answers, he could.

While running through the gallery one day, I noticed Norvyn Meneses enter. As usual, he was mobbed by well-wishers, people who needed favours and those who just idolised him. He was, to many, a demi-god, a symbol of their own misery. He'd been released from the prison because of his generosity to the church, and to this day, he is a benefactor - always coming to the prison to champion the causes of the forgotten. Norvyn Meneses was a true saint. For some, that wasn't a laughing matter. I saw Norman go into the church and fifteen minutes later emerge to give me the nod. One of the church guys came and told me Norvyn would see me now; I was to go through the church office to the supply room in the back and he would meet me there.

I followed his directions and didn't have to wait long. Speaking in English, this articulate man of average build with a tanned, healthy complexion asked, "What do you need? I can get anything you want - visits, telephone calls, name it and I will have it done for you. I know who you are and I'm very familiar with your case. As you know, I spent six years here in this same gallery, so I know what you are going through".

"I need only this: I need to know who is responsible for putting me here. It's something I can't find out on my own. I need to know this so I can sleep easier". I looked directly into his eyes, searching for truth.

He understood that it was one thing to be sentenced for breaking the law - you know you have a certain amount of time to serve. But it was quite another thing to be put here knowing that you had committed no crime, not knowing when you may be freed, and not knowing who was responsible for placing you in a situation where you could be killed at any time.

"You know who was responsible for putting me here, don't you", he said. "That same person is working for the DEA. You're in here; he is out there - what does that tell you? Chipita, Danilo's wife, is coming here this week; she will be staying at my ex-wife's house. I will find out what I can. I also have police sources who can give me information. It will take about two weeks for me to gather the information for you. I can tell you this right now: the word is that you are a free man, just be patient. This is Nicaragua - everything takes time. I will see you in two weeks. Until then, anything else I can help you with, let me know".

"Okay", I said. "Thank you. This means a great deal to me".

Norvyn turned and walked back to the throng of people who all wanted a few minutes of his time. I felt satisfied that, finally, I was going to find out who was responsible.

It was exactly four months to the day since my arrest. The prison was going to explode - there was a tension in the air. During the day people scaled the walls to steal clothes from the laundry lines, or anything that they could reach inside to take. Protecting your belongings from these bands of thieves became a daily necessity. The guards were indifferent to it. I think they were trying to embarrass Dr. Frech publicly in order to regain control over the prison. I didn't care what they did, as long as they left me alone. I was close to going home now. I had my special Sundays to look forward to. Between seeing Ivonne and hearing from Grant, I had all the encouragement I needed to stay positive and see this nightmare through.

Chapter Nine

"BITTER DISAPPOINTMENT"

Saturday was the usual noisy start to a typically boring weekend. The gallery was alive with the sounds of basketballs rebounding off the backboard, and a particularly raucous game of volleyball, where bets were being placed on the outcome. Damien and I turned the television up to try to drown out the noise but that was only a quick fix. Finally, we retreated to the church to escape the noise. We brought our dominoes with us to play the afternoon away. I was becoming a fair player; being taught by a master helped. He would still clean my clock. The best I could accomplish was to control my frustration and not quit. During the course of our play, our talk drifted to the huge downpour and lightning show we'd had the night before. At this time of year, this usually signalled the start of the winter season and the hordes of mosquitoes that came with it.

"What happens if a mosquito bites one of the fags across the way, then flies over here and bites one of us?" Damien wondered.

"Chances are, we would contract AIDS from those guys", I replied. "The problem with mosquitoes is that they can carry and distribute any of the diseases that are prevalent in here.

It's sort of like playing Russian Roulette - sooner or later, the gun goes off".

"Too bad we can't bubble wrap the entire cell", he said.

"Damien, we can hardly breathe as it is, even with an open window. What are we going to do when we put plastic it in?" I asked.

"I don't know. I just know, I'd take the worst prison back home and gladly trade places with someone there", Damien stated.

"The prisons in the States are better than here?" I asked.

"Shit, no comparison. You don't have to worry about some diseased mosquito going to come and kill you. The food you can at least eat. And back home, you know the exact day you're going to be released!" Damien looked down at the dominoes, selecting one of those in his hand. I countered, hoping that I would make him draw. When I finished my play, I looked up to see Norman coming into the church. He joined us and stood by, smoking a cigarette and watching our playing. Damien invited him to join in, but Norman declined, saying he'd only come to tell me that he had finished reading over my transcripts. Come over to his cell, he said, when I had a moment. I told him I'd be over after I finished my game, and he left us.

Damien beat me yet again, but I had done slightly better. We put the dominoes away and Damien returned to our cell to start supper while I went to Norman's to get my transcripts. Norman shared a cell with an inmate who was clean and willing to give up some of the available space for Norman to do his artwork. Norman fixed up a couple of those special coffees for us before getting down to business. When we were comfortably situated, he passed over the transcripts and said he had read them over thoroughly and had made some notes. We talked of the contents and I clarified some points for him, but he told me nothing more than I knew already - our appeal was expertly presented and the lawyers had put time and effort into the document.

I asked him if he would like to join us this evening to watch some television and partake of some English conversation.

Norman agreed, saying he needed to practice English. He arrived just in time for the evening news. There was unrest in the streets. University students ripped up the interlocking brick on a major thoroughfare and set up barricades to protest the rise in gasoline prices. Ironic really, when I considered hemp's potential role in this particular market. As it happened Nicaragua was 100 percent dependent on imports for its oil. The students were in solidarity with the bus owners, who were threatening to shut down public transportation. This was very serious. It would mean traffic would grind to a halt, both coming into the city and going out. The spokesperson for the transportation co-operatives was calling for a shutdown of all services by midnight.

Daniel Ortega (leader of the, now opposition, Sandinista party) the seized the moment to expound to the public. The cause of this great inconvenience, he said, was caused by the "thieving Liberals, who now won't let you go to work!" The trouble with that claim was that the people calling for this strike action were his people. If he truly cared for his people, he would order them back to work to keep the country running. The last thing this country needed was to have what trade and commerce they had left shut down. Politicians the World over are cut from the same cloth - I thought - they only use such moments to drum up support, rather than coming up with constructive methods of improvement.

The three of us had a mini forum after the newscast, discussing the events taking place. Damien's stance on this issue was one of disbelief - how had this demonstration of public anarchy been allowed to get so carried away? Where were the police? Why weren't the protestors arrested for destroying public property? Norman remained aloof; saying that events like this occurred a couple of times a year. If the police intervened now, before any violence erupted, then the government would be accused of heavy-handedness, an accusation the present government could ill-afford. The Somoza era was still fresh in the peoples' minds; the last thing they wanted was another dictator! It is no wonder that people all over the world are disenchanted by their political 'leaders' – the whole system lacks credibility.

My only worry about all this was how it was going to affect me. Ivonne depended on public transportation to come to the prison for visits. Without her support, I would have to rely on the food here for sustenance. That was not good; I had lost enough weight! I asked Norman, who grew up during the Somoza dictatorship, what life had been like here before the Revolution.

"Nicaragua was prosperous", he said. "The people had pride in their work. You could leave your things in your yard and no one would steal from you. The Aleman and Ortega families lived in the same neighbourhood; we all grew up together, knew each other. Daniel's sister and I had a child together".

"Then came the revolution. With it came the destruction of Nicaragua. I was a medical student before the revolution. At the beginning, I was in charge of security for the Sandinistas. We rounded up Somoza supporters and took them to Casa Cinquenta to be held until transport could be arranged to bring them here. Some of them were friends of my family. I couldn't stand by and watch this without doing something to help them, so I arranged to help them flee the country. I was found out and tried as a traitor. I thought that I would be shot, but my life was spared. I was sent here.

"While trying to escape from here, I was shot in the leg". He pulled his pant leg up to reveal an entry wound; the projectile was still embedded in his leg. Dropping his pant leg down, he rose and pointed at the television. "Daniel and I are no longer friends; we have gone our separate ways". He sighed.

He turned to me and asked, "Aren't we going to have a coffee and a cigarette before the movie starts?" Damien answered by putting the water on to boil while I retrieved the packet of cigarettes from the stash in my pillow. Each with a cigarette, we sat back and watched the movie.

In the morning, the newscasts showed pictures of buses lined up along the Caretera Masaya, not moving. The next day, the start of the workweek would be disrupted – Managua's traffic would be cut off. I knew that Ivonne would not be coming for our visit today. I could only hope that this strike wouldn't last long. The public unrest had escalated overnight and continued into the day. The police were called out and the battle lines were drawn. Skirmishes with the police developed all over the city. The reports came live to us over the television. We at the prison were not to be outdone. In the afternoon, the young offenders had broken out of Gallery Seven. They were armed with clubs and makeshift weaponry. From our vantage point, we could see them storming the yard and driving back the prison officials. They gained control of the Bar, smashing doors open and looting the commissary. On their way back out, they met with resistance. The riot patrol had arrived and now advanced on the young offenders.

The shout went out to prepare for tear gas. I soaked my shirt in the water bucket and told Damien to cover up any food that we wanted to keep from the gas. I thought how lucky I was that Ivonne hadn't come today. The worst of the riot was taking place in the exact spot where we'd sat under the lemon tree. Once we were prepared, we went over to the window to watch the action. Down below us, I could see a guard pointing out to the kids which window to rob. I couldn't believe it - here was a guard assisting in robbery! The roof of our gallery reverberated with the sounds of people running across it. Shots were fired; the gas filtered into the gallery. There was nowhere to go! This was the second time I was gassed and it was no better than the first. My eyes and throat burned something awful. I just have to get out of here soon, I thought, this is bullshit.

The following day, when the violence had died down, the Captain came to the gallery. I asked him about my Spanish courses. I got enough special privileges, he told me, and denied permission for the courses. I wondered how I would get over to Dr. Frech's office. He might have an open door policy, but to get to his door, you had to pass through several other doors, all manned by military personnel. Midweek, the Canadian Consul came to visit. They had been talking with our lawyers and reported that Talavera was indeed working hard. The amount of backlogged cases at the appeal court was staggering. I was case number 91 in 1999. The court could only hear twenty-four cases a month and that was only if the magistrates were all present. Talavera had managed to have my case moved from somewhere in the pile to the top of the pile. They told me to expect a resolution before the fifteenth of the month. That was only a week away!

Again I could feel that unmistakable feeling building in my gut - could it finally be over? I thanked them for coming with this fantastic news, adding that the next time I talked with them, it would be in their offices at the Consulate. I again reminded them that I was counting on them to have all the paperwork completed for Ivonne. Under no circumstances would I leave Ivonne behind.

At the end of the week I received a special visit from Ivonne. She was worried and wanted to make sure I was okay. Every day, the media reported the unrest in the prison and showed confiscated weapons and prisoners being beaten and gassed. She brought food with her; the transportation problems left her uncertain of when she could get back here again. She told me an appointment was set for the CAT scan during the next week, and her passport was ready. She confirmed that everything was ready for my release - next week, the lawyers were saying. We only had a ten-minute visit, but God willing, she would be back in two days for our scheduled Sunday visit. We said good-bye and I thanked her for coming under such chaotic conditions.

Later that night, I had another attack of stomach pain. I was anxious to have the problem dealt with. Whatever caused this much pain had to be stopped. It was frightening to know that for the next four or five hours I would be in excruciating pain. I was tough, I told myself; I would survive. That's how I dealt with the pain. The medication I was taking only dulled the rough edges, leaving me to deal with much of the pain mentally.

Sunday - finally, the day I was waiting for! Ivonne was on time. We sat in our favourite spot under the lemon tree and discussed our plans for our future together. We knew that it was only a matter of a few weeks before we would be together in Canada. She was full of questions about life in Canada. This would be her first trip out of the country, and what an adventure this would be for her! All this talk of a life of freedom made me thirsty. I asked Ivonne if she would like something to drink from the Bar, and she requested a rojita, or a cream soda. When I placed my order at the Bar, Marvin said he would have "the kid" bring the drinks to us. The kid brought our sodas and Ivonne, with her love of children, soon had him talking. His was a truly shocking story. This boy was only seven years old and was sentenced to ninety days in here! What a world we live in.

Saying good-bye was not as hard now that I was having visits with Ivonne almost twice a week. We joked: any more visits than that, and she might as well move in here. We both knew that the appeal decision was only a week or so away, and all of this would soon be over. But none of it could ever be forgotten. I tried phoning Canada later in the evening. The guards, as was usual, made me wait till they felt like coming to take me out to the phone. I let the phone ring until the message machine answered. I tried twice, both times reaching only the machine. It didn't disturb me too much because I knew that I would be going home soon. I told the officials on duty that I was finished and ready to be taken back to my cell.

At our next conjugal visit, Ivonne said she would be back the following morning to take me to the clinic for the CAT scan. What a relief that was. I'd needed this to be done last month, but better late than never I suppose.

In the morning, I was called out and met by two police officers who escorted me out of the prison and into a waiting taxi, a beat-up Lada. Ivonne sat in the passenger seat, while I was sandwiched in-between two policemen in the back. Apparently the journey was going to take some time. There is no such thing as a street address in Nicaragua. Your directions might read "one block south of the hospital, two blocks east, in front of the pool hall". To complicate matters, you are given a district, called a barrio to look in, only to find out that the pool hall isn't there anymore. Getting lost is easy and that is exactly what happened. The taxi driver, the policemen and Ivonne had no idea where the clinic was, so we drove around for a couple of hours. I didn't mind too much, it felt good to being out, seeing the City. But I could tell the policemen were getting annoyed, especially when our astute driver pulled a U-turn on a busy street, managing to get pulled over by the cops. The two sitting beside me had a little explaining to do in order to get us on our way without an incident. I watched to see if they didn't slip the other cop some money to look the other way. It is common practice here to give a little gratuity to your local constabulary to keep you on the road.

We finally found the address we were looking for and walked into an ultramodern facility. It was like stepping through the doorway from one world and into another. I didn't have to wait long. I had the impression that having us in the waiting room wasn't good for business. I was told to lie on the examination table while they performed the scan. It didn't take long to find the problem; I had gallstones and needed to have my gall bladder removed. I asked the technician if she had a photocopier here in the clinic. I needed to have copies of the diagnosis made for the prison hospital, the Canadian Consul, and for myself. She gladly obliged, and then we were on our way back to Tipitapa. The police did not allow Ivonne and I any time to converse privately, so we parted, both thinking that the next time we saw each other, I would be free!

The next day, Norvyn Meneses came to the gallery with the church group. On his way out he took me aside and said he had information for me. The word was that someone had gone to the police with damaging information that the crop was marijuana! He believed that someone to be Danilo Blandon, after being pressured by the Americans to do their bidding. After all, he was controlled by the DEA and their highly politicised (and internationally illegal) directive on Cannabis is one of non-distinction within the species. It was a US conspiracy, which involved someone I considered a friend and who was himself a partner in Hemp-Agro! What the hell did the yanks have on Blandon to make him do this!?

Meneses also said that I was as good as free. The Appeal Tribunal was to make a decision today, and my release would be announced. Norvyn gave me his business card and said that if I needed any help when I got out, not to hesitate to call. I thanked him for his help. I told Damien that I was going out, that the appeal court was to make their decision today. This time I knew I was going home for sure because everyone else believed that it was truly over. I was excited at the prospect of freedom! I could hardly contain myself and began to pack away my personal effects so when they called my name, I would be ready.

I lay on my bed, thinking over what Norvyn had said to me. He assumed that it was Danilo who went to the police, but that didn't make any sense to me. I knew Danilo; he was my friend and associate. He had nothing to gain from this. He, like all of us, had everything to lose. No, it was definitely not him. He loved this project, he realised that a better future for his country was through the project. He believed, like me, that we had the ability to change the course of agricultural history and bring prosperity to this nation through the development and industrialisation of hemp. Danilo was a Liberal supporter and was friends with many top-ranking Liberals who had supported our project and understood what we were trying to accomplish. They had given us written authorisation to work on the project in this country. I didn't believe he was the one who had gone to the police. Although he may have been guilty of gross stupidity when it came to his understanding of DEA policy regarding Cannabis cultivation and he was apparently – for whatever reason – in their pocket. Shit!

I believed our disgruntled employee, Jorge Vega, feeling jilted, had gone to the police. All the pieces were fitting together. His family had close ties with the Sandinistas, who seized the opportunity to once again scandalise the Liberal government. He had once bragged to me that he had family members working at Interpol. But there was still the question of the DEA. They had clearly been protecting Danilo by ordering him out of the country at Christmas time. It would have resulted in bad publicity, perhaps even a scandal if one of the their operatives were involved. Did they orchestrate the whole affair? They would have known that 15 tons of Hemp seed had been imported here from China. After all, the seeds were checked and cleared by US customs in California. Could they have set this up 'to bust' from the offset using Blandon for information on the project's development?

I recalled my meeting with the DEA "translators". One of them, a guy called Joe Petrauska, was also Blandon's "case handler". He knew about the hemp project but he also made clear that this was a "Nicaraguan decision". In his view, the DEA had nothing to do with it. The Nicaraguan government, in following international law on the issue, decided it was legal – they had granted us the required permits and licenses, all from the top levels of the relevant government ministries.

It was the US Ambassador, Lino Gutierrez, who had instructed the company not to go public following Hurricane Mitch. Perhaps he thought that all the industrialists and farmers campaigning for hemp cultivation in the United States would be pissed to discover there was a successful hemp project in Nicaragua being funded by Canadians! Or perhaps it's just more of the same bullshit. The "war on drugs": consistently used to undermine the legitimate hemp industry in North America and to increase US arms sales in Latin America.

I couldn't dwell too much on it. It would only drive me crazy. After all, I told myself, I will be free soon, and then I'll have all the time in the world to think about these things!

The only thing I liked about weekends was that I got to see Ivonne and I got to talk to Grant. I lived for Sundays, and this Sunday I was really looking forward to speaking with Grant.

When Sunday rolled around, the visit with Ivonne was great. We both knew that our ordeal was over. Now it was a time to rejoice; now we could get on with our lives. My call to Grant was filled with both happiness and relief. Grant said, "Pack your bags. The three magistrates have signed off on the appeal and you're coming home". That was music to my ears – freedom at last! He told me that the tickets for Ivonne and I were waiting for us at the airport. We had definitely won the court decision.

I continued with my exercise program to keep my mind occupied and my stress level low. I had my laundry done, and I planned on giving Damien everything in the cell. I would be ready to go when they called. Maybe it was from the stress of waiting - I had another stomach attack that again lasted into the night. By this time, the medic had convinced the prison officials that it would be wise to leave my cell door open so I could get up and walk the gallery if I had an attack. I was administering my own injections; that way, I didn't have to disturb anyone in the middle of the night. The fly season had arrived and the garbage dump outside my window was one big breeding ground. It was so bad that I could not write in my cell or, for that matter, remain in my cell during the day. There were hundreds of them; the ceiling was black with them. The prison had a remedy for this though.

Unfortunately, we were not warned when they came and sprayed. Men in protective suits sprayed a thick cloud of pesticide that choked off any available oxygen. I ran into the church to get away from the chemicals, but it was no use - they came in there too. It was horrifying, being gassed like that - they didn't have the common decency or intelligence to take us out of there beforehand. We had to throw out any food and water that had been left out during the onslaught, which really hurt. Since I was going home, I wasn't going to receive any more barco.

By the following Sunday, I was getting apprehensive. Why wasn't I going home? When I talked to Grant, he was just as mystified. Talavera was supposed to bring my release papers to the prison. What could have gone wrong now? Grant promised to get to the bottom of this, and told me not to worry. The problem was, I was getting that let down feeling again.

That night I was in severe pain. I think the added stress wasn't helping my medical condition - instead of occurring monthly, the attacks were coming weekly and yet another month was drawing to a close. I could feel my hopes of freedom being shattered once again. The lawyers didn't have the decency to come and explain to me what was going on, the lying bastards!

Ivonne missed the conjugal visit, which only added to my developing depression. Her missing a conjugal visit meant that she was having problems, most likely financial ones. This month the scheduled visits came back-to-back, so the very next day Ivonne made it to the gallery visit. She could tell I was tired and unhappy. It was becoming increasingly clear that it was all bullshit, there was not going to be any freedom. I asked her to phone the Canadian Consul to find out why I was still here. Ivonne said she'd do whatever it took to get me released and told me she'd arrange a special visit to bring me whatever news she could gather. I was certainly glad of Ivonne's visit. Between the two of us, we would fight it out; we were determined to win. They could not beat us no matter what they did to me. I felt that beautiful feeling of hatred again. I began to unpack all of my personal effects under the watchful eye of Damien.

"What are you doing that for? I thought you were going home", He said.

"I'm not going anywhere".

"You receive bad news from Ivonne today?" he asked.

"No, not from her. I just know that I'm not going home. Those lying lawyers aren't finished milking me, I guess", I said.

"They will never let you go free. It's cheaper for them to keep you here".

Damien might be right, I thought. They might not let me go.

The next month started with a bang. I had another gallbladder attack. I had to address the problem soon, but my prospects of having the operation done at home in Canada were slim. I adopted a "wait and see" attitude: I'd believe I was being released when I was actually released, and not a second before. I was tired of having my hopes built up, only to be let down - talk about an emotional roller coaster! That didn't mean I'd given up, only that I took everything they told me with a grain of salt, neither believing nor disbelieving. The only time I would truly believe that I was going home was when I walked out the door and into the world beyond.

The next day, Dr. Frech was on the newscasts proclaiming that some prison officials would be replaced. Among those he named were Commandant Molina and Freddy. I was sorry to see Freddy go, but his alliance with Molina made him a casualty. Molina's replacement was Captain Marcia, the same woman who had talked bad about me to the Narco Jet guys. She would be no help to me; it was a good thing I had Dr. Frech on my side or I would be in trouble around here.

At the end of the first week of June, an article in the La Prenza newspaper had announced that the plants were growing again at the Sabana Grande research site. Officials were collecting more samples to be sent to El Salvador for testing for THC content before the site was burned again. A true show of survival from the most useful plant on Earth - I thought, they won't beat hemp either! This also indicated to me that the case against us was very weak. They were grasping at anything to justify their outlandish charges. They just could not accept the fact that they were wrong and somebody had to claim responsibility for the mistakes that were made. The downside to this was that I would be here until the tests were completed and decisions were made. No one could tell how long that would take!

On Sunday, Ivonne came early for our special time together. We knew the duty officer so he allowed us out in the yard for a six-hour visit, our longest visit together yet. Our Sunday visit was the focal point for me - I lived from Sunday to Sunday. Ivonne was positive that somehow I would be free soon, and it was this positive feeling that kept my spirits high. It was always nice to see her smiling face, a reminder of the life I once knew. In here, nobody smiled. There was absolutely nothing here to be happy about. We walked together over to the concession stand to buy soft drinks and cookies to munch on. She told me her mother was concerned for my safety when I am released, but I would be welcome in her home. We walked hand in hand back to our bench under the lemon tree. It was idyllic; the warm tropical breeze blew gently, caressing our faces with cool relief from the searing sun. I wished these moments could be frozen in time. All I wanted to do was keep walking, right through these gates! But I would have to be satisfied with a few hours of togetherness.

"The medication has run out", I told her. "I used the last of it on Tuesday. The pain was so intense that, besides the injection, I borrowed a pain pill from one of the guys. I'm afraid I will have to get operated on here".

"I will talk to Norman and ask if he can recommend a stronger medication", Ivonne said.

"Find a place where they do laser surgery. Marion Chamorrow had the same surgery done; she will know where to go and how much it will cost". I explained to Ivonne what I thought would be the best type of medical surgery. I would never forget that my best friend Sergio had died in their care. He'd had a bleeding ulcer; when the doctor arrived, he'd administered blood into his system too fast and exploded his heart. If I was going to undergo surgery here, I wanted to be sure that I'd be in competent hands. The six hours together seemed like moments. Before we knew it, the official came to let us know that our time was up - I had to be back in the gallery before count. We said our good-byes and Ivonne promised to be back for visit day.

Back in the gallery, I settled into my routine until Norman showed me the La Tribunal newspaper. It contained an interview with Jorge Vega. Jorge told the reporter that I'd sold cocaine to keep Hemp-Agro going through some difficult financial times. I just about fell over. This was all I needed right now! The lying bastard! But in this country, all that was needed was supposition in order to detain someone. I looked over at Norman and inquired, "Does this mean I could be charged for this?"

"No. It is only one man's word over another's. Am I correct in saying that no proof exists that this is true?" asked Norman.

"Yes".

"Well then, you have nothing to worry about. This is nothing but hearsay. It appears that you have an enemy. Do you know this man?"

"Yes, he used to work with me, until he was let go. He felt jilted over six hundred dollars that he thought was owed to him after his separation from the corporation. I believe that many of our problems stemmed from that man. He started something that he soon lost control of; his lies to the authorities were convincing enough that someone of importance actually believed him! At the lawyer's office in Granada there's a false document, a labour agreement between Hemp-Agro and this Jorge Vega that had my signature forged at the bottom. He tried litigating me in an attempt to extract money from the company; when that didn't work, he set his focus upon the company. This, I believe, is his last-ditch attempt to keep me here. He must fear reprisals when this case is resolved and I'm released".

Norman was listening intently, evaluating the legal aspects of what I said. "You know the group of ladies that come to the gallery?" he asked.

"Yes, the lawyer Lisa Smith (not her real name, obviously) and her team of professionals".

"Well, you need to talk to her", said Norman. "I know her. She used to be a magistrate but found private practice more lucrative, especially with her connections. I have an appointment tomorrow to see her. When she comes here, I will tell her to see you for a moment".

"I have lawyers already", I countered. "I can't see that having another one is going to help any".

"Look, your lawyers have lied to you. They don't even visit you to let you know what is going on! You need someone out there to work for you", he stated.

"Okay, set up the appointment with her. Maybe she can go to the court of appeal and find out for me how far my case has progressed".

I left Norman to walk the gallery and think. What he'd said about this woman lawyer was true. She was good; she'd gotten one of the Colombians out of here. She was also the German's lawyer. All were major cases. She was diligent - a trait I respected here, because it was uncommon to find a lawyer who didn't just take your money, but worked for it!

The next day Smith and her team came to the gallery for interviews with clients. There seemed to be no shortage of them. Norman and I waited in the church to be called. Norman went in first to present his case. After he had finished, he summoned me and made introductions. She was acquainted with my case, she told Norman, but wanted to know how she could help. Norman was invaluable to me; he not only knew her but also helped with translation. Spanish legal terms were difficult for me and I didn't want any mistakes in the translation. I explained to her that the appellant tribunal had supposedly signed off on my case, but I was still here. I needed her to find out the real status of my case. At Norman's urging, I explained to her about the Jorge Vega affair. She told me she could get in touch with the lawyer in Granada if she needed to, but first she wanted to find out what had been done on my case.

I then told her of my medical condition, and that I needed to have an operation - could I be allowed to convalesce at the home of Ivonne's family in Granada? She said that she could look into it. With that, the interview was over and I was dismissed. Norman stayed behind to talk further with her and her staff; I think he was probably making a play for the buxom stenographer, who had been making eye contact with him throughout my interview. Good for him; that was something that could occupy his mind for a while. For me, it was back to my prison routine - waiting for the next Sunday!

Sunday transformed me into a happy man once again. The visit with Ivonne was, as always, a highlight, as was my call to Grant. It was nice to hear what was going on back in Canada; it made me feel like there was something there for me when I returned. When you are suddenly faced with deprivation, it becomes necessary to have something to look forward to. I think religion in the prison served the same purpose, combating the hours of hopelessness. In the face of adversity you need strength of character, great resolve, and determination. You understand who you are, for better or worse.

My evening call to Grant was an important one - after all, I should have been free. It was time to get to the bottom of this and find some truths. Grant was incredulous that this could be happening. The information being directed to him was conflicting and misleading. The truth lay here, with the lawyers and the appeal court. Grant believed that the three magistrates signed the document but did not submit the finished document, possibly due to the damaging newspaper article in La Tribunal. I suggested some action be taken against Jorge Vega to show the public the damage he'd caused with his slanderous lies. I neglected to tell Grant about the meeting I had with Lisa Smith. I would wait until I had the facts to present to Grant. I told him I would phone again next week; with any luck we would have positive news.

A week passed uneventfully. I spent my time carrying water to my cell, exercising, reading, and of course, writing in Spanish. My Spanish vocabulary had improved considerably, but I feared it would grow no further. Chavarria, the man with the dictionary, had been released, and his dictionary went with him. There was still no running water. I was surprised that there had not been any fistfights down at the water tap. I think this was due to the fact that everyone was resigned that the water problem would never be fixed. The human being is such an adaptable animal; all the grumbling concerning the water issue had been forgotten; the situation was now accepted.

Dr. Frech had not been at the prison since the rioting. He was in Miami, supposedly because of health problems. This was worrisome to me; my authorisation ran out at the end of the month, and I knew getting a renewal would be difficult without Dr. Frech. I petitioned the gallery Consejo, but since Chepe had left, the job had fallen to people with lesser administrative skills. I could only hope Dr. Frech would be back in time to reissue the permission. Without my special Sundays, time would slow to a crawl!

Ivonne and I had no new news to exchange during our next visit. We were on hold, waiting on the lawyer Lisa Smith for information on my promised release. My phone call to Canada was also uneventful. I guess no news is good news. The next day I was called out to the visit room along with a German national who was charged with counterfeiting American Visas. He had retained Lisa Smith as his legal counsel. Another prisoner, a Colombian national who also had her as counsel, joined us. The three of us stood talking while Lisa Smith and her assistants talked with the other inmates. She really had something going on in here. One after another, prisoners came to see her, all putting their faith in this woman to perform a miracle. We three were the last to be addressed. First she explained the situation to the German; he would be going to trial by jury that week.

Next she told me that she had gone to the court of appeal to learn that there were no signatures on any document, because they had not heard my case! Just as I suspected, we were being lied to - I was no closer to going out than I'd been last Christmas. She said that getting me out on a medical leave to have an operation was an option. I would then have to go to the Atlantic coast to be flown back to Canada. The Colombian was a pilot; he could fly me in his Lear-jet to Montreal. I looked from the lawyer to the Colombian, realising that they were indeed serious. I told her I would have to think about it; Ivonne would inform her who to contact in Canada to arrange the financing.

Leaving this meeting, I had much to think about. Was I being set up to take a long prison sentence? That I'd been lied to made me instantly aware that there was more to this than was apparent. Was I being dealt away by my lawyers? Could I afford to take a chance on believing my lawyers when they'd lied to me so often? Smith provided me with an alternate solution - granted, it came with a high degree of danger, but so did staying here for the next thirty years!

On the 23rd of June, I'd been in Tipitapa six months. Damien's television broke down that day, which was a serious blow to our independence. We were used to watching our own television programs when we wanted. Having the television repaired would be no easy feat. Getting the television out of the prison, repaired, and then returned to the prison all required separate authorisations to accomplish. It was much easier to buy a new television - that required only one authorisation.

The last Sunday of the month was also the last date on my visit authorisation and I was worried that they still had not issued a new one; the rumours around the prison were that Dr. Frech was not coming back. At our visit, I told Ivonne to go and ask Captain Marcia for an extension on our authorisation. Perhaps a woman-to-woman chat would accomplish the task. My call to Grant was a little difficult because I had to assume that the call was being monitored. I had to watch what I said. I related to him my displeasure with our lawyers. I now knew that the Court of Appeal had not even heard our case, let alone signed off on it, and since the lawyers had lied, they could not be trusted. They did not even bother to come to the prison to talk with me, to keep me current concerning the criminal proceedings. I was facing serious time here. I deserved the right to be informed.

I then told him about my talks with Lisa Smith, and that Ivonne would be in touch with him to discuss details. I could only describe to him part of our conversation, for any leak would put our plan in peril. I told Grant of her ability to accomplish what she said, that she could get me out to have my operation. I also explained that she had a proven track record around here, that the Colombians were using her as legal counsel. It was time to change lawyers.

I received barco from Ivonne just in time; she had an uncanny ability to know when I was getting low on supplies. Wrapped in plastic amongst all the supplies, she had enclosed letters for me to read. She had talked to Grant and Danilo. They said the magistrates needed more information from the United States Custom officials who had inspected the seeds while the ship was docked in Long Beach, California. Those documents distinguished the cargo as hemp seed, allowing the cargo to proceed to Puerto Quetzal, Guatemala. This request was the final one that would win the case for us. This sounded good, albeit absurd – the yanks can apparently distinguish hemp and marijuana seed; a much harder task than differentiating the grown plants themselves! At least it was more positive; I felt that I was getting a little closer to the front door.

I continued reading through the letters. Ivonne had seen Captain Marcia to request a special visit for today. She was told flat-out that there would be no special visits for me, and that included Sunday visits. The only visits I could have were the gallery visits. That pissed me off. I knew she didn't like me and that I could expect nothing from her, but perhaps Captain Roche could intervene on my behalf. This was Friday afternoon - I was out of luck till he returned Monday morning. The weekend was going to be terrible, stuck in here. Damien and I would wear the dots off the dominoes.

On Monday the Canadian Consul came by for a visit. I told them I'd been unable to get my authorisation for visits and phone calls on Sundays reinstated and asked if they could talk to the prison authorities on my behalf. They had come to ask me when I wanted to have surgery performed. The sooner the better, I told Marion. I suggested she phone Grant to arrange the financing. I did not volunteer the information that I had been talking with Lisa Smith. I didn't want anyone to know about those negotiations. I didn't like the idea of skipping the country. I felt that would be an admission of guilt, and would prefer to win the case on its own merits. I was innocent, damn it! The flip side of the coin, though, was whether I could trust that I'd get a fair trial. I had to make a decision: do I try and run, or do I stay? I sensed that this decision would have to be made soon.

As always, Marion brought books. This time they were mystery books and, as always, much appreciated. Whenever I saw her digging out books, I knew our interview was over, so I stood and thanked her for coming. I watched as she and her driver made their way to the front gate, then turned and headed for the gallery. I went directly to my cell to put away my books before going to the Consejo's office to find Captain Roche and see what he would do to help me with my Sunday visit. He invited me in immediately and I stood before him to present my case.

He listened, taking in what I said before slapping the old, decrepit desk and saying, "No problem, of course you can have them. I will sign the authorisation and take it over to administration to be ratified".

"When?" I asked.

"Three days, and it will be here in the office".

"Thank you". I turned to the door.

"Just a minute", he said. "This week we are changing people's cells, so expect to be moved later in the week".

"All right. That's fine with me, just as long as I get my Sunday visit with Ivonne", I said with a smile. He returned a weak smile. I closed the door behind me and strode through the office, not stopping to talk to all the gossipmongers who hung out around the office.

I wanted to be alone in my cell to compose some prose for Ivonne. I was feeling philosophical as I looked out the window at the mountains on the distant horizon. The beautiful sight drew me closer to the woman I loved and to a nation I had adopted. The words flowed from my pen hand as I wrote. What is there in life besides the person one adores and the life one can build with that person?

The sky had darkened and I could tell we were in for a storm. I thought I'd better put dinner on before we lost our power. During the winter, every day around four in the afternoon, there was rain. Judging by the looks of this sky, we were in for a lightning storm. Sure enough, just after Damien and I finished our supper the thunder and lightning came, first with a crack followed with a zigzag streak that threatened to tear the fabric of the sky. It was impressive. We both stood at the window watching the spectacle until one last lightning strike left us without power. We were now limited in what we could do. Luckily, we had candles. I suggested to Damien that we play some dominoes. I was getting better now; I could hold my own and in fact, the tables were turning - it was Damien who was getting frustrated. When they couldn't get the auxiliary generator going, they came and locked us down, just in case any of us decided to walk off.

I told Damien what Captain Roche had said about moving at the end of the week.

"I hope they don't split us up", he said. "That would be

the shits. I don't want to share a cell with someone I don't know".

"Well, I don't think so, but around here, you never know. Whatever you think is logical, expect the opposite. I even heard that they're thinking about putting three people in a cell", I said.

"Shit, ain't that 'bout a mother fucker. Where the fuck could we put another man in here?" demanded Damien.

"I'm glad that I'll be walking out that door soon".

"Don't count your chickens before they're hatched. You're liable to be here for a long time more". Damien scrambled up the dominoes and selected seven pieces.

We played until the candle burned out and decided to call it a night. Lying in my bed listening to the frogs croaking, I transported my mind to another place and another time, closed my eyes, and drifted off.

True to his word, Roche posted the names of the inmates who would change cells on the bulletin board. Damien and I were moved to cell thirty-seven, about halfway down the gallery. We didn't like it, but at least we were still together. The move was scheduled for Friday. In two more days we would be living in a new cell. Damien suggested we go and have a look at it. We asked the current occupants if we could look around the cell that would be our new home. In the bathroom we found handprints - it looked like someone had slit their wrists in the shower! There were pictures pencilled on the walls in the 'living area' - drawings of ugly naked women, the kind of artwork commonly seen on shithouse walls accompanied by phone numbers for blow jobs. It didn't take us long to get out of there.

Out in the gallery, we looked at each other. One look said it all.

"This is terrible", I said. "I don't think twenty coats of paint is going to help that cell".

"They definitely don't like us gringos", Damien said.

"Lets go find Captain Roche and see if we can get a different cell. That one is not going to work; it looks like somebody died in there". I pointed over my shoulder at the cell we had just left.

We found Captain Roche in his favourite spot, sitting behind his old beat-up desk, signing authorisations. He invited us in and asked us what we wanted. When we told him we weren't happy about the move and wanted another cell, he just looked at us and said that was not his worry; the gallery Consejo made all the cell changes. He'd side-stepped that issue; I knew we were shit out of luck and stuck with the change. I asked him if he had heard about my authorisation, if my Sunday visits were reinstated. He fished through the papers on his desk until he came up with one that had my name on it. Passing it over to me, he said, "I am sorry, but you have been denied your Sunday visit. But you have the authorisation for your call to Canada in the evening".

"Thanks". I spun around with the refusal in my hand and left the room before I blew my top. Once I was out of earshot of the rats that hung around the office, I let out a string of profanities. Now they were taking away the only day that I had to look forward to. Please, I thought, let it be true that I'm going home!

On Friday morning I was called to go to the prison infirmary - the doctor wanted to see me. This doctor was remarkably young; he reminded me of a Doogie Howser.

"How are you?" he asked pleasantly. "What brings you here today?"

"Listen, you fuckin' asshole, you're the one who wanted to see me". I felt like telling him to go piss in a bedpan and let me go back to the gallery.

Digging through his files, he pulled mine out and began to read it. Several people barged into the room to ask him mundane questions while he read, but he finally looked up and told me that I needed to change my medication to something stronger. I agreed; the injections I was taking didn't do much for the pain. He wrote out a prescription and told me to watch my diet.

Hot tip, Sherlock, I thought - he should eat this food and watch what crawls around his plate!

Back at the gallery, I had to pack everything up to move.

When you move cells you have to move everything: laundry lines, electrical lines, even the tape used to suspend things from the wall. The hardest part wasn't the move itself - there isn't much to move from a five by ten cell - but cleaning the shit-hole we had to move into was a task and a half. Damien got back from teaching early to give me a hand in putting the final touches on home sweet home. I spent that first night in a strange cell tossing and turning, trying to escape the buzzing of the mosquitoes. I knew Damien was having an equally bad time of it because I could hear him swearing at the mosquitoes. In the morning Damien awoke to find he was one massive mosquito bite. This was a nightmare month for insects - flies by day and mosquitoes by night, and not just a few; there were hordes of them.

The weekend was starting, and our cell was situated right next to the volleyball court. We'd have to find a place to go to get away from the noise. Perhaps I could do some letter writing down in the church, I thought. Damien liked to watch cartoons on Saturday morning and went to the cell of a friend with a television. After we had finished up breakfast, I heard my name being called. I wasn't expecting any visits so I wasn't going to hurry. Two off-duty policemen came to my cell door and told me to come with them. I asked them where they were taking me. Outside, they replied. My mind was scrambling; what was this? The only reason I could think of was that they were here to escort me to the hospital - perhaps it was time for my operation. I began to pack some toiletries, but one of the policemen said not to bother, just come with them. Now I really didn't know what this was all about.

They led me beyond the prison walls and into the open arms of José Talavera. He clapped me on the back, laughed and invited me into his Land Cruiser. I was still bewildered as I climbed into the back seat between the two policemen. A woman sat in the front seat reading a fashion magazine; I assumed she was Talavera's wife. She was in her forties and very pretty. I didn't inquire where we were going; I just sat back and enjoyed the ride. The tinted windows allowed easy viewing while filtering the harsh sunlight. The air-conditioner provided cool comfort from the sticky heat, and the seats, covered in soft leather upholstery, were very comfortable. I was quite content. I only hoped that José would keep driving all the way to Canada! José pulled up at the first cantina beside the road and everyone climbed out. We entered the open-air rancho, selected a table, and sat down to wait for someone to serve us. José, digging in his pockets for coins, asked what music I would like to hear. I told him I had no preference. He nodded and walked over to the jukebox. Soon he had a Country ballad playing - fitting for the surroundings we found ourselves in.

The waiter arrived with the menus and wanted to take our drink order. José asked if I wanted a beer or a bottle of rum, which started an argument with the police. They didn't think I should be drinking. José countered by threatening to phone their superiors. That dispelled any further arguments. They reluctantly backed down, looking at each other sullenly, like beaten dogs. They settled back into their chairs. After all, José revealed, this was a victory celebration! He explained to me that a little later, we would see a lawyer who could translate for him. For now, I was to relax, knowing that we had won the case. The beers tasted good. It had been a long time since I'd had such a pleasant meal. When I climbed back into the Land Cruiser, I felt a little closer to freedom.

We arrived at the house of the lawyer who would translate what José had not already explained to me. This lawyer worked at the United States Embassy, in what capacity was not made clear to me, but his expertise lay in international law. He explained that the Court of Appeal was waiting for the Long Beach documents. When they received them, they would rule in our favour. After all, if the American authorities inspected the cargo and took samples of the seed when the ship was docked at their port, the Americans knew that this was hemp seed stock. Otherwise, the shipment would have been detained and not been allowed to proceed to Nicaragua. This would clearly exonerate us from any wrongdoing.

I asked how long I would have to remain in prison. I had been living this emotional nightmare day to day; I needed to know for sure when I was going to be released. José said that it would be in a month; at the end of the month they would make a public announcement. I could feel that old feeling of hope awaken once again. This time it just had to be true!

The ride back to the prison was one I didn't relish. After that little taste of freedom, this was the last thing I wanted. I knew that it was for just a short time, though. The next day was Sunday, and I wouldn't be getting a visit from Ivonne. That bummed me out. I had so much to tell her. This ordeal was almost over; soon we could start putting our life back in order. Damien was happy for me, but he was sceptical. He had seen so many empty promises of freedom that, to him, this was just another one. I had to agree with him, but in my mind, I just knew I was going home. Everyone felt that I would be going home. We'd won this case due process, and it would violate international law to detain me any longer. Not that the whole episode wasn't a gross violation of international law in the first place. Those responsible will pay, I reminded myself – you can run from justice, buy politicians but you cannot hide from the truth: sooner or later.

At least I still had my call to Canada. Grant confirmed what Talavera had said the previous day - we were waiting for the documents to arrive in Nicaragua. I left the telephone convinced that these were to be my final days of incarceration; Ivonne and I would soon be returning to Canada.

In the middle of the week I felt sick. There was a dengue outbreak in the prison, but for now it was contained in other areas of the prison. I thought my symptoms were nothing more than a common cold caused by the continual dampness. By Friday the fever had broken, but left me with aching teeth. Norman gave me something to apply that soothed the pain, making eating possible once again. For some reason, I felt violent. I wanted to lash out at anybody that came around. Perhaps it was because of my aching teeth, or just wanting this over with - or a combination of the two.

I was antsy, tired of being cooped up. I decided to go talk to Norman. He always had something interesting to say. I wanted to run an idea by him, to see if I was taking the right direction. I planned to have an interview with the La Prenza newspaper to explain to the Nicaraguan people what Hemp-Agro was all about. It would have nothing to do with the criminal proceedings. I would talk about the nuts and bolts of what we were doing here as a corporation, what we were trying to accomplish, our aims and objectives. When I explained this to Norman he said, "I think it is extremely important that you tell your side of the story, you have been slandered by the press since your arrest. I think that it is a good idea! Can Ivonne go to the newspaper and have them send a reporter out here to the prison?"

"Yes, as soon as I can get word to her", I said.

"Tonight is a good time to use the phone. They're going to allow anyone who wants to call home to use the phone after count, because this weekend marks the twentieth anniversary of the Revolution".

"So that means this is a long weekend".

"Right, the Sandinistas will be partying all weekend. Everything will be closed till Tuesday. Tomorrow evening the Sandinistas in here are going to have a party to commemorate the day they seized control", Norman said.

I excused myself and went looking for the Consejo to have my name added to the phone call list. I had to tell Ivonne what she must do. If I could have the newspaper article coincide with my release, the impact would drive home the point that Hemp-Agro was the innocent victim of a political campaign to scandalise the government, unwittingly or otherwise implemented by the DEA via incompetence and the unlawful Federal directives they were following. The Consejo added my name and told me to come down to the office right after count.

I made a beeline there right after count and, surprisingly, we were taken out to the phone immediately. My luck held. I reached Ivonne. I explained as much as I could about my current status in five minutes. She'd been following events as well; she had been in constant communication with Grant and Danilo. I told her of my plan to go public with the truth, to reveal the side of the story the public had never heard. She promised that the day after the long weekend, she would go to the editor of the La Prenza and tell him that I wanted an interview. She would bring good news with her on the next visit day, she told me, and added an admonishment to stay safe; we would be together soon. Hanging up the phone, I felt confident that she was right - we would be together soon!

The next day was Saturday, the beginning of the long weekend in celebration of the Revolution. The television aired footage from the war years and broadcast coverage of parades from around the country and entertainment that played on into the night. It was a carnival atmosphere and the inmates in the prison were not to be outdone. The Sandinistas were preparing a fiesta in the gallery. They obtained special permission from Captain Roche to bring in streamers and posters, assorted baked goods, fresh juices and sodas to drink. During the day they set about adorning the walls of the gallery with posters proclaiming the revolutionary slogans.

One look from Damien said it all. We retreated back to our own domain to wait out the storm. We knew that tonight was going to get loud, and it would most likely last until Monday. We would have to subsist, paying dominoes, reading and writing for the weekend. That evening, after count was taken, they started playing old revolutionary songs, which drew the Sandinista supporters to the banquet area. Some of the guys were old enough to have participated in the war - men like Captain Carillo Hernandez, who were trained military men. Others were the idealists, the revolutionaries, the freedom fighters, and still others present were too young to recall the rigors of war but old enough to know of its impact.

I was lying on my bed reading when one of the organisers of the fiesta came and invited me to join them. I accepted graciously; I knew how important this day was to these people. There were many old memories that needed to be remembered. For me, it was like going back in time, reliving the past with those who had lost much. In war there are no winners; everyone is touched by loss. I was deeply moved that they would include me, an outsider, to participate in these sombre moments. I listened to speaker after speaker recounting their personal tales of the day when the airport was seized and they had Somoza on the run. The most moving tales were the ones told by the idealists. One such narration was delivered by Norman Cuadra who spoke of men like the fundamentalist Carlos Fonseca - of how ideas can be transformed into reality and of the ultimate cost of that transformation.

There was a benediction given commemorating the loved ones lost, followed by a moment of silence. This was not what I had expected at all; this was not the party event that I'd thought it would be. Rather, it left everyone a little more humble. Me - an outsider, walked away with a different perspective. When one is a revolutionary, it is not merely a matter of belief, but also a matter of how the public perceives you. To many people, a revolutionary is a romantic character, a person who believes in a vision of the future and is willing to risk his or her life for it - but that is only the public perception.

I waited for visit day to see how Ivonne had made out with the newspaper. I was anxious to have this interview; the time was well overdue for the public to know the truth. Someone must be held accountable for this shit awful mess – my incarceration the demise of the corporation, and the impact this had had on the people of Nicaragua, who I believed had lost the most. All eyes were on Ivonne when she walked into the visit hall. Dressed in a black and white pantsuit, she was stunningly beautiful. Her radiant smile sent chills through me. When Ivonne is happy, nothing bothers me. Her smile is so disarming it's lethal, and today, she was deadly!

She had been to the La Prenza newspaper and they had expressed interest in doing a feature story, but first they wanted to confirm with the appeal court. She also had good news from Canada and the Canadian Consul: my release would come at the end of the month. We were extremely happy. We agreed that this should be our last visit; Ivonne would never have to come here again.

My teeth were still giving me problems. Thanks to Norman and his cotton swabs, the pain was kept to a dull ache, but by the end of the week I needed to see the prison dentist to fill a hole in one of my molars. I was taken to the hospital to see her Friday afternoon.

The dentist took one look and said, "I will have to extract the tooth".

"No, you won't", I said. "I am about to be released. I need something temporary, just to make it back to Canada". I wasn't going to settle for anything else. I had heard nothing but horror stories about this woman, which included pulling the wrong tooth.

"See that cement?" I said, pointing to a jar of white cement that was standing on the counter. "Just fill the hole with that!"

"That tooth of yours needs to be extracted. I don't want you back in here next week, complaining of a sore tooth".

"I promise I will never come back here again", I replied.

I was thankful to get out of there with all my teeth; that girl had a tooth fetish.

On Sunday my call to Grant confirmed that the documents had arrived here in Nicaragua. I was to be released later in the week. Grant said that they'd run out of excuses. It was time for them to let me go. The next week was agonising. Every day, my eyes were glued to the television news reports as I waited for the announcement of my release, but none came.

Chapter Ten

"STALL TACTICS"

AUGUST STARTED OFF badly. The thought of freedom was in my mind every waking moment; it was driving me crazy. The fact I was receiving no news of my status was not helping. I stepped up my exercise program; that always helped to relieve the stress. My writing stopped. I just couldn't put anything positive down on paper. All I had was my exercise and the thought of Ivonne's visits to keep my sanity intact.

It helped having Norman around. He and I talked of philosophy and pyramid power. Norman was a master of both the construction and the esoteric qualities the pyramid is known to possess. He showed me how to chart personal biorhythms and explained how biorhythm can aid in the art of negotiation. He and I would walk and talk until one of us broke off to pursue other endeavours.

Another interesting man that I became acquainted with was the prison psychiatrist, who was serving a sentence but was working, counselling inmates with psychological disorders. Believe me, there were many of those; his caseload was enormous. He showed me the steps to insanity. Just by walking around, you could see men in each phase of mental duress in the gallery. It was interesting to note that the progression to insanity was a surety once the person gave up and succumbed to hopelessness. I believe that spirituality is a necessary ingredient for a person's well being. I saw the power of God working, saving many of these men from despair.

Eleven days into the month, we received notification that Damien and I were being moved once again, this time across the gallery to cell number nineteen. The nice thing about this move was that, on that side of the gallery, you could look out over the top of the prison walls and see the volcano, Santiago. The steady plume of volcanic gases rising into the atmosphere is a constant reminder of the activity occurring underground. Being in such close proximity to the volcano, it was interesting that the water we drew from the tap was warm, suggesting that this area was very fragile. Santiago could very well spew forth its lava once again and put an end to this place. It is one thing that man forgets – we are inconsequential as far as the biggest picture is concerned. Call it God; call it Nature, same difference.

The view also afforded a glimpse of the surrounding land, some of the best farmland in Central America. Its rolling hills of fertile soil were like gentile waves on the ocean. The breeze from the west came directly through our window and provided relief from the humidity. With any luck, the breeze would be strong enough to drive the flies from the cell. The previous occupant was Carillo, so there was very little cleaning for us to do. Looks can be deceiving, though. Carillo told me that this was the worst cell in the gallery; when it rained, the water ran down the walls. He advised me to pull the bed away from the wall and not to leave anything on the floor, or it would get wet.

This was just great. What was I going to do with all the books? I couldn't leave them on the floor to get wet. Damien suggested that we put the books in a duffel bag so we could move them to a dry spot when it rained. We'd been storing the books in a cardboard box, but that wasn't such a good idea - we found out that a particular insect liked to nest in the box and feed on the paper. Every week we had to take the books out of the box and vigorously shake it to get rid of the bugs. When they were scurrying across the floor, we had to run around stepping on them so they didn't get into anyone else's cell. Perhaps with Damien's duffel bag, the books would be protected from the insects as well as the water.

That night I invited Norman over for coffee and conversation to celebrate our new lodgings. He accepted, saying that he would be over after he finished his exercise routine and showered. Around eight o'clock, Norman showed up at the cell door and for the next two hours, Damien and I were captivated by his storytelling. Many years ago, before the Revolution, when Norman was a medical student in Mexico, he was approached by a French national to join him on an expedition deep into the jungles of southern Mexico in search of Mayan ruins. He offered to pay Norman a huge salary to be medical officer on a team comprised of European nationals. Their mission was to search the Mayan ruins for antiquities. It was dangerous but lucrative work, stealing these treasures.

Norman accepted the invitation and soon found himself deep in the Mexican jungle. They had air support for the ground crew, which was composed of twenty-four men. Their job was to locate and seize the treasures before the Mexican authorities were alerted to their presence. If found out they would have been executed, and their bodies left as a reminder to leave the antiquities alone. At one of these sites, the helicopter alerted the ground personnel that the Feds were closing in on the operation, and it was necessary to evacuate. The helicopter was loaded with the precious cargo and flown off, leaving those on the ground to fend for themselves. There weren't many options. They would have to make their way through the jungle into Guatemala, hoping that the Mexicans would give up the chase when they crossed the border.

Norman described the arduous journey through the jungle. After a week of forced march, they were still being pursued. The Mexicans had followed them into Guatemala - at least, they thought they were in Guatemala. Since there were no markers, they could never be sure just where they were. Many of the men were exhausted. They just simply gave up and sat down, unwilling to go on. The group had been whittled down to eight men, and by this time, they were subsisting on monkey meat because it was the easiest food source obtainable. Norman described how they caught monkeys: A hole six inches deep is dug, and two sticks are inserted across each other. The monkeys are inquisitive. They understand that an intruder is in their midst, but they watch to see what is going on. When the trapper finishes digging the hole, he stands back, allowing ample room between himself and the hole. A monkey will climb down off a tree to see what is in the hole. When he sticks his hand into the hole, it gets caught. Instead of using its other hand to free itself, it starts squawking. That's when the trapper approaches from behind and grabs it by the neck, snapping it quickly. Voila, one dead monkey for the barbecue!

Norman and the other tattered remnants of the expedition limped into Belize after walking through Guatemala. They had no idea where they were. The jungle can be an easy place to get lost and forfeit your life; there are many unforgiving things in a tropical rainforest.

It was getting close to count time, so Norman wished us a good night. We thanked him for the entertaining story and said we'd see him the next day.

During the next visit day, Ivonne reported that she had talked with Talavera and he told her that only one signature was still required for my release. That reminded me of the position the Narco Jet guys had been in, so many months before. We were both becoming despondent. It was always necessary to wait for this or wait for that. We were waiting for something all the time! No matter what - we told each other - we would continue to struggle through this and in the end we would be victorious.

The next day was Friday the thirteenth and, as the superstition says, a bad day. The Consejo told me that, due to Dr. Frech being replaced with another director, the authorisation for my call to Canada was being revoked. It would be replaced with a new authorisation that would be current. I was angry. Everything was being taken away from me and I knew that when I gave this paper up, getting another one was not going to be easy. I needed to call Grant this Sunday; this was an important time to remain in contact. The Consejo said that he would personally assist me in getting my call this Sunday. He said that the permission was logged in at the administration office; it required only a telephone call to get approval. Reluctantly, I gave up my authorisation. I could only hope that the Consejo would keep his end of the bargain.

There were to be changes to the military personnel. Molina was being reinstated in his old job. It appeared that the military had won this little power struggle over the prison system. On Sunday, the Consejo did, in fact, assist me in gaining permission to phone. It wasn't easy, though. It was difficult to get a guard to phone his superiors, but after persevering for two hours, I was finally allowed to use the phone. Grant was waiting for the call. He assured me that on Tuesday I would be coming home - it was finally over. The positive news was nice, if only it could be true. I jokingly told him that I had been packed for four months, waiting for the next week!

On Tuesday, the 17th, there was a news conference shown on the popular broadcast 100% Noticia. It announced I'd been found not guilty and would be released on August 31st. I was becoming used to the delays concerning my release, but this nagged me. Why were they waiting for the end of the month when I'd been found innocent?

The frequency of the gallbladder attacks seemed to be increasing. I really needed to go home to have surgery. I had toughed this thing out, but it was increasingly hard to bear. The flies were also increasingly active. There was no way I could stay in my cell in the afternoons. It made my reading and writing routine difficult - I had to escape to the church, the only place in the gallery where there was a cross breeze that seemed to discourage the flies. It was in there that I composed a letter to the editor of the newspaper La Prenza. I made it clear to them that I wanted my letter printed in their editorial section. I stated that I was concerned with the negative reporting of the case, and I believed that the Republic of Nicaragua needed to have information concerning the role of Hemp-Agro and of hemp in Nicaragua. I expounded that I had recently been declared innocent of all charges and that my freedom was imminent.

I included a brief, easy to understand synopsis of the plant's history, its physiology, and the benefits that hemp agro-business could bring to Nicaragua. I described our company objectives and followed this with a brief statement of my observations and conclusions. One of the inmates who taught in the computer room typed the letter out and put the information on disk. His mother worked at the newspaper and she was coming this weekend for her weekly visit. She would take the disk with her and personally give it to the editor. I could only hope that this document would rally some public support and put some pressure on those resisting my release.

The next day, my case received a setback. José Cuadra, a deputy of the Nicaraguan Legislature and a close relative of the President of the Court of Appeals, was gunned down outside his coffee plantation. This sent the country into mourning. As required, government activity was suspended till after the funeral services. A further setback occurred at the end of the week. 100% Noticia reported that my release would be postponed till September 15th because one of the magistrates had been hospitalised for surgery. This really delivered a major blow to me. Ivonne and I had planned to celebrate our birthdays together. Her birthday was on the eleventh and mine was on the fourteenth. First we'd had Christmas and New Year's robbed from us, now we had our birthdays taken away from us!

On Sunday I talked to Grant. He was as furious as I was. They were using every stall tactic available, but the real kicker was that the magistrate was hospitalised for liposuction surgery. The justice system had ground to a halt because this person had to remove some fat from her body! Whatever happened to good old diet and exercise, I wondered incredulously. Grant also reported to me that the Canadian Consul was pressuring the appeal court to uphold its ruling. One of the magistrates had retracted her signature from the document; that was what was keeping me in here. Again, I was incredulous. How could you sign your name to a legal document one day, and then decide to take it off the next day? The following day, Lisa Smith was busy. Both her clients - the German and the Colombian - were on their way home, and with them went my hopes for catching a plane ride back to Canada. Well, it was better this way. I was proving my innocence. Now, though, I had all my eggs in one basket.

Chapter Eleven

"A TRADEGY STRUCK"

I STARTED SEPTEMBER FEELING resigned to the possibility I wasn't going to be leaving here any time soon. The Narco Jet guys had resorted to having family and friends picket the Court of Appeal and staged a hunger strike in order to pressure the lone magistrate to sign off on the declaration. These tactics were extreme, to be sure, and whether they had done any good was debatable. I knew that I could only sit tight and be patient, or, as the Latinos say, tranquilo.

The second day into the month, a lieutenant came to see me. He said he brought a message from the outside and asked if I knew Lazaro Urbina! Lazaro had worked for me. He replaced Jorge Vega when Jorge quit the company. The lieutenant had my attention. I had wondered what had become of Lazaro.

"Yes, I know Lazaro", I said. "How is my friend Lazaro?"

"Just fine. He is working every day he can, but in this weather it is difficult, no? Rain every day. Rain is impossible to work in - too much water on the field. Lazaro is my good friend. He asked me to see you, to arrange a visit with him, but first I need your permission. Then I can arrange the visit".

"Of course, it will be very good to see Lazaro, Lieutenant. It has been a long time since we've talked. When can you arrange this visit?"

"I will begin today and possibly arrange for him to attend the next family visit".

"Thank you, Lieutenant", I said, and with a nod he was off, marching down the gallery towards the door. It would be good to see Lazaro again. I had a few unanswered questions; perhaps he had some answers.

On Saturday my friend from the computer room came back from his visit with information concerning the editorial I had prepared. His mother had relayed La Prenza's stance: since there had not been a formal confirmation from the Appeal Tribunal that the case was concluded, they would suppress publication until a verdict had been made public and my freedom assured. This didn't help me at all. I was counting on the power of the press to put pressure on the Tribunal to make a resolution quickly!

Early in the week, the maniacs downstairs in Two Baja broke out. Another gallery soon joined them and a full-scale riot ensued. For the next four days, police in riot gear dispensing tear gas besieged us. In one day, thirty people were hurt, with one death. The media converged on the prison like flies to dead meat, all reporting on the horrors of Tipitapa Prison. This occurred just days before the Independence Day celebration. I thought; if these guys are this carried away now, what's it going to be like during the long weekend?

On Friday the Canadian Consul came to visit and make sure I was okay. They had been listening to the news broadcasts. I assured them that I was hanging in there. They were doing everything possible to get a resolution on this case, they told me, but this was, after all, Nicaragua.

The next day was Ivonne's birthday - Saturday the eleventh - and I had planned to have the celebration of celebrations! She certainly deserved it, more than I can even put into words. As

I stood at my window gazing out across the fields, my eyes came to rest on the majestic Santiago. Standing proudly, its steady stream of sulphurous smoke attested its might. The sight could not appease my sadness as I thought of the hardship this ordeal had caused Ivonne and her family. Today should be a day of happiness for her, I thought, not a day of sorrow! Ah, mi amor, I have only two days to wait before seeing you for a conjugal visit - the day before my birthday. I turned away from the window, breaking the mood - facing reality.

My Sunday call to Canada was a real morale booster. Grant was out of the country, but my sister Patricia was there to receive my call. I hadn't talked with her in a very long time, so it was a welcome surprise to hear her voice. This call was truly a birthday present - to be able to talk about the family made me feel a little closer to home. Near the end of the call, the prison SWAT team, dressed in their riot gear and armed with shotguns, ran past me on their way to address a problem somewhere in the prison. I told my sister to keep talking for a little while longer. I didn't want to walk into a hotspot. When I saw the police return, I knew the trouble was under control and I could safely return to the gallery. I thanked my sister for staying on the line, said good-bye, and headed for the gallery.

A conjugal visit with Ivonne the day before my birthday - I could not have planned it any better. I was disturbed to find out that she had been sick, though. She had come down with a case of dengue; if left untreated, this disease can kill. Her brother, being a doctor, was quick to respond; he gave her proper treatment. I didn't feel that good myself. There was an outbreak of malaria and dengue in here due to the mosquitoes, and I was experiencing the symptoms. I didn't tell her. This day was too important to spoil. Later we lay in each other's arms, talking of a life together beyond the prison walls - together, forever! Since our dreams of having our birthdays together were not realised, we set our sights for Christmas 99'. If I were to be released before then it would just be icing on the cake.

The two hours seemed to pass in a snap of the fingers, and we found ourselves once again folding the sheets and packing them away in the garbage bag, a ritual that by now was mechanical. Saying good-bye and watching Ivonne leave was horrible. You would think I'd have been used to that by now, but no. It was something I could never get used to.

When I returned to the gallery, I found the medic and took some malaria pills. I didn't want to come down with a full-blown case of either malaria or dengue.

The next day I celebrated my birthday with a gallbladder attack that lasted into the night. I don't know what set it off. Maybe it was the medication I took for the malaria. I was falling apart. I needed to step up my running, I decided - maybe I could sweat this out of me - but I couldn't tie my shoelaces. Bending over proved to be too much. I lay in my bed and slept off the effects of the medication. Damien came back to our cell in a state of excitement. He told me that he had just talked to his mother in California, for free. When I asked him how he'd accomplished that, he said a guy who had just been transferred here from another gallery had told him how to do it. It was easy, Damien claimed; you just punch in the numbers and the call is placed free of charge.

I told Damien to set up a meeting with this guy. Perhaps he and I could work something out over this phone thing. Damien left and within the hour came back and said, "Let's go and I'll introduce you to him". I followed Damien to where the guy was waiting. Damien introduced us and then left us alone to talk. The kid was in his twenties, tall and thin almost to the point of emaciation - this guy could not afford to lose another pound. His pallor testified to the rigors of this place.

"Damien tells me you're good with the telephones", I said.

"Yes, anything with a computer chip in it, I can break the code. I worked writing programs for Southwest Bell in Costa Rica, so telephones are easy, especially cellular".

"Look, I've been trying to call Canada since I first came through the door, and it cannot be done", I stated.

"We'll go out together to the telephone, and I will show you how it is done. Then you can call to Canada anytime", he said.

I thanked him and told him to be ready to go with me on the next call day. As he walked away, I thought, if this kid can do what he says he can, he is worth his weight in gold.

I found Damien back in the cell, reading. He looked up when I entered. "How did your meeting go with Canda?" he asked.

"Just fine. Tell me something, Damien. What do you know about this guy?"

"Not much, other than that he is good with that telephone".

"He doesn't look like no criminal to me. What did he do to end up in here?" I asked.

"He's one of those computer geeks that rob banks", said Damien.

"Well, next phone day that computer geek - what's his name again?"

"Canda", Damien replied.

"Funny name for a funny guy. He is going to show me the secret to the telephone", I said.

"That telephone thing saves my ass!" Damien said. "My wife just had a telephone restriction put on her phone because I've been calling home too much, so this is a Godsend for me".

I had to agree with him on that. Damien had no support from the American Embassy. Getting a letter was impossible and sending one was worse. He needed that phone to call home; it was the only lifeline to his family.

The press was here at the prison almost daily. There were reports of widespread, contagious diseases running rampant. One gallery was quarantined. There were no fewer than six infections running through the prison system. One day they would run an article on AIDS and tuberculosis, the next one on malaria and dengue. This was a biological soup pot of contagions. Getting sick was a sure thing - your only hope was that it wasn't deadly!

Everyone in the prison was waiting for Saturday, for the big fight between Oscar De La Hoya and Trinidad, and the betting was rampant. Gordo 'the diner' was giving odds and he had lots of takers. The favourite was Oscar but Gordo was laying it all on the line for Trinidad. When Saturday arrived, the prison officials gave permission for the inmates to stay up to watch the fight in its entirety. Boxing was a huge sport in this country and was followed fervently - the prison would erupt in violence if inmates were prevented from watching the fight. When Trinidad won, there were a lot of unhappy faces. The fortunate few who had bet on Trinidad were smiling. One of these was Gordo. He pulled in a mitt full of cigarettes, enough for him to be on easy street for a while.

The only word I had on my case was that the last magistrate still had not signed her name. What she was holding out for was anybody's guess, but I assumed it was in accordance with the political party line. My conjugal visits with Ivonne were of higher importance. I was sick of being told this bullshit of freedom next week, freedom tomorrow, freedom next month. I was not going to be set free until they were good and ready to set me free. I had to control this roller coaster, at least in my own mind.

My conjugal visit was on the twenty-second of the month and I was once again feeling a little under the weather. This also was the day for the telephone, so right after the visit, I had to race to find Canda and then arrange for both of us to go to the phone. There was no logic to having a visit and a call on the same day, but who said they were logical. I found out from Ivonne that they were still talking about my release in five days. It had become a joke for us because we knew it was all empty promises; the best we could hope for was release before Christmas. We knew that these interludes were special for us; this shared time was what held us together.

After the visit we are led away for the customary strip search. The sky had darkened and was preparing for a tropical monsoon. I looked up at my window and realised I had left the plastic rolled up, exposing the open window to the elements. When the clouds eventually opened, the rain fell in a torrential downpour that deposited inches of water in mere minutes. I knew that our cell was soaked, between the open window, the wall that leaked and the locked door that prevented anybody from entering to roll down our protective plastic window covering for us. Sure enough, on returning to my cell, I found the contents waterlogged. I stripped the mattress of its cover and hung my wet bedding up on the laundry line. I hoped the foam mattress would dry before nightfall, or I would be sleeping on the floor. Next I took the books out of the duffel bag and inspected them for damage. The ones I found the slightest bit damp, I laid out on my bed to dry.

I was racing against time. When your name was called for the telephone, you had to go or you would lose your privilege. I mopped up the floor just before I heard my name being called. Locking the door once again, I went in search of Canda. He was in his cell waiting for me. He was to tell the officials that it was necessary for him to assist me in making an international call because I didn't speak the language very well. The officials accepted this story and, after the usual wait, we were finally allowed out to the phone.

He tried every variation of numbers he could think of, but it was to no avail - he couldn't break the code. I waited close by, hoping that he would be successful, but our allotted time passed and we were sent back upstairs.

"This puzzles me", he said. "I'll work out the code and then we can try again".

"Don't worry about it; you gave it a good shot. Canada is a difficult country to call from here!"

I noticed a disturbance outside our cellblock. Three guards appeared to be trying to control an inmate. They had managed to move the prisoner away from our door and had him against the far wall. One guard came over to let us in to our gallery. He fumbled around with the keys, trying to find the right key; he was clearly agitated. Out of the corner of my eye, I saw the prisoner outflank the guards and come straight at me. I could see that this guy was a nut. He yelled at me to give him cigarettes and reached for my pocket. I stepped back to avoid his hand and saw a flash of bare metal. With his other hand, he had pulled a modified weapon from his waistband, a sharpened paint scraper.

As he lunged forward, I connected with an overhand right that hit him right between the eyes. It wasn't a preferred spot, but he had walked right into it and my fist connected solidly. Somebody behind me grabbed me by the shirt and pulled me into the open doorway, away from the danger.

"That was close! Are you okay?" Canda asked.

"Yeah, just lovely", I replied, still somewhat shaken by the encounter. It had happened so fast. I felt terrible; all wanted to do was lie down in my bed, but I couldn't do that because my bedding was still drying. I went down to see Norman for a cup of coffee while I waited for my mattress to dry, but I couldn't hold down the coffee. I returned to my cell and cleared the books off my bed. Taking down my partially dried mattress, I laid it out on the bed. Just doing that made me vomit. I knelt before the toilet and retched up the contents of my stomach. When I was sure there was nothing left, I splashed water on my face and made my way to the bed, where I lay for the remainder of the month. The diagnosis was malaria.

Once you've had malaria, it is something you never want to have again. I was bedridden for several days, followed by more days of weakness. My old acquaintance Denis Lopez was transferred to the gallery. It was good to see him. He had kept himself in reasonable shape, a little on the slender side, but healthy. There was talk of moving the older inmates out of the gallery and replacing them with troublesome cases, men with suicidal tendencies. They thought that since we had the medical professionals residing in our gallery, they could watch over them. These moves were to take place early in the week, because on Wednesday, Cardinal Obando was coming to the prison to give mass and any dangerous offenders must be locked down somewhere away from the dignitary's eyes.

After the weekend, these rumours were proven true. On Monday the women were taken from their gallery and shipped out to more suitable accommodation at the women's federal prison. They were being replaced with the senior citizens in the facility, most of whom resided in our gallery. To fill the vacancies in our gallery, they moved all the remaining teachers and Internationals onto our tier. One of these was my old enemy, the Cuban, Angel.

Much fanfare heralded the arrival of the Cardinal. There was as much pomp and ceremony as the prison could afford. It wasn't often that dignitaries like this visited the prison, but they were here to give speeches not so much to us as to the television cameras that would broadcast the words of these caring political figures to the far reaches of the Republic. Finally, after hours of sitting in the sun, we were allowed to return to the gallery.

I don't know how she perceived that I needed supplies of both food and medicines, but Ivonne brought me barco. Maybe it was the divine passage of the Cardinal. It was like a Christmas present, opening the barco to find letters, food and my much-needed medicine. Ivonne was receiving the same information I was: any day now, my freedom was assured. Luckily, we weren't holding our breath.

The Canadian Consul came to visit on the last day of the week. They told me that all three signatures had been gained; my freedom was imminent. Bullshit! Why was I still here, then? I didn't say that, of course. I sat there with my hands folded in front of me and said how nice it was to know that I was finally believed. After ten months of maintaining my innocence, weathering personal and professional slander, and enduring the most horrific situation of my life, finally, my innocence was being taken seriously.

The day that I had awaited finally arrived - visit day with Ivonne. It was October eleventh, Canadian Thanksgiving Day. There would be much to eat around my mother's table and that was where my thoughts were - eating a turkey feast with my family and friends. I told Ivonne what Canada was like on this day when families celebrated the bountiful fall harvest and gave thanks for the food we ate. Ivonne smiled at me, knowing that I longed to be away from here, in a place very far away.

"Sounds beautiful, this fiesta, but why do you eat birds on this day?" she inquired.

"We sometimes eat ham - cured pork". I remembered they didn't cure pork here. "Turkey is symbolic, from our past". I changed the subject, not wanting to get involved in a history lesson. For the next four hours we talked of our life together in Canada. We dreamed of our own house, with a great big backyard for our gardens. This visit picked me up; Ivonne had a knack for doing that. She was a great morale booster, always remaining faithful and conjuring for me visions of a life somewhere other than my current hell.

It was becoming increasingly easy to just let go and be sucked into this quagmire. In the absence of hope, insanity replaces the empty corners of your mind, until you lose all thoughts of an existence beyond these walls. It's like a cancerous growth. The visit with Ivonne gave me a real boost to continue. I put hours into my routine of working out. The physical endurance, the therapeutic effect it had on me was an added bonus to just passing the time. I felt that every passing day I was getting stronger both physically and mentally. The only setback was when my body reminded me that I had an ailment. The gallbladder attacks were always a possibility; I knew that just when I felt good - wham! - another attack could come.

On the fifteenth, Ivonne came to the conjugal visit with renewed hope for my release. The lawyers had said that today held a good possibility of release. Immediately after the visit, Ivonne was going to the lawyers to follow up on this latest development. Our passion for each other was heightened by this prospect. I had a bounce to my step when I returned to the gallery. The Consejo was waiting for me at the top of the stairs. He pulled me aside and directed me away from the walkway into a corner where we could not be overheard.

"What's up?" I asked.

"The Captain asked me today for a conduct paper on you", he said.

"There is nothing on the report, is there?" I asked, wondering why he was telling me this.

"No, I took all the stupid shit out before I gave it to Roche. He gave you a good report. I know; I was there when he signed the paper. You know what this means, amigo", he said.

"Yeah, thanks for the information". I turned away and

headed for my cell.

For most people, being told that their conduct report had been requested was a welcome sign, but for me - I wasn't too sure. Instead, this message warned me that something was not right. I lay on my cot thinking, now what? There was no doubt in anybody's mind as to my innocence. The appeal court had made their judgement, all three magistrates had signed their names on the declaration, but I remained in prison - a free man held against his will.

The fact that a conduct report had been requested was a mystery, because this report was not required if I had been declared innocent. The only time the report was asked for was when you were going to a jury trial in the lower court, and that was a bit unnerving. I knew that I would be hung if taken before a jury. Orietta Benavides would gladly hand me a life sentence! The lower court system was like playing a deadly game of Roulette; because of jury tampering, you could never tell what would happen. Also, I had to consider another avenue of thought: what if the police, having been stymied on this set of charges, were waiting to recharge me on other crimes that would hold me here longer!

The humidity, along with the growing frustration I felt at this new development, made the sweat form on my brow and begin to run in rivulets into my eyes, stinging them with the salt. I rose to splash some water on my face, to rinse the sweat away and hopefully wash away that nagging feeling of despair.

On Sunday I anxiously anticipated my call to Grant. Perhaps he could enlighten me. I knew from Norman that it took a maximum of four days to be released; I could only conclude that somebody was lying. I raced to the door, only to wait for them to check my authorisation, then wait for the officer in charge to come and take me out. I had been following this same procedure every Sunday; I would have thought by now that they knew my face! This particular Sunday, I felt an urgency to get to that phone; my patience ran thin. I started calling them names, daring them to open the door so I could pop one of them. Finally I grew weary of this and changed my tactic. I resigned myself to the fact that nothing was going to change their protocol. They were the cats and I was the proverbial mouse.

An hour or more passed. I was standing in a pool of stagnant water - the water barrel had overflowed and no one had bothered to mop up the water. As always, it was a give or take situation - the water was better than the customary ants crawling over your feet. Finally the duty officer led me to the phone, where the official behind the desk told me the phone was out of order - the lightning storm had knocked out the phone service. I could feel my blood boil. I stepped back and took in a breath of air. Smiling, I said, "Thank you very much. I will try again next week". I was then taken back to the gallery. As Damien would say, "Ain't this 'bout a bitch!"

The next afternoon a guard smuggled me in a letter from Ivonne. She said she had phoned the lawyers and they had told her that twenty-two days from now, I would be free. She was to pick up the release order and bring it to the prison. I should have felt elated, but I could not. Why the twentieth? Why not today?

On the twentieth, I waited all day. I knew that this was just another false hope and I should not feel disheartened, but there was always a flicker of anticipation and then a letdown feeling. Towards the end of the week, I resigned myself to routine and put freedom out of my head. This, however, did not last long. Talavera and Sequiera came to visit me. This was the first time I had set eyes on Sequiera. He was in his late forties or early fifties, very elegant in both dress and mannerisms. Talavera was, as always, his smiling, congenial self. I cut to the chase and asked them what the hell was going on. Why was I still here?

Sequiera asked me to be patient - one more week was all it would take. He said the courts had to transcribe the court proceedings into the books. These inscriptions must be handwritten, and due to the length of the documents, it would take a week. He said not to worry, I'd been found not guilty - there was nothing that could stop my release. I returned to my cell none the wiser. Other than putting a face to Sequiera's name,

I had heard only excuses. Damien and I had quite the laugh over this. Both of us knew how the lawyers worked here, so it was no surprise - anything was possible, as Damien was soon to find out.

Damien's lawyer had been working on his appeal for a sentence reduction and this procedure was soon to be realised. Then the shit hit the fan. His lawyer was arrested for cocaine possession and an arsenal of weaponry, including rocket launchers. Newscasts showed him being led out of the courtroom weeping, after testifying that the drugs and weapons belonged to the Colombian left wing guerrilla group, FARC. They had left the stash with him for safekeeping. He implicated the Colombian who had previously offered to help me fly out of here, naming him as the leader of the group dedicated to procuring armaments for the guerrillas.

Everyone was coming over to our cell to rib Damien, saying things like "Paul is going home and your new cellmate will be your lawyer". Damien could relax though; his lawyer had managed to secure his appeal. Damien had his sentence reduced by half, which meant he would be going home soon. It was now the end of another month and a week since the lawyers had come to visit and tell me that I would be free by now. As always, it had been bullshit.

The lieutenant who had told me my friend Lazaro wanted a visit came by to say that all the paperwork had been done and Lazaro was free to visit. He explained that Lazaro had been working and was unable to get away, but would attend the next family visit. I thanked him and told him to tell Lazaro that I would be expecting him. It would be a welcome visit, for I was sure he could fill in some missing pieces of this jigsaw puzzle.

A new month and as the jailhouse saying goes, Una dia mas una dia menos - one day more, one day less. That is how I felt. It was getting closer to Christmas. Who would have thought I'd have spent a year in this place? What does it take, I wondered, to gain freedom? Perhaps Damien was right; they would never let me go. In the first week, Ivonne brought me the dreaded but likely news that one of the magistrates did not sign the appeal. If this was true, they wouldn't be able to hold me here as an innocent man, not even in their system. I told Ivonne to get hold of Marion and have her put the squeeze on this magistrate to make her sign. She could not hold out indefinitely; there had to be a time frame for these magistrates to follow.

I just had to get through this weekend. Monday was visit day and possibly the beginning of a good week. The days were slowing down. It felt like a weight was attached to my shoulders - the burden of this place was taking its toll. All the weekend noise in here was driving me nuts. When Monday morning rolled around, I was ready. I had my freshly laundered blue jeans and shirt on. I borrowed some of Damien's hair gel to slick back my newly cut hair. When they called for visit, I was the first one standing at the door waiting for it to open, but as always, I had to wait. Once inside the hall, I took my usual place to wait for Ivonne. Norman came to join me and we talked about our favourite topic: freedom. He was as close to it as I was, but close doesn't win you any cigars. Even when you are standing at the outside gate, they can haul your ass back inside for one reason or another.

The hours ticked by and I knew Ivonne would not be coming this day. Just as I was thinking about getting up and finding the official to take me back upstairs, I saw my friend Lazaro walk in. I waved to him and he made his way through the tables to join me.

"How are you, my friend?" Lazaro said while grasping my hand in a firm handshake. His other hand gave my shoulder a strong grip.

"Just fine. You look good! I can tell you have been working - you're darker than usual". I thought he looked just the same as the last time we'd seen each other, but it seemed so long ago. The last time we were together was at his farm, loading the seed into his metal shed for safekeeping until we could process it. Lazaro had overseen the cultivation at Malacatoya. We had left some seed out there and it was this seed I was interested in, because with this seed, I could start over again.

"You look skinny! You need some food. I have some money;

let's go buy whatever you need". He pointed to the Bar.

"They don't have much there, other than cigarettes and pop".

"Let's go and have a look", he said, pulling at my arm. "Come on".

"Okay". I knew better than to argue, so we went and he bought. I think he bought one of everything behind the counter. Returning to the table with a few shopping bags full of sundries, we settled in to sip Cokes and have a quiet conversation. After we had talked about families and friends, we got down to the nuts and bolts.

"What happened to the seed?" I inquired.

"After your arrest they came to the farm here in Tipitapa and seized all the seed in the storage shed. I thought that would be the end of it, then about a week later, the police came and arrested me. They took me to Granada and held me for three days. Every day, they asked me about Malacatoya and where the seed was. Finally I told them the location of ten bags of seed. They knew the number of bags we had out there, but they didn't know the location. When I told them, they took me out of the interrogation room. I had to pass through the station, and guess who was sitting there with the police? Jorge Vega!" Lazaro exclaimed.

"That son of a bitch!" I said. "He caused more problems, that guy. I cannot understand why no one questioned that liar! The damage he has caused - that stupid, insignificant piece of shit!" I could barely contain the rage I felt for Judas Vega.

"Yes. He is a snake, to be sure - a very dangerous one. So now you know, my friend. I fear I have let you down but I could do little, they knew I had seed. Jorge told them. Withholding that information would only make me guilty of something as ridiculous as these charges of yours are".

"You did right. I'm glad that you never found yourself in this situation", I said. The buzzer sounded, ending another visit time. Only this visit was special; not only did I see my friend but he was able to provide me with useful information. He promised to visit again on the next visit date. Then he gave me a hug and turned to leave. I felt a hodgepodge of emotion as I watched him go out the door and disappear from sight.

Back in the gallery, I discovered we'd received a new inmate, a German national by the name of Peter Weiss, who was proficient in three languages. He was recruited by the Cuban to teach German in the school, which had qualified him to be transferred to this gallery. I could tell at our first meeting that he had a lot of business savvy, being a precious commodity dealer, primarily in jewels and antiques. After this first meeting, we would often get together and talk of gemstones whenever he wasn't preoccupied with his girlfriend. Everyone in here had baggage and he was no exception. I had a fascination with emeralds only because I had good connections in Columbia and Panama for the stones. Peter was knowledgeable and I was an apt student, learning as much as I could in a short period of time. This was not only beneficial to me as a learning experience but also filled some of my idle time, affording me the chance to forget my situation momentarily.

I hadn't seen Ivonne in some time, so when the conjugal visit on the twelfth rolled around; it was a very happy day for us. There was no news and I suppose to an extent that was good - we could just be satisfied with what we had together. I had tried to get a four-hour visit but had been turned down; they liked to piss me off, I thought. We made the most of our two hours together and like every time before, it was over much too early.

After the loud yet boring weekend we were all given the welcome news that Orietta Benavides was leaving. Today was her final day as judge of the second court. The reason she gave for stepping down was that she wanted to have a family. The reason didn't matter. Cheers went up in the gallery; she had put as many innocent people as guilty in prison. The reign of the glamour judge was over, to the relief of the inmates. Perhaps some cases could be reviewed and some people set free. On Thursday I was called out for a visit. Finally, someone had come; perhaps now I could discover the status of my situation. I was led to Molina's office, so I suspected that my visitor would be Marion. I was correct. She had in front of her a Toronto Star and a bag containing what I assumed to be books. Her demeanour was as ever businesslike. She waited until all prison personnel were out of earshot before proceeding with any conversation. I too, remained silent, sitting back in the chair, absorbing it's luxurious comfort. When the coast was clear, Marion leaned forward and said quietly, "Sequiera is, at this moment, talking with the magistrates at the Appeal Court". Reaching into her pocket, she produced a cellular phone and placed it on the table. "He will telephone me directly to inform me of the outcome of this meeting. He sounded confident that today they would grant him the decision. If that's true, we can have you out of here today!"

"That would be great, but how many times have I heard this, Marion?" I countered.

"I cannot stay long today, as there is a function I have to prepare for, but the minute I hear any news from him, I will phone the Director to get word to you", she said.

"Thank you for coming. It is, as you can probably realise, very difficult for me to be waiting for my freedom. Having to rely on the press for information is extremely difficult!" I rose from the chair's comfortable confines and pointed to the newspaper on the table. "Did you bring me a Canadian newspaper, Marion?"

"Yes; I also brought you a couple of books".

I took the bag of books from the table and glanced at the date on the paper. Of course it was out of date. Smiling, I thanked her once again, then walked over to the door and opened it for her and her driver. We stepped out into the sunlight. As they walked away from me, heading for the front gates, I had time to reflect.

What a crock of shit! If she was so certain that today was my last day, why bring the reading material? This sounded to me like another stall tactic. Grant was putting pressure on Sequiera and the Canadian Consul - what else could the guy do but buy some time by lying? Somebody was certainly lying – again.

An official demanded that I return to the gallery under his escort, interrupting my musing. I followed him back to the gallery, eager to read the news from home, even if it was a month old. The next day one of the guys said that Radio Ya had announced that a decision on my case was to be made next week. Not freedom, just a decision. This could mean anything. I was no better off now than I'd been a month ago. The only thing that was constant, that I could depend upon, was my visits with Ivonne. And I had two more days to wait for the next one.

On visit day I was blessed with both Ivonne and Lazaro's presence. We had our pictures taken together for twenty Cordoba, or about two dollars. A man took our picture in front of a mural depicting a revolutionary theme; it was a nice service for families with loved ones in the prison. We had Coca-Colas together and reminisced about the three of us during better times, having beers instead of Coca-Cola.

Lazaro assumed a serious look and said, "Have you heard any news on your release?"

"No, it is always one more week, one more month, one more day - I don't think anybody knows. I do know this though: it will be soon!" I said, breaking into a grin. Ivonne started to laugh. We had been saying 'soon' for a long time. But one thing was certain, if we continued to say my freedom would come soon, one day it would.

"What will you do when you get out of here?" inquired Lazaro.

"First, I must return to Canada to see my family. After I get some investment money I will return - not to here, but perhaps Belize. They were also expressing interest in hemp agriculture. We have proven, Lazaro, that hemp acclimatises well to this environment. The future for hemp production in the tropics will be a lucrative one for whichever countries want to adopt it", I said.

"Keep me in mind, amigo. I know this; anyone who has agriculture in his or her blood cannot help but like this plant. I will work for you anywhere, any day, my friend", he said.

"I sure will keep you in mind", I replied.

"I will get another round of Cokes", Ivonne offered. As she rose, I couldn't help but notice the gentle sway of her hips. It reminded me of a gentle breeze through a palm-filled oasis - hot, yet sort of cool.

When she returned, Lazaro and I were talking agriculture, and continued until Lazaro looked down at his watch and realised he had a tractor to pick up. He excused himself and said he would come to the next visit day, weather permitting. We stood facing each other. "Stay safe, amigo", he said as he walked off in the direction of the gate. A moment later he disappeared from sight.

"He is a good man", Ivonne said.

"Yes, he is", I agreed, sitting down beside her. It felt good, her closeness. We chatted quietly, just being happy together, shutting out our surroundings, and being alone with each other. As always, the bell ringing brought our semi-idyllic state to an abrupt end and cold reality set in again. We parted, exchanging each other's letters.

Once back at the cell, I lay down to read the letters she'd given me. I marvelled at her resilience; most would have given up on me as a lost cause. When Damien returned from school I put the letters away and started getting our supper together. We always had a good dinner after a visit. I cooked steak and potatoes on this day. Damien and I ate until we couldn't eat any more. After putting away the dishes and after count had been taken, we settled in for a night of dominoes. One of the guys next door came racing over to our door. "Cañamo, you're on TV!" he said, beckoning me to follow him.

I joined the crowd that had gathered in front of the television. Behind the announcer was a clip showing me being led from the courthouse on that fateful day eleven months ago. The announcer was saying that the Appeal Court had made a ruling on my case. It was a unanimous decision - all three magistrates declared Hemp-Agro innocent of all charges! I was to be released on the November 30th, a week from today. Some were clapping me on the back; others appeared to be less than enthusiastic about the news. Some just can't bear the thought of someone other than them going free - I would be careful of them. Later that night, while Damien and I were playing dominoes, we were constantly interrupted by a parade of people asking for my bed, my clothes, even my underwear. I told them that when I went, everything was Damien's. Hell, I wasn't any closer to that door. I'd heard it all before, the "one more week" syndrome.

On Friday I had a conjugal visit with Ivonne. At this stage, after what we had gone through, we'd lost the ability to believe in anybody. Ivonne said prayers daily for my release in time for Christmas and it was on this that we set our sights. Later that night the Channel Two newscast announced that my case, along with two other cases, would have a solution on December 3rd. It didn't say release; it said solution. That could mean anything, so I did my best to suppress the build-up of anxiety I was experiencing. I would talk to Grant on Sunday; maybe he knew something I didn't. Sunday came and I was anxious to speak with him. After going through the usual wait, I made the call to Canada. Grant answered and asked why I hadn't called in a while. I told him that the telephones had been broken down and I could not call out. He told me he had some bad news. I wondered what could be so bad - I didn't think it could get any worse. Then I thought of my mother. She was eighty-five and her health was failing.

"Do you want me to tell you the good news first?" he asked.

"No. What's wrong, Grant?" I asked.

"Your son, Christian, was killed in a car crash. I'm sorry, Paul. I didn't know if I should tell you".

Everything sort of stopped. I couldn't grasp the information; my ears must be deceiving me. My head stepped into nothingness.

"Paul . . . Paul, are you there?"

"Yes, I'm here", I said slowly, still trying to get back to earth.

"I'm sorry I had to tell you this, but I thought it better for you to hear it from me than somebody else", he said.

"Yeah, thanks Grant".

"My father and mother drove there to lend support; you

know, helping Isla with the funeral arrangements. They said it was a large funeral; he was a well-liked kid. . . . . "

He kept talking about what, I don't know. My thoughts were a million miles away, in that little prairie town where Christian had grown up. I visualised my sister and her husband being there, helping with things. They were both always there for me; my brother-in-law, Mark, so strong in character, would see that everything was done all right. That was reassuring.

". . . and the lawyers are confident that, two more days, and you're out of there", Grant was saying.

His last words brought me back to the conversation.

"Well then, with any luck, I will be seeing you soon", I said.

"Don't let anything happen to you, now. Stay safe, brother", he said.

As I hung the phone up, I felt like I had a heavy weight tied around my neck. I felt my shoulders sag under the weight; my walk was a trudge. The pain was numbing. It was a long walk back to the gallery.

Chapter Twelve

"FREEDOM IS BITTERSWEET"

THE FIRST DAY of December brought a visit from Ivonne, and with her she brought a renewed sense of hope. Ivonne had been talking with the lawyers and they seemed to think that on the third I would be going out. She said the radio reports were confirming the date - they said no later than the end of the week. I told her of my call to Grant and of the news of the death of my son. She had heard this also and was saddened by my loss, but no matter how sad this situation was, nothing would bring him back. It was necessary to remain focused enough to get out of here alive. At the end of the visit we exchanged our letters and while holding her in my arms, I said, "Let this be the last time you have to come to this place."

"Only two more days." Her smile was infectious. She broke away from my embrace and, taking my hands in hers, she said, "*Te amo*, Paulie."

When she reached the exit door she turned and raised two fingers into the air. I waved back, one last time before she vanished from my sight. After the strip-search, we were led back to the gallery to begin unpacking the goods that family and friends had brought.

Later in the afternoon, around four o'clock, the guards came up to our gallery to call names for release. This was unusual; months would go by without anyone from our gallery going free, so everyone stood out in the gallery listening for their name. I stood with my fingers crossed. Norman slid up beside me and wished me luck. I knew that he, too, hoped that his name would be called. On this day, only three names were called; Norman and I were not included, but surprisingly, our German friend Peter Wiess was. He went from a state of disbelief to one of sheer joy. He'd been caught totally unaware. He ran around crazily, giving away his meagre possessions before running down the gallery to join the waiting guards.

The three lucky recipients of freedom left with the guards, leaving the rest of us to get on with our routines. Like vultures, others swept down upon the vacated cells to take whatever could be gleaned. In about four or five minutes all the articles were dispersed throughout the gallery community. I had just returned to my cell when I heard my name being called. I rose from my bunk and went to my door to see what the racket was about.

There was Peter, yelling out, "Paul, they want you, not me. Hurry! Hurry! Before they change their minds."

"What are you talking about? They called your name, not mine," I said.

"No, they mixed your name with mine. You had better get going," he said.

I turned to Norman and asked him to take the keys for my cell. Damien had not come back from school and I knew he didn't have his keys with him. Looking around, hopefully for the last time, I knew that if I were to leave here today I would never forget these surroundings. They would be burned into my mind forever - I would take these memories with me to my grave. I had only a few things; after all, I had been packed, ready to leave, since May! I said good-bye to Norman and then I was off down the gallery. My acquaintances, the men I had lived with this past year all came out to bid me farewell. I didn't delay. I walked straight out of the gallery without looking back. I looked only forward, to the future.

I joined other prisoners at the administration office. We were lined up in single file to wait for our walking papers. I'd been standing there for about fifteen minutes when I saw Damien come out of the computer room. He saw me in the line-up, so he walked over.

"Going home, eh, doc," he said as we hugged each other, knowing that quite possibly, this would be the last time we would see each other.

"Take care of yourself, Damien. I hope you get out of here soon. I gave Norman the key for the cell, but you're going to have the vultures come for handouts. Everyone knows that you own everything."

"Hope to see you around, Paul," he said. Then he turned and walked away, heading for the gallery. I watched him disappear from my sight. I raised my eyes up to the window of the cell I'd called home, and made my last look a cold hard stare before being called in to receive my discharge paper. I didn't say a word, just stared at that little piece of paper that I had waited for, for so long. I rejoined the others outside and once more we had to call out our names, just to be sure they had the right people. When they were satisfied, we were marched out to the gate to wait through one more identification procedure. Finally we were all cleared and allowed through the portal, out into the free world!

José Talavera was there to greet me. After the handshakes and backslapping, we climbed into his Land Cruiser for the first stop - the offices of *El Nuevo Diario* newspaper for an interview. Being free at last should have been a happy occasion, but it wasn't. I felt that at any time, someone would yank my string and I would find myself going back to the prison. Another thing that disturbed me was the absence of Ivonne. I wanted her to share with me these first moments of freedom; especially after all we'd gone through. She should have been here to celebrate this moment. No, oddly enough, it wasn't as happy a moment as I'd imagined - a bit of a letdown after the months of anxiety. Next we went to see Mario Sequiera, our other lawyer, to notify him that I was indeed free. After congratulatory drinks, we retired to José's house to spend the evening. I inquired when I could go to Granada to pick up Ivonne. I didn't want her to hear of my release before I could see her first. José said he would drive me to Granada tomorrow, after first going to the courthouse. That was okay by me, as long as I could be in Granada by noon.

The next day, after José concluded his business at the courthouse, I felt that I was being paraded around and shown off like a trophy. As the time passed, it became evident that going to Granada was not a priority with José. I repeatedly told him that I wanted to be in Granada at noon. Ivonne would be waiting and I would be there! I don't think he took me seriously, but I was tired of his games. At twelve o'clock, I waited for him to stop the vehicle for a red light and jumped out into the noisy, polluted atmosphere of Managua, where even crossing the street is hazardous to your health. The heat hit me like a blast wave. The hot air combined with the carbon exhaust from the diesel motors made my eyes burn. Dodging the cars that honked at me, I made it to the roadside, where the street vendors hawked their wares.

Once I got my bearings, I set off walking. I realised that I didn't have a cent to my name and all my belongings were at José's house, but for now that didn't matter. I could phone him from Granada. What did matter was getting to Granada. I walked up the highway to Masaya. The next city past Masaya was Granada, which sat on the shores of the great Lake Nicaragua. I was in good physical shape, but I estimated that this would be a fifty-kilometre jaunt - a daunting task in this heat, without water. I must have been nuts to attempt such a thing. I picked up my pace. The people driving by me must have wondered what a gringo was doing out here, walking in the country. One such vehicle stopped and gave me a ride. I think it was a Toyota pickup truck, but there were so many different body parts on the thing, I couldn't distinguish the make. This was a typical farm vehicle, used to transport people from the outlying farm communities who were bringing their goods to the marketplace in Managua. I climbed in the back and joined the people who were already standing there, gripping the makeshift racks. They were of all ages, from infants to elderly.

The youngest passenger looked at me wide-eyed; the child had probably never been this close to a gringo. The oldest stared off into the blue skies, indifferent to an outsider. They had made this trip too often to care who I was or where I was going. The inquisitive ones were of working age, both male and female. In Nicaragua, the women worked alongside the men, and in most cases, they outworked the men. The men were asking questions and the women were snickering amongst themselves. I had employed many people such as these; they were good, hardworking people, proud of their families and homes.

As the truck moved down the highway, it was great to feel the breeze. It cooled and dried my sweat-soaked shirt. My fellow passengers had shared their water, the ride, and conversation with me, so when I jumped out of the truck I waved and thanked them for their kindness. The truck ambled off down the dusty side road that led to their village, leaving me alone once again. I felt refreshed, but even after that ride I knew I had better hurry if I wanted to reach Granada by nightfall. I ran and ran; the highway seemed to go on forever. If it weren't for the road signs telling me how far I'd gone, I would have turned around. The worst part was watching the buses passing me, all of them going to my destination. For a lousy three Cordoba - about thirty cents - I could have taken a ride and been in Granada by now.

I was nearing Masaya when a taxi pulled alongside and the driver asked if I needed a ride. I told him I didn't have any money; if I did, I would take a bus. He asked where was I going. When I told him Granada, he must have thought I was crazy. He invited me into his cab and said he would help me out. He drove me to where the bus to Granada stopped; reaching into his pocket, he produced money for the bus fare. Thanking him, I ran off to catch that bus. In Nicaragua you don't have to wait long for a bus, as one comes every ten minutes or so. Once I got on that bus, I was elated. I would be with Ivonne soon!

The bus arrived in Granada in one piece - no small feat. Every time you climb on a bus here, you're taking your life in your hands. The bus park was within walking distance of Ivonne's family home. It felt good to be on familiar ground once again. Passing the century-old hospital gave me a chill; it always gave me an ominous feeling of dread. The architecture suggested a mausoleum more than a hospital, lending itself to the macabre. I could see the corner of the street now. I was only a stone's throw from the house. Anticipation quickened my pace. As I rounded the corner of the familiar street, I noticed the neighbourhood hadn't changed at all - time had stood still here. The same children played in the street; the same old people sat on their chairs outside their homes.

When I reached the house, the gate and door were closed. I had just put my hand up to knock when the door flew open. Ivonne must have seen me coming from the balcony. Our eyes met, first in surprise at this chance meeting then melted into longing. We embraced. Locked in each other's arms, we gave thanks, for we knew that our yearlong ordeal was finally over. Shouts rang through the house: "Paul is here! Paul is here!" The sound of running feet broke our embrace. I followed Ivonne into the house to be met by her parents, who had also stood by me one hundred percent. This welcome was everything I had imagined it would be. Ivonne's brothers, Ricardo and Norman, brought over some beers to add to our merriment.

We had a quiet little family party. It was relaxing, but at the same time exhilarating to know that I was truly free! It was just beginning to sink in that I didn't have to return to prison. The next morning, I called Grant to let him know that I was out and things were fine, and to ask him to wire some money down to me - walking back to Managua was a more than ridiculous notion! After I placed the call, Ivonne and I had a couple of hours to wait for Western Union to open, so we took the time to walk through the ancient city. The architecture in Granada is the most beautiful in all of Central America. Walkways led through the Central Park. Adorning the park like jewels on a necklace are a band shelter and a fountain; on hot, sultry nights, it is a fine setting for romance. Surrounding the park are some of the most magnificent buildings comprising the city core.

For those who would like to sip a cold drink and watch the comings and goings or to just pass the time of day, there is the Alhambra Hotel, where I had hung out with the expatriate Americans to watch football and chat. It is a pleasant venue to sit and reminisce of good times past, or look forward to good times in the future. We picked up the money at the Western Union office in record time. Usually you have to wait, as Western Union is the busiest business in all of Nicaragua. We returned to Ivonne's parents' home to tell them we would be going to Managua for a few days to get our paperwork together, ready for our trip to Canada.

While Ivonne packed some clothes, I sat and talked with Ivonne's mother. When Ivonne reappeared with the luggage, I excused myself to find a taxi, leaving mother and daughter a few moments alone together. Hailing a taxi is no problem, there are plenty of available taxis around, but trying to find one to take you out of the city can be difficult. The fare is negotiable, and should be negotiated beforehand, or a gringo will be overcharged. I was fortunate to find a driver that would take us to Managua for thirty dollars.

Ivonne and I said our final good-bye to her family while the taxi driver loaded the suitcase into the trunk of the car. After one final wave, we watched the house disappear from sight. We were on our own now, with a bright, sunshiny future to look forward to. We checked into the Margot Hotel, the very same hotel I'd tried to get to on that fateful night one year ago. We were shown to a sparse room with Seventies-style furnishings - what you would expect at a Holiday Inn from that period. There was a balcony that looked out onto the street, not much of a view and kind of noisy, but for the price we were paying, it was a bargain. The service was superb and the beds comfortable - what else do you want – I was free!

Feeling the effects of the alcohol consumption from the previous night's party, I decided to have a shower to wash away the hangover. Stepping into the shower stall and being able to turn on a faucet for water was a luxury. I let the water beat down on me. It felt good; how I had missed one of life's simple pleasures - having a shower! Stepping out of the shower and towelling myself dry, I looked at myself in the full-length mirror for the first time in almost a year. I had lost a lot of weight, but I was sturdy from the daily exercise. I left the bathroom and that mirror behind - vanity was never part of my character, made even less so by my incarceration.

Ivonne was stretched out on the bed. The television was on, but she could not care less - she was only looking at me.

"Come here, Paulie," she said, patting the bed. "We have not been reacquainted yet. You have been out of prison for quite some time. I thought all men coming out of prison were sex starved."

"I have to make a few phone calls first. Why don't you have a shower, I'll make the calls, then we can go have a nice, romantic dinner and come back here, where I'll show you just how sex-starved I really am!" I jumped on the bed and rolled on top of her. While trying to get out from under me, she said, "I'll scream rape and they will take you away again. Now, let me up right now! If you don't, I'll scream!"

Letting her up, I watched her walk into the bathroom. I waited till I could hear the water running before I left the room. I went to the front lobby in search of a newspaper; I wanted to see what was being said about my release. I bought a copy of each of the dailies. On the front page of the *La Prenza* was an article that stopped me cold.

The headline read "Canadian could be re-arrested." I felt that cold chill again. I walked back up the stairs to my room. Once inside, I sat at the desk and read the article. It seemed the Prosecuting office didn't like the decision handed down by the Appeal Court. I thought that any decision from the Appeal Court was final! Where is José now, I wondered, when I need him?

Ivonne came out of the bathroom wearing only a towel. Her feet made soft squeaking noises on the tile floor. Looking over at me, she saw my concerned expression. "What is the matter, Paul?" she asked.

"The papers say there is a possibility that they will recharge me. I need to phone Talavera. Do you have his number?"

"Yes, I have it in my purse."

While she rummaged around in her purse, I had time to weigh the possibilities. The situation was just too unpredictable; nothing here was what it seemed to be. This was the land of "what is isn't and what isn't is!"

"Here it is!" She handed me the scrap of paper with Talavera's number written across the top. As I dialled, I was thinking what I was going to say to him. The worst-case scenario would have been us fleeing the country without the correct papers.

"Shit, he's not home. I got his answering machine. Do you have the Consulate's number?" I asked.

Ivonne recited the number while I dialled. On the second ring someone answered and I was transferred to Jack Adams. Those at the Consulate were as concerned as I was over my safety; that was reassuring. Jack said that a car would pick me up outside the hotel in fifteen minutes. I needed to have passport photos taken and Canada wanted me to call right away. Hanging the phone up, I looked over at Ivonne, who was clearly wondering what was going on.

"I have to go to the Consulate. They are sending a driver over to pick me up to take me for passport photos. Grant has called and wants me to return his call. By the time you get dressed and your face done, I will be back. Then we can go for a nice dinner."

"Don't be long, okay? I don't want to be here alone," she said.

"Wild horses couldn't keep me away. I will make this as fast as possible." I smiled. The one thing Ivonne hated was being left alone.

I opened the doors that led to the balcony and leaned over the railing to see if the car had arrived. Sure enough, the car was parked in a no parking zone with the motor running and the tinted windows rolled up tight. That had to be a government car. We kissed and I repeated my vow that I would be back as fast as I could. Shutting the door behind me, I could hear the voices on the television as I walked down the hall to the stairs. I opened the car door and met a blast of frigid air from the air-conditioning. They kept their cars too cold for my liking. I almost needed a sweater for the ride to the Consulate. I was whisked right through the security doors. The woman behind the information kiosk directed me to Jack Adams' office and told me to go right in - they were expecting me.

Jack was talking on the phone when I entered the office. He motioned for me to come and sit down. I assumed he was talking with Canada. I heard my name mentioned. Holding his hand over the receiver, Jack said, "I have Foreign Affairs and Grant Sanders on a conference call. They wish to speak with you." Turning his attention back to the conversation he said, "Yes, I will put him on now." Jack gave me the handset. "It's Grant, I will be outside if you need me." He rose and motioned for me to sit in his chair. "You may as well make yourself comfortable," he said before leaving his office.

"Hello Grant."

"Hi, how are you? Have you seen the newspapers?"

"Yes."

"We've been discussing this turn of events, and we believe that you have to get out of there before something happens," Grant said.

"Who's we?" I asked, not liking where this conversation was heading.

"I have Foreign Affairs Ottawa on a conference call," Grant said.

"Hello, Mr. Wylie, this is Sally Marchand, Foreign Affairs Ottawa."

" Hello Sally."

"Grant and I were just talking about this recent turn of events. We feel that for your own safety, you should leave there right away, before they can re-arrest you," she said.

"Do you remember where we used to buy crocodile skins?" Grant interjected. "You could cross over to Costa Rica, to your friend who has that cattle ranch. You have got to get out of there now! Jack can get you a travel document and you can be on your way within the hour."

I couldn't believe what I was hearing. Not only was this dangerous, but this would mean leaving Ivonne behind, something I could not do - after all these months of separation, to be separated again! We had been through enough, and now this!

"Paul, are you hearing me?" Grant said.

"Yes, I hear you, but it doesn't mean I like what I hear. You understand what you want me to do."

"Mr. Wylie, we, the government, can only advise you. The decision rests solely with you. I can't imagine what you have already endured, but we are very much concerned over your present safety," Sally said.

"Paul, get out of there now! You can be home tomorrow. The risk of you staying there is far more dangerous than a jungle crossing," Grant urged.

"Okay, I will phone you from Costa Rica, Grant," I said reluctantly. I would have to break this news to Ivonne. That would be far worse than a jungle crossing.

Hanging the phone up with a heavy hand, my mind raced through the necessary preparations for the border crossing. It would have to be done at night, and I would have to pass through the military boat patrols that were frequent along the San Juan River, whose ownership was being disputed by Nicaragua and Costa Rica. Great care would have to be taken. I shuddered to think what would happen if I was caught.

I left the office to let Jack know what I had to do. There was no doubt that he was already aware that I'd be leaving the country immediately. However, the details would remain secret, known only to me.

Marion was there. As usual, she was efficient, proposing that we prepare a travel certificate that would ensure travel one-way to Canada. The first step was obtaining a passport picture to be embossed on the certificate. When the certificate was in order I thanked both Jack and Marion for the help they'd given me in the past year while I was in prison. They supplied me with a driver to take me back to the hotel. When the car dropped me off, I could see our balcony door open and the drapes fluttering in the breeze - Ivonne never did like air-conditioning. It was a slow walk to the front door of the hotel, as I tried to come to grips with what I had to say to her. I did not like this one bit.

I sighed, then took a deep breath before entering the hotel room.

Ivonne was lying on the bed, watching the television. She rose to greet me. Seeing that I was upset, she said, "What is the matter, Paul?"

" Ivonne, please sit down. I have awful news to tell you." Once she was seated I continued. "I spoke with Grant and the Canadian Foreign Affairs representative. They think I should leave the country immediately."

"When?" she asked.

"Within the hour," I said.

"Oh..."

I then explained in detail what had transpired while I was away, leaving out what I was preparing to do. That would have worried her, and secrecy was important, if this was to work.

"When will you send for me?" asked Ivonne. Tears were welling up in her eyes. I had to look away before I became too emotional as well.

Gathering my composure, I looked into her soft brown eyes and said, "I will not rest till I have you in Canada, I promise you that! We have fought this together and we will continue to fight this until the day that we can be together, to have our life without worry or trouble."

"I love you, Paul. If this is necessary, then so be it, I only want what is best for us. I will wait for you to call. Go now, okay? Prolonging this will only be more difficult for me."

Ivonne was right. The longer I stayed, the more opportunity I'd have for second thoughts. I couldn't afford second thoughts. I had a little daypack in the suitcase. In it I put the blue suit that I would change into when I crossed the border. That was all I would take: the suit, a change of socks, shirt and underwear.

"That is all you are taking?" she asked.

"Yes, I'm travelling light. Do me a favour, phone Talavera

and get my personal effects from him. You can bring everything with you when you come to Canada. Whatever you do, keep our letters safe. One day they will be a valuable resource when I write a book!" I said.

Reaching into my pocket for a roll of bills, I counted out the money and divided it in two, giving her half. "Here, take this. You will need some money until I can get to a Western Union in Canada," I said. She nodded. No words could be said; it was too sorrowful. We came together in an embrace, holding tight our love for each other. I will never forget that last look into her eyes. It told our whole story, all the pain and sorrow that had been prevalent in our relationship thus far. The final farewell kiss made my knees weak. My head swam with emotion, my heart felt stabbed with pain.

We broke apart. Grabbing the daypack, I was out the door before I had any doubts. Down the stairs I went, two at a time. I had this compelling urge to get this show on the road, to leave this sadness behind.

A taxi stand was just across from the hotel. While hailing a taxi, I looked up at the balcony to see Ivonne standing there, looking down at me. No words were exchanged, for none were needed. Climbing into the cab, I turned and waved for the last time before the taxi sped off.

"Where to?" the driver said in the characteristic manner all cabbies have, the world over.

"Wembley," I replied half-heartedly, not really paying much attention. My mind was still back in the hotel room. Wembley is a bus station of sorts, but it is also one of Managua's marketplaces. You can barter for anything from soup to nuts; quite truthfully, anything can be found there, including trouble. Gringos are targets for all types of hustlers - some annoying, some downright dangerous. It was advisable to keep valuables out of sight of would-be thieves. My journey would begin at Wembley. From here on in, I would have to be wary - until I boarded that plane that said "Canada" on it!

Paying the driver, I stepped out into the mass of people. Confusion was everywhere. Children tugged on my shirtsleeves, looking for any change that I could give them. The little street urchins offered to guide me for a few pesos. I walked through the children and entered the market. Shop merchants called out their wares to the throngs of people walking along the narrow aisles. Shoppers stopping to barter at the stalls made the going tough. Finally, I broke through the mob of shoppers and found myself right where I wanted to be: the bus terminal. I spotted the sign reading "San Carlos" in large bold letters down at the far end. That was the town where I was headed, the last town on the frontier. After that, it would be by water into Costa Rica.

I only had a fifteen-minute wait till the next bus departed to the fringes of no-man's land. Spotting a beer sign, I made my way toward it for a cold one. I was thirsty; two or three of those would hit the spot and, maybe, act as a sedative for the long and tiresome trip. The buses are antiquated contraptions belching black exhaust fumes. The exhaust, mixed with the high humidity, leaves an ever-present film on your skin. I shudder to think what it does to your lungs! When the bus arrived I had just finished the last of my beer. I was satisfied to see that few people were taking this bus. Perhaps I could get some sleep. I was going to need all the sleep I could get; tonight would be sleepless. Boarding the bus, I took a seat roughly in the middle. I knew from previous experience that was the best spot. Usually these buses were overcrowded. Being close to the exit doors was maddening, always having to move for people coming on and off with their supplies and animals. For most people, this was the only form of transportation. If you are not used to travelling like this, it is an experience of a lifetime. I have witnessed some unbelievable sights. They show total disregard for public safety.

The driver closed the door preparatory to departure. I could tell he was a seasoned veteran. A bottle of water stood upright on the motor cowling. Beside the water were his music tapes. These were the two prerequisites for a long drive. His short arms could hardly reach the steering wheel. His belly was resting on the bottom of the wheel. I don't know how he could drive like that. His helper, a boy of about fifteen, was selecting the music to be played. Their discussion over the selection became animated. Finally the boy won out, and I heard a scratchy version of a Michael Jackson tune: "Just beat it..." I thought that's exactly what I want to do - beat the hell out of that cassette player.

Maybe if I closed my eyes, I mused, sleep will come. But that was impossible. The bus stopped and started constantly, letting people on and off. I would have to wait till we got out on the open highway. A woman who appeared well kept occupied the seat next to me; judging by the parcels she had with her, she was returning home after shopping in the city. The window seat provided me with an unobstructed view of the countryside. The flat valley floor seemed to stretch endlessly on, bordered by mountains on one side and water on the other - Nicaragua was an agricultural paradise. The steady drone of the diesel motor, mixed with the salsa music and my fatigue made me drowsy. I drifted off to sleep.

The shadows of late afternoon gave way to night; it was dark when we arrived in San Carlos, a frontier town. Disembarking, I looked around at the squalor - this was the (incredibly) poor Nicaragua. I spotted a taxi and headed toward it, hoping that it could take me to my associate's house. It had been quite a while since I had last seen him. Ronald McDonald (clearly not his name) crocodile hunter extraordinaire, dealt in reptiles: snakes, crocs, frogs, and iguanas. He raised them at his farm; you had to be careful where you walked - it wasn't a petting zoo! He'd been the first person to take me croc hunting, and tonight I hoped to go back on the river. This time, instead of shooting crocs, it would be for the purpose of transporting me into Costa Rica.

The taxi driver knew where to take me; Ronald was well known in these parts. I must have looked a little out of place, the only gringo in town, going to a reptile farm - not exactly ordinary. It was a bumpy ride. We followed a cart path until we came to a fork. One way led down to the river, the other way led to Ronald's farmhouse. The driver expertly manoeuvred up a driveway that wound through the tropical greenery, coming to stop in front of a typical ranch house with its wraparound porch. I paid the driver in local currency, making sure to give him a large tip. Where I was going, I wouldn't need that currency.

The lights were all on in the house, suggesting that Ronald was at home, but you could never be too sure. He could be on the river. Night is the best time for hunting, when the crocs are aggressive. It is when they feed on their unsuspecting prey. You hunt them by shining a light on them, then you move up close to shoot them between the eyes with a little 22-caliber. The tricky part is putting them in the boat.

I heard the screen door open and then I heard his unmistakable voice call out into the night, "Who's there?"

"It's me, the Canadian, Ronald," I answered, walking from the cover of darkness into the subdued light of the porch.

"Look at you, my friend! I thought you would be back in Canada by now. I heard that you were released from the prison, but I did not expect to see you here. I think that you are not here for the skins." His eyes stared hard into mine, as if in search of the truth.

"No, I'm not here for the skins, but I need your help to cross over to Costa Rica," I told him. I returned the stare; we held steady for a moment, each of us weighing the implications. Without him, the crossing would be impossible. I couldn't go it alone, but for him, his life would be on the line if caught; at the least, he'd get a prison sentence.

"Come on inside. You remember my wife, Maree, and my sons. Michael is home; he will be happy to see you." Ronald took me by the shoulder and steered me toward the front door. I knew by way of that invitation that he would take me, for a price. That would have to be negotiated, after the mandatory food, drink and small talk.

His wife Maree met me at the door. "Hello, welcome. You must be hungry after that long ride. I will fix something to eat."

"Thank you, Maree, that would be fine. You look as good as the last time I saw you," I said, smiling. Maree was a little on the plump side after three children. A transformation seems to occur in Latino women; their once-shapely posteriors change, their hips widen to accommodate fat deposits. Maree's face still retained her adolescent beauty, though. She must have been a real looker when she was young.

I took the proffered seat at the kitchen table while Maree scurried around the kitchen preparing the meal. Ronald went to the cupboard to get the rum. He placed the bottle of rum, Coca-Cola, and a dish of ice on the tabletop. Only when he was sure that everything was under control in the kitchen did he bring the glasses. Then he sat down and toasted to my newfound freedom. We had a few drinks before Maree brought the food to the table. She was an able cook. The meal consisted of Gallo Pinto, *Tostados con Quesos,* and blood sausage. This was the typical fare that I had grown accustomed to and enjoyed. I didn't realise how hungry I was. This was the only food I'd had all day.

Michael came into the kitchen to say hello. He had filled out in the last year. Michael was seventeen and was already an accomplished riverman - his wide shoulders and thick arms attested to that.

"Hello Michael, you have gotten bigger since the last time I saw you," I said, smiling. I had always liked him; he was always good-natured and courteous to me.

"Hello, what brings you back? More skins, I hope; I have two hundred salted, ready to go!"

" Michael, is there fuel in the boat?" asked Ronald.

"Yes, Papa."

"Good. Help your mother with your brothers and then meet us outside," Ronald said. "Come, Paul. We talk outside. Bring the bottle; I think we could use another drink." Ronald pushed himself up from the table. He took the glasses and the mix, I took the bottle, and we walked out onto the porch.

The night breeze felt cool. It was a clear night. The moon was shining full, providing lots of light - perfect for croc hunting. It was time to talk. I knew he had me over a barrel. I had to pay him whatever he wanted because he knew I needed him; I didn't have much to negotiate with.

"What you ask is very dangerous, Paul," he said. "The military patrol boats are on the river checking every boat. Everybody watches that river, since the American DEA gave money to the police to fight drug smuggling. The Nicaraguan authorities want to make these huge busts to show the Americans that they are doing their job. The Costa Rican authorities are stopping all the illegal immigrants from Nicaragua and sending them back. Costa Rica wants the river - Nicaragua wants the river for the proposed canal. Whatever country controls the river controls the canal, and it would mean a richness beyond our country's expectations." He downed the rest of his drink in one long swallow.

"I have to get to San José tonight, Ronal. They may recharge me tomorrow morning - that is why I must go now." My voice conveyed my urgency.

"I can get you across, but the place I take you can be dangerous for you, my friend." His smile suggested that this wasn't going to be an easy trip. "I want one hundred dollars for taking you. This is, I think, a reasonable price, considering the degree of difficulty. You don't have a passport; if we are stopped for questioning, Michael and I would be in serious trouble for aiding in your illegal border crossing."

It could very well be difficult to hide from the patrol boats, but I also knew that Ronald knew these waterways as well, perhaps better than anyone. He would not put his son Michael in harm's way, this I was sure of. He wanted too much money, but I didn't have the time or inclination for bartering, so I agreed with his price and produced a bill from my pocket.

"Thank you for helping me, Ronald," I said as I handed it over to him.

"Don't thank me now, you haven't made it across. Thank me the next time we meet," he said, patting me on the back.

He left to get Michael and the two of them readied themselves for the trip down the river. Maree took my daypack and pressed my suit, saying that I must look good for the trip to San José. She neatly folded my clothes and wrapped them in plastic before repackaging them into the daypack. She then put a packet of cheese and bread in the pack, telling me that by morning, I would be in need of food. Saying good-bye to Maree, I left to join Ronald and Michael and help them take the supplies down to the boat, a short walk from the house.

We were travelling down the river in the guise of croc hunters, so we took the tools of the trade along, in case we were stopped by a patrol.

Down at the boat launch we stowed our gear aboard. Ronald set the forty-horsepower motor on the transom and Michael began to prime the motor with gasoline from the two five-gallon steel tanks. When we were all set, Ronald sat at the back controlling the motor while I sat in the middle with the rifle across my legs. Michael gave us a push off the beach and then deftly climbed aboard without making a sound. The boat was an eighteen-footer that had a wide girth, a typical riverboat used here to haul supplies from the city to the indigenous people living along the river. The San Juan River was, in many respects, the border with Costa Rica, as it started here and went out to the Caribbean at a town called San Juan del Norte. In most parts, the river was wide and quite deep. This was where the proposed canal would go. It was far more logical than the Panama Canal, a lot shorter and less costly.

At this time of year the water current was fast, just beginning to recede from the winter rains. From here on in, there would be no rain. The dry season lasts till May, then the rain begins again. Ronald said the waterway was dangerous at this time of year because of the floating debris. At night, getting hit by a log could puncture the hull and sink the boat, which was why Michael was in the front, keeping his eyes on the river. He shone the light on anything suspect to identify what was coming at us.

Ronald kept the boat close to shore. Under cover of the shadows as the moonlight could give us away to the authorities. This part of the river was where the patrol boats were. If we were lucky, we could slip by between patrols. Once we were off this waterway and into the tributary that would take us deep into the jungle, where we would we be out of danger from the patrols. I couldn't wait to get off this river. Only the steady drone of the outboard motor broke the stillness of the night. It was making me edgy. The time went by slowly, like watching a clock. I don't know how long it was before Ronald turned the boat down a tributary leading into the jungle. We all let out a sigh of relief. Getting this far and escaping detection was one hurdle crossed.

As we travelled further into the bowels of the jungle, the waterway grew progressively narrower and significantly shallower. In some spots, if it weren't for Michael's observant eye, we would have grounded out. It became necessary now to use poles to make our way. Ronald raised the motor, as the motor leg was too long - it kept getting snarled up with debris. I knew we were in crocodile habitat. This was getting into their prime territory. In the upper reaches of the river where we had just come from, the water is cooler, fast flowing, and is usually clear of silt. Here in the lower reaches, the water is slow moving, warm, and it provides adequate cover for the crocodile. Crocs like shallow waters that receives abundant sunlight and therefore abounds in rooted and floating plants that in turn support a diverse fauna. They rely on both land and water for their activities. By day they will be found on shore, basking in the sunlight, but at night they are in the water, where the temperature cools slower than that of the air.

This swamp forest we had entered was croc heaven. As I shone the flashlight around, I saw various sets of eyes watching as we glided past. In the beam of light the crocs' eyes glowed red. Even then, they could be submerged under a jetty or a tree, waiting for the unsuspecting. For the unwary, death is never seen, only felt. Crocodiles cannot chew so they tear off pieces and swallow these whole. The victim is usually submerged and shaken vigorously to dismember it. If the pieces are too tough, a comrade will come to assist, using the prey in a tug-of-war contest.

"We are here. This is where you get off, my friend." Ronald stood in the boat and pointed to land. "See where I'm pointing to?"

My eyes followed the direction indicated by his hand. I could see nothing, only the blackness of the mangroves.

"Follow through there till you come to a trail. It is well travelled. The ranchers use it to drive their cattle from the water. Make sure you stay to your right. Follow the trail; you will come to a hill crowned by two eucalyptus trees. At the top of that rise is Costa Rica."

"Okay..." I said, not too sure at all about getting out of the boat.

"Amigo, watch that you don't become dinner for them!" Ronald laughed. "I want to see you again. Just remember, walk steadily but slowly, and keep a lookout for nests. If you see one, take care to walk around - do not disturb. There will always be a guard close by. Be very careful, Paul. This is breeding time." Ronald's voice held sincerity that I knew to be genuine.

"Take care, my friend," I replied. "I will be back to drink a bottle of rum with you." Turning to Michael, I clasped his hand and said, "Take care of your father, Michael, and thank you, my friend."

Grabbing my daypack from the floor of the boat, I slipped over the side into the waist-deep water. The vegetation threatened to suck me deeper into the quagmire. I moved away from the boat, my feet making sucking noises as I made my way into the gloom of the mangrove swamp. In some places the debris was more stable, so the going was faster, but that would only be for ten feet or so, then I would find myself waist-deep in the water again. As the time wore on, so did my nerves. I kept a vigilant eye out for crocodiles, always conscious that they were in the vicinity. My nerves were tighter than guitar strings - ready to snap whenever I encountered a nest or saw a hungry pair of eyes. It became increasingly difficult at each encounter to hold my fear in check and stop myself from running. The fear was so uncontrollable at times it brought bile up into my throat.

I knew to run would be certain death. Crocs are territorial so defensive behaviours are more pronounced during the breeding and nesting season. Running would show as an act of aggression, triggering an attack. The most I could hope for was that they were well fed and too tired from mating to care about my intrusion. Time seemed to stand still. Every minute was an hour. I didn't know what time it was or how much further I had to go. My mind reeled with the possibility that

I had lost my way. My surroundings hadn't changed - it all looked the same. I felt the panic well up from within me and had to stop to collect myself. Taking in three deep breaths, I exhaled slowly, placing my mind in a state of forced calm.

After several moments I felt fine again, and all the more determined to get through this. I hadn't come this far, only to die in a swamp so very far from home. It was with this new resolve that I pushed forward into the night. The full moon cast ominous shadows through the jungle canopy. The terrain was drying out; swamp vegetation was giving way to the thick vegetation of jungle. I had made it through the crocodile habitat, now I must find the pathway.

There are incredible noises in the jungle at night, which reach a frenzy near morning. I knew that it was nearing daylight because the noise of the birds and monkeys was maddening. Stumbling through the jungle, I watched the branches overhead for snakes. These parts were known to host the deadly Bushmaster and Anacondas that were as thick as me!

The panic returned, but I pressed onward. "Where is that damned path?" I muttered. I began to run; the urge to leave the jungle cries behind me was too great. "I have to find that pathway!" Slipping and stumbling, I soon realised how futile running was and slowed down to a walk. There was no sense in injuring myself by being foolish. Night gave way to daylight and the jungle took on an altogether different look and brought forth in me different feelings. Gone was that urgent need to escape. It was replaced with a sense of wonderment; this was nature at its most prominent, a magical world filled with a spectacular array of plant life. The filtered sunlight pooled on the jungle floor; the surrounding forest framed these spots.

It was in such a spot that I chose to rest. Sitting down on a decomposing mahogany log, I opened my daypack and took out the packet of food Maree had provided. I ate slowly, contemplating the night I had spent in the swamp. It gave my nerves time to adjust. I needed to be in control. I wasn't out of here yet; I still had not found the path that would lead me out of here. Eating the last bite of cheese, I stood up, refreshed and ready to travel on. Taking bearings was impossible. I just went in the direction opposite the one where I'd entered the clearing. After walking for an hour or so, the symphonic music made by the buzzing bees and wasps, with percussion from the crackling vegetation, disturbed my nerves. Anywhere snakes, bloodsuckers and other crawling organisms abound, it is hard not to feel fear! Nevertheless, I drew from the storehouse of my prison experience the strength to face this fear and welcome it as a friend. It would keep me wary and keen of mind.

Finally I saw the path through the foliage. My heart surged, pumping adrenaline through my veins like crazy. I took leaps and bounds through the vegetation until I stood on the pathway.

"Yes! Yes! I've made it! I screamed, jumping up and down. Relief flowed through me. For a while, I'd thought myself lost, destined to walk forever in circles. I could now pick up the pace. Turning to the right as I'd been told, I walked on. The pathway took me downward; the foliage became more swamp-like as I descended toward the valley floor. I kept on the path till I arrived at a river crossing. This must be where Ronald said the cattle were watered. Markings clearly indicated that several had been down here recently. Looking in either direction for anything that could make a meal of me, I waded into the stream. It wasn't deep, only a foot or so, and only twenty feet across.

Trying not to step in the cow pies, I walked on up the path. I rounded a turn and there, right in front of me, was the hill that Ronal had told me about - cresting the hill were two towering eucalyptus trees that dominated the skyline. I ran towards the top of hill and into what I hoped was Costa Rica. What a sight! Standing at the edge of the pasture, I could see the cattle grazing. From my vantage point, I could look down to a gravel roadway in the middle distance. Time, I thought, to abandon the clothes I was wearing and put on my clean suit. Back down to the river I went, to wash myself and change clothes. After hiding the discarded clothes, I made my way back up the hill and started toward the pasture.

I was glad that night was over and Nicaragua was behind me! I now felt warmed by the sun and looked forward to my prospects at San José airport. I felt confident now. I had the documentation from the Consulate for Proof of Nationality; if I was picked up now as an illegal, I would be sent home to Canada - perfect! I was out of danger of being re-arrested, but I still didn't know where I was. For all I knew, I was still in Nicaragua. I followed the gravel road downward, around switchbacks that zigzagged across the mountain. From these switchbacks I could see the valley below and the highway. There was no doubt that this was Costa Rica and that highway would lead me to the nation's capital, San José.

I came onto a plateau where the ranchers kept their cattle during the dry season - this would explain the cattle I saw, left unattended. I hadn't seen a car or a truck since I started out. That was good; I had no explaining to do as to what a gringo was doing walking around out here wearing a blue suit! It was getting hot, so I took off my suit coat and slung it over my shoulder, hoping to cool off some before hitting the highway. I knew from experience that the temperature would rise dramatically once I got on the tarmac.

In Latin America there is always a bar or a restaurant situated at every junction, and luckily, this highway was no exception. The sign on the exterior façade claimed the name "El Rancho del Fuego." It looked to me like this place needed a fire to burn it to the ground; it was a real hole in the wall. But at this stage of the game, who cares? I wasn't walking a step further. I was tired, thirsty and ached everywhere. I had my priorities; I would have to wait for a hot bath and clean sheets, but I needed an ice-cold beer and a thick steak to fill the void in my stomach.

The interior wasn't much different than the exterior; it was just as weather-beaten and run down. The furniture was 1940s-style, pedestal tables with cracked Arborite tops. The chairs were all homemade; they looked to be fashioned from packing crates. They were strewn around the room, left just as they were – I imagined, from the last bar fight. It took a moment to get my eyes accustomed to the darkness, then, squinting, I let my eyes wander the room, looking for a sanctuary away from any action. I picked a table under a ceiling fan that afforded me a view of the front door and the bar. At this time of the morning the place was nearly deserted. Besides the bartender, there were two teenage girls with high heels and the skimpiest hot pants that all but showed the cheeks of their posteriors, bent over a jukebox, discussing their next selection. Over at the bar, two old men sat engaged in conversation and drinks, seemingly unaware of my intrusion.

The bartender, seeing a stranger, smelled money. He wasted no time in getting to my table. He was middle-aged; lines hardened his face, telling a story of a life of hardship, but his manner was friendly, almost apologetic. I ordered two beers and a steak - this being ranch country, the meat should be good. When he returned with the beers I asked him when the bus to San José came by. There were two a day, he said; one in the morning and the other at night. The morning bus was due in an hour. I thanked him and sat back in my chair to wait. The ceiling fan sounded loud, groaning with every revolution. I suspected the bearings had long ago dried up, but the cool air was welcome. The jukebox played a mixture of romantic salsa tunes. The two girls were dancing with each other, giggling and laughing; it was entertaining to watch.

The bartender returned with a plate of meat and two refills. Draining the last drop of beer from the bottle, I passed the empty bottles back to him. Quite possibly, that was the best steak dinner I had eaten in a long time. I devoured the whole plateful of steaming meat, savouring every bite. Once I was finished, I sat back in my chair. The fatigue I had felt earlier had vanished, replaced with a desire to get on with the journey.

Paying the man, I walked outside to wait for the bus. It was due anytime now, and the last thing I wanted was for it to go by and not stop. I didn't have to wait long. The bus stopped right beside me. It was one of those tour buses, the kind that you can stretch out in. Between the air-conditioning and the comfortable seats, I was soon lulled asleep in my seat. I never heard anything until I felt a hand on my shoulder. I woke with a start. My senses screamed "danger," but one look around reassured me that I was in safe surroundings - unfamiliar, but safe. Disembarking, I entered the blast furnace outside. It sucked the air out of my lungs. The unmerciful sun was high in the sky and the sunlight bore down on me hard. That is one reason I didn't like air-conditioning - it was damn hard on your body. Adjusting from extreme temperature changes is a good way to become sick.

Spotting a taxi stand, I walked over and asked a driver for a lift to the airport. The airport, like those in most countries, was located outside of the city. This gave me time to waken properly. The sleep on the bus was the first relaxed sleep I'd had in quite some time, and I was still groggy. When we reached the airport, I paid the man in U.S. dollars and went in to purchase a ticket to take me home. The lady behind the ticket booth told me that there were no direct flights to Canada. I would have to take the next available flight to Mexico City, then a connector to Montreal, then another to Toronto. I told her that would be fine. She asked me for a passport. When I produced the travel paper that the Consulate had provided, she had to get her supervisor to look at it. I had no other identification. I could only hope that I would not be refused.

The supervisor arrived and, after one look at the document, he smiled and said, "Have a nice flight." And that was that. I had only two hours wait. I decided to phone the Canadian Embassy here in San José to check in and say I was okay. Finding a telephone was no problem; in Costa Rica they are everywhere. I dialled the number that Marion had provided. I was finally told a representative would come to the airport to talk with me, and I thanked them and hung up. I went to wait for their representative in the lounge. I couldn't think of a better place to sit.

A smartly dressed, blonde woman entered the lounge and I half-rose to get her attention. She was the Ambassador's assistant. I had seen her previously; she had accompanied the Ambassador on his visit to see me in the prison.

"You look much better than the last time we met," she told me. "How was your trip here?"

"Just fine, it was a walk in the park." I smiled and raised my hand to the waiter, then asked, "Would you care for a refreshment?"

"Yes, water please."

When the waiter arrived I placed our order and we carried on with our conversation. It was relaxing to talk to a fellow Canadian. We talked a little about everything. The waiter arrived with our refreshments, breaking off our conversation. After I had paid the man we resumed where we had left off until my flight was announced over the intercom system and it was time to depart. The time had passed swiftly. Thanking her for her time and for being courteous, I left for the boarding gate.

In no time at all I was strapped in and the plane was taxiing down the runway in preparation for takeoff. I could hear the engines rev as the plane gathered speed. The next moment, we were up and airborne, leaving the airport below. When we had reached cruising speed and the plane had settled in to the proper altitude, the stewardesses came by with the drink cart. I asked for a beer and settled in for the flight to Mexico. I looked out the window. We were over land, and I wondered if it was Nicaragua. The Captain came over the intercom to inform us of our cruising speed, time of arrival, and current geographical position. I didn't need to wonder any longer; below was Nicaragua. I tipped my beer in salute to the country that I would remember for the rest of my life, for good and for bad.

Sitting back in my seat, I closed my eyes. The emotional upheaval was crushing. Somewhere down below me, in a town called Granada, I had left a part of myself. I was both happy and sad to be leaving; my freedom was bittersweet. I had not planned any of this, especially being - yet again - separated from Ivonne. I silently looked out the window and repeated the vow I had made to her: "I will not rest till I have you in Canada. I promise you that!"

Chapter Thirteen

"THE WAY FORWARD"

It wouldn't be right for Hemp Conspiracy to end with Paul Wylie flying home to Canada with a beer in his hand and a longing in his heart. After all, this isn't Hollywood and it is certainly not the end of the story. Forced to return to Canada without Ivonne and his business in ruins, Wylie was given a quiet resolve and fearless desire to share the truth – that you have just read. As passionately as he resisted the fate imposed on him in 1998, Paul Wylie continues working on a reinvigorated project aimed at securing long-term industrial Cannabis (Hemp) production in Nicaragua. This project will be implemented as part of an integrated strategy to address climate change, air pollution, unsustainable land management and poverty. The only ending is that of the Hemp Conspiracy itself, creating a future that promises to be considerably greener and more prosperous – especially in Nicaragua.

On the basis of all the evidence, Nicaragua's highest Court of Appeal exonerated Paul Wylie in the year 2000. Wylie is not only suing the Nicaraguan government over his yearlong (illegal) incarceration and the destruction of Hemp-Agro;

there is an even more exciting plan to be implemented as part of this settlement for the direct economic and environmental benefit of Nicaragua – and without exaggeration, the entire Planet. It is also the case that the Nicaraguan authorities owe the Hemp-Agro employees their 1998 Christmas money and their jobs back. Actually, the US government and DEA do, but these events took place in Nicaragua and by law that is where the quest for justice must begin.

Before going into the basic idea of this project, and indeed the wider legal implications of Wylie's case, it is worth taking a brief look at the facts and 'confusion' that surround industrial Cannabis (or hemp) production.

Like Humanity, Cannabis is a diverse species, and while all plants within the species can interbreed there are also several genetic and man-made differences, such as those characteristics determined by the cultivator. However, the most important fact is that industrial Cannabis production is permitted under the 1961 United Nations Single Convention On Narcotic Drugs while other varieties, such as Cannabis Indica or marijuana, pot, smoke, gauge, ganja, and herb are clearly not. The 1961 United Nations Single Convention on Narcotic Drugs states that, 'this convention shall not apply to the cultivation of the Cannabis plant exclusively for industrial purposes (fibre and seed)'.

Despite the fact there are substantive genetic differences within the species, such as the naturally varying amounts of delta-9-tetrahydrocannibinol, or THC - the chemical responsible for the species 'narcotic' status and reason we inhale - humans also influence these factors during the cultivation process. These are choices determined by the desired end use of the plant.

To be absolutely sure, the methods of cultivation for narcotic (THC) quality Cannabis and fibre/seed quality Cannabis are mutually exclusive. So even while there is a natural genetic difference recognised, or at least implied, in the current (UN) legislation, it should be explicit that one cannot produce a good quality fibre/seed crop and produce a high market value narcotic at the same time. It is impossible because many

Cannabinoids - consisting of 60 chemicals unique to Cannabis, but especially THC - concentrate themselves in the reproductive parts of the plant. In order to grow it must be allowed to complete the reproductive cycle.

The reason for these chemicals concentrating in various degrees around the plant, particularly on the female flowers, is simply to protect the plant from excessive UVB radiation, water loss and to repel pests, such as Bill Clinton. These mechanisms help to secure reproduction and seeds are the main product of this process, creating - as they do - the next generation of species. In making this transformation, seeds containing no THC replace the flowers of the female plant.

Someone cultivating Cannabis in order to manufacture hashish, for example, (more likely for export) will ensure that their seeds came from a generation of plant selected for a high THC content in the first place. They will graciously tend the crop, snipping the odd bud while removing male plants to prevent fertilisation. Other than sheer stupidity, there are two very obvious reasons why the industrial fibre and seed producer would not even consider these options. Firstly, to do so would ensure an extremely low fibre yield and secondly, there would be little or no valuable seed with which to make oil, food (see hempconspiracy.com for more detail) or indeed plant the next crop.

To cater for these mutually exclusive ends, the cultivation processes of each are very different. The industrial fibre or seed producer can plant vast areas at extremely high densities without worrying about crop manipulation. If growing Cannabis for fibre and seed, 10 to 40 plants per metre-square is desirable. With a specific fibre crop, anywhere between 50 and 750 plants is good. Cannabis has a naturally occurring sex ratio of 1:1 – perfect for multipurpose (fibre/seed) industrial production but a great inconvenience for the illicit 'herb' grower. As a result, the illicit 'industrial' producer will cultivate only relatively small areas at very low densities (1-4 plants maximum per square metre) to make the removal of male plants a more realistic possibility and to conceal his or her rather obvious work from the authorities. All illicit

Cannabis production in Nicaragua is for domestic consumption; and located, with some discretion, in the beautiful, mountainous regions of the country – not outside Managua, visible under the flight path of an international airport and sign-posted 'Hemp-Agro Nicaragua S.A'.

So, although both (legal and illegal) methods of cultivation are economically beneficial they are very distinct. Let me give you one final and definitive example. As you are aware, Paul Wylie's company purchased fifteen tons of Cannabis Sativa L (Hemp) seed from China for 22,000 (USD). The equivalent market price for that quantity of Cannabis Indica or good quality 'marijuana' seed would be around two billion (USD). According to the DEA, Hemp-Agro's crop tested at 1.6 percent THC or several percentage points below useless as narcotic grade Cannabis. The latter should have a minimum of 10 percent THC and can reach a dizzying high of 30 percent - if you grow it professionally as the UK government is now doing to produce analgesics for cancer, AIDS and multiple sclerosis sufferers.

It is also worth mentioning that despite hundreds of billions of tax dollars fighting a global 'war on drugs', Paul Wylie still had the privilege of meeting the 'Narco Jet Guys'. Some people maybe 'liberal' on economics, but they are very sparing with the truth. Let us make one thing absolutely clear. The 'war on drugs' has been an utter failure in terms of vastly increased numbers of drug addicts and our swelling prison populations, benefiting only a privatised prison system (visit investigative journalist, Greg Palast's website: see Wackenhut Corporation) and its political advocates. Why should people be allowed to profit from this industry?

Global militarisation and millions of dead people are the only real legacy of the 'war on drugs' because before this 'war', there was no drug problem, or indeed weekly shootings in our inner cities. Our 'war on drugs' served to open up the global arms market from Latin America to Afghanistan and beyond, while the proceeds from the illicit trade in opium and cocaine more often than not funds the purchase of weapons.

There are some rather disturbing linkages. Shortly after

the bombing of Afghanistan, that country was restored to No.1 global opium producer. Under supervision of the United Nations Drug Control Programme, the Taliban regime had virtually ended all opium cultivation, leaving only 7000ha controlled by the Northern Alliance. That is not to say the Taliban regime was "good". They lived off the proceeds of stockpiled opium, butchered farmers to prevent opium cultivation and received area per ha payments for from the international community for not growing any. However, the US led 'victory' or 'liberation' of Afghanistan increased opium production by 657 percent in 2002 to between 45 and 65,000ha: worth an estimated 2-300 billion US dollars. Afghanistan is once again supplying 80 percent of world heroin 'demand' and one third of total global narcotic turnover, some of which accrues to the same CIA that protects cocaine production in Latin America – hence the 'Narco Jet Guys', and investigative journalist Garry Webb's book, 'Dark Alliance'.

So, while the CIA-protected international trade in drugs is a $500 billion dollar annual industry, the legal hemp industry (although recovering) has been reduced to a stagger from what promised to be an utterly brilliant start in the 1920's. Instead of hemp-based fuel/gasoline, paper, plastics and building composites being a global multi billion-dollar industry: oil, drugs, timber and the guns used to control these resources form the base of global industry at the dawn of a new millennium - why?

An equally significant question is why the distinction between Cannabis for industry (fibre/seed) and a narcotic (THC) should actually be a point of international law? Answer: Cannabis Sativa L is scientifically and industrially recognised as one of the single most useful natural fibres and sources of raw cellulose on the Planet, and has been since the early 1900's. Cannabis fibres can be used to produce a vast range of textile products. It can also be processed into high value particleboard for the construction industry, environmentally friendly cement and is an excellent source of paper pulp. Cannabis has around 25,000 documented industrial uses.

Cannabis has a cellulose content comparable to that of a

tropical hardwood. This fact – considering also the speed at which it grows - makes industrial Cannabis the most practical raw material for cellulose-based ethanol production: a liquid fuel that can be used to power the internal combustion engine, minimising toxic emissions by up to 98 percent. Humanity currently has the technology and legislation (Kyoto Treaty) to make this a global reality. Today's cellulose-to-ethanol technology is a highly sophisticated and refined industrial process compared to that of the 1920's or 30's.

The possibilities are fantastic. We can cultivate a plant in order to produce locally required, clean fuel. Ethanol can also be used in existing oil and gas fired power stations for electricity generation. Not only would rural areas have a new high value industry, we would all benefit environmentally and economically. Afghanistan and Colombia, for example, would have an economically viable alternative to narcotic cultivation and the perpetual state of war and foreign occupation that accompanies it.

Arguably, the most important aspects of industrial scale Cannabis production are the direct environmental benefits. There is a large body of scientific and industrial literature detailing these facts at hempconspiracy.com. It is an excellent rotation crop - both cost effective and low maintenance; requiring fewer chemicals than most other domesticated crops. Industrial research in the European Union confirms that it can be grown effectively without any chemical inputs. Industrial Cannabis can be grown successfully using no herbicides or pesticides. Spanish research has demonstrated that planting Cannabis in rotation with Wheat crops can increase the yield of the latter by up to 40 percent using only organic fertiliser and nitrogen, presenting another reason why we must surely question the "need" for genetically modified crops.

Since the main 'arguments' in favour of GM crops are 'reduced chemical input' and 'improved yields'; would it not make more sense to employ people in sustainable agriculture using rotation crops with huge industrial value - fuel - already proven to perform these functions without damaging the environment?

GM technology is very controversial. It has the potential to be both creative and destructive. In truth, however, there is no such thing as an environmental 'experiment' with this technology. We either have it inside a laboratory or we have it outside in the environment and should probably ask ourselves some fairly basic questions as to why the scientific community is seriously divided into an 'inside until later' and 'outside now' camp. Scientists are clearly not 'Luddites', Mr. Blair. But there is a lot of money at stake and well-funded biotech industry lobbying organisations, such as Science Media Centre, do not exist solely for their investors' passive amusement.

A grand component of the Hemp Conspiracy is (deliberate?) ignorance and never has this been more apparent than when we tried to engage a global agricultural organisation in our work. The Consultative Group on International Agricultural Research (CGIAR) appeared to be the kind of organisation that would have an interest in our hemp-for-fuel project. CGIAR has a proven record in conventional crop breeding, while promoting 'sustainability' via offices throughout Latin America and Africa, working with a collection of indigenous - but not so financially independent - policy and agricultural research groups. CGIAR shares a head office location in Italy with the United Nations Food and Agriculture Organisation.

In early 2002, CGIAR advertised 'calls' for sustainable agriculture-based proposals and so we submitted our work well in advance of the deadline under the proposal category: 'Beat the Heat: climate change and rural prosperity'. It would be fair to assume that because the hemp project fulfils every recommendation set out by the largest group of international researchers on the topic of climate change (The Intergovernmental Panel on Climate Change), that we could expect a reply or perhaps an acknowledgement of receipt. No communication was entered into by this organisation, despite this work being professionally translated into Spanish and distributed to every regional office in Latin America.

There could be a rational explanation. CGIAR promotes chemically dependent agriculture, such as herbicide-coated seeds for resistant maize varieties and genetic modification

– methods seriously questioned by industrial Cannabis cultivation within our proposed strategy of (real) sustainable agriculture. CGIAR would appear to have bought the silence of the scientific community on two Continents (Africa and Latin America).

CGIAR is chaired by Ian Johnson and also receives most of its funding from the same World Bank that employs Mr. Johnson - to whom we sent a courtesy copy of the project. Do we conclude that the same corporate interests who sought to prevent industrial Cannabis production in the 1920's are continuing to do so via an institutionalised bias in favour of chemically dependent agriculture, fossil fuel consumption and the outright control of foreign markets though a highly politicised global financial system that benefits only an elite of corporate interests at the expense of our Planet, our health and our economic security?

It is a very serious problem. How can anyone be allowed to develop when the objectivity of science is removed by vested interests and when these same interests have only one desire: to sell and market products to which they own patents? And lastly, why do these interests not appear pleased to discover that industrial Cannabis production is challenging the status quo of environmental degradation and endemic poverty through the application of scientific objectivity and a desire to create independent domestic industry for the World's poorest people?

Despite a wealth of natural resources (soil, land, water and climate), Nicaraguans are disproportionately very poor. So-called 'Structural Adjustment', including the re-named versions of the same IMF and World Bank prescription, has been an utter disaster for millions of people in Latin America. For Nicaragua, this means cheap labour, poverty, minimum state spending on health and education with industry geared primarily to export markets in cigars, crocodile skins, coffee and fruit. Regardless of the price you might pay for a cappuccino in the City Centre, the poor farmers in Nicaragua receive less than 8 cents for every dollar spent – and that is on the wholesale price. In the last year alone over one hundred coffee farms have been seized by the banks in Nicaragua, tens of thousands of people are without work many of whom are begging – or getting involved in the cultivation and sale of drugs to feed their families.

Nicaraguans experience a level of poverty associated with the poorest countries in Africa - they have insufficient health care provisions, one of the most brutal and financially starved prison systems in the World and a high level of adult illiteracy. Like the nations of sub-Saharan Africa, Nicaragua is an unnecessarily poor country. It seems fair to suggest that the only long-term solution to this crisis is through the creation of sustainable domestic industry using the available agricultural and climatic resources. We must put an end to the development of dependence.

A cellulose-based fuel economy using industrial scale Cannabis production would also help mitigate the problem of climate change. Due to a high-cellulose content and rapid growth cycle, industrial Cannabis cultivation would sequestrate large quantities of Carbon Dioxide from the atmosphere, making our air more breathable while helping to combat climate change in the long term. Combine the unique - immediate - agricultural and environmental benefits that make Cannabis a far superior source of fuel than starch based crops, such as corn or sugar, with direct fossil fuel replacement and we are onto something - right?

The Nicaraguan government certainly thought so in 1997, solely on the basis of an initial plan to use Cannabis for wood product substitution, textiles and seed oil – never mind petrochemical equivalents. Industrial Cannabis cultivation has the potential to be the largest, most environmentally and socially beneficial industry on this Earth. That is a fact.

So why exactly was Paul Wylie imprisoned? According to the court transcripts, the DEA (United States Drug Enforcement Administration) supplied the 'evidence' or 'advice' on which the Nicaraguan authorities acted. Under US Federal Law, administered in this case by the DEA and according to one US Embassy spokesman to Managua daily, Nuevo Diario,

"All cultivation of Cannabis is illegal . . . I believe it is this way for the Nicaraguan authorities too".

Incorrect. US Congress enacted the Comprehensive Drug Abuse and Control Act in 1970, replacing the old Federal Bureau of Narcotics with the Justice Department's DEA, which stated that all drugs,

". . . will be controlled in conformity with the [UN 1961] treaty or other international obligation". Sounds good; however, the 'confusion' rests in the House Committee Report on the same 1970 Act by concluding that, "marijuana would be prohibited except . . . for the emergency production of hemp". [my emphasis]

The question is: do we blame ignorance, stupidity or a very deliberate action on the part of the US legislator, going back as far as the 1920's to prevent competition to the petrochemical and timber industries? Since these people were neither ignorant nor stupid we must assume the latter to be correct. In fact, considerable time and effort has been expended investigating the political motivation behind the 'war on drugs' – see hemp-conspiracy.com. Incidentally, the 'emergency production' of industrial Cannabis refers to instances when other industrial fibre and fuel supplies are interrupted i.e. during times of war.

Over the course of a Century, the World has been deliberately addicted to polluting fossil fuels while being stripped of bio-diverse natural forest resources - much of which remain unknown to science. Hemp-Agro of Nicaragua was perfectly placed to assist the sustainable rebuilding of homes following Hurricane Mitch – instead; the relief workers had to cut down trees. It is a global tragedy. United States Federal Law has been in breach of the United Nations Single Convention on Narcotic Drugs since this legislation was internationally ratified in 1961 – a fact reflected in DEA policy since that Administration was formed in 1970. The US government ratified this international Treaty but refuses to respect it.

The court transcripts of Wylie's 'trial' contain a direct reference to "the study on the Cannabis Sativa plant taken from the Drug Manual of D.E.A" by the prosecution - and, as is apparent from Wylie's personal experience of Hemp

Conspiracy, the DEA were involved from the offset. How can this administration function when the laws that govern it not only breach those of the United Nations but all common sense? The Cannabis plants at Sabana Grande were planted at high density, they grew to around seven feet in height, were laden with valuable seed and had a THC content well below useless. According to the DEA 'Drug Manual', that is a 'marijuana' crop. Although, if it's a state of 'emergency' for Uncle Sam's fuel and fibre supply, it's conveniently called 'Hemp For Victory'. That is what US Federal Law on industrial Cannabis amounts to – a sick joke, choking on it's own cynicism.

Every country is bound to the 1961 UN Single Convention on Narcotic Drugs. Almost every developed country in the world, especially in the European Union, is currently researching and commercially producing Cannabis as a renewable resource. Following intense agri-industrial lobbying, the UK government re-issued industrial Cannabis licences in 1995. Other countries, such as France, Spain, the Netherlands, Russia, China and India never stopped production. But it would appear that if the United States does not like it (for whatever reason), they can prevent others from trying and are not only breaking their own constitution by preventing US farmers growing this valuable and renewable resource; they are severely infringing the sovereignty of others; especially their considerably poorer - oil and 'aid' dependent – neighbours in Latin America.

Farmers in the United States cannot get licenses to grow Hemp unless they are extremely lucky. For example, in the State of Virginia (1999), some small scale, experimental industrial Cannabis cultivation was eventually permitted not only by the Secretary for Agriculture but also the Director of the Drug Enforcement Administration and Director of the Office of National Drug Control Policy - a viable and LEGAL industry unlawfully strangled by several miles of highly politicised red tape. In the face of this absurdity, Hawaii has been trying for a very long time to get a viable Hemp industry started. In 2002/3 Don E Wirtshafter and the Hemp Industries Association continues to be embroiled in a lawsuit against the Bush administrations (DEA) recent attempt to ban hemp-based products via a new and equally bizarre 'war on health food' - or anything made from hemp. The DEA claimed that trace amounts of THC in the seed meant it should be illegal - a move that would kill the industry completely. Apparently the DEA do not mind the higher trace levels of opiates found in the poppy seeds of your breakfast roll. At the time of writing, the United States Court of Appeals for the Ninth Circuit ruled in favour of the Hemp Industries Association's petition that the DEA's attempt to ban the seed be declared "invalid" and "unenforceable" but this issue is far from settled yet.

These events follow the seizure and holding of 50 tons of Canadian hemp seed by US authorities in August 2000 - for five months. It is a blatant story of repetition. Exactly the same tactics were used in the 1920's and 30's when life was made so difficult for the Hemp industry that most reluctantly gave up trying. Several Canadian Hemp growers and processors are now facing bankruptcy for trying to grow a very useful renewable resource. It is a disgrace.

What is the point of international law if it is not applied and/or administered equally? Paul Wylie's case will undoubtedly address this important 21st Century issue and from the evidence, the ongoing litigation will also demonstrate how the Nicaraguan government, depending as they were on US 'aid' following Hurricane Mitch, denied their participation in the project - their complicity aided by initial newspaper reports branding the Hemp-Agro crop a 'marijuana bust' and the shareholders 'narco-traffickers'. These Nicaraguan officials, having granted their documented permission under international law, had a moral and legal obligation to defend Paul Wylie, Hemp-Agro and their employees' income.

Although the Hemp Conspiracy has never before been the subject of an autobiographical book - many have "disappeared" - it does have an 80 year-old history, also available at hempconspiracy.com. Nicaragua did not begin the Hemp Conspiracy and Nicaragua has absolutely no vested interest in its continuation - quite the reverse. The only losers at the end of the Hemp Conspiracy are the corporate interests responsible for the bulk of 20th Century environmental degradation, including the politicians that these interests have traditionally supported and quite often made outright purchases on. The most recent and obvious example being George W. Bush's Administration, which has shown utter contempt for the Kyoto Treaty and the collective will of the international community to seriously address climate change - all in favour of the corporate interests who funded the 2000 'election' campaign.

Of course, it should be pointed out that not all petrochemical interests would lose out to a cellulose-to-ethanol industry. Some, such as Royal Dutch Shell Plc, have already invested heavily in cellulose-to-ethanol conversion technology. In this case owned and commercially operated by Iogen Energy Corporation of Canada.

Nicaragua was perhaps an unwitting participant of the Hemp Conspiracy during the late 1990's and has a strong case for recourse against the US government. Paul Wylie will get the justice he deserves, but it is only fitting that this conspiracy ends in Nicaragua, marked by the beginning of a new era of sustainable agri-industrial development and justice for all the people. It could realistically be the beginning of the end for poverty in Nicaragua and will definitely provide a striking example to other agricultural economies as to the benefits of industrial Cannabis production. The United Nations Africa Recovery Programme has already expressed an interest in this work.

The project awaiting implementation in Nicaragua will immediately reduce the national oil import requirement by 10 percent, rotating industrial Cannabis on less than 10,000 hectares of land – most of which is either under-productive, non-productive, partially degraded and therefore a source of poverty at the present time. Cannabis fibre will be processed along with all suitable agricultural waste i.e. the parts of food crops we do not eat, using commercially proven technology to produce ten million gallons of ethanol per year from the offset. It will employ thousands of additional people in sustainable agriculture and fulfils every policy recommendation of the Intergovernmental Panel on Climate Change (IPCC).

Even at this early stage, the project will remove - via oil replacement, carbon sequestration and sound land management - a minimum of 300,000 tons of atmospheric carbon per year that would otherwise be adding to global climate chaos. Direct oil replacement, including ethanol-gasoline blends in transportation, will proportionately remove airborne toxins that cause respiratory illness and premature death among the population.

Paul Wylie's incarceration and extraordinary survival has certainly not been for nothing. Both are the catalyst for a new beginning. It is more than justice - it is the start of something that promises to help create a better World for all our children and as such we would strongly encourage you to support this work further by visiting our website. All the information is free. You can personally examine the project for Nicaragua and all of the evidence at your own leisure. This website includes political, journalistic and a wealth of scientific information, along with photographs of all the original documentation pertaining to Paul Wylie's experience of Hemp Conspiracy.

Please finish by signing our international petitions. These will be formally presented to the United Nations and the United States of America Federal Government. The United Nations is being petitioned to strengthen the 1961 Single Convention and oversee the implementation of a global climate change mitigation strategy using industrial Cannabis as a primary renewable resource in fulfilment of the Kyoto Treaty and all practical recommendations of the Intergovernmental Panel on Climate Change.

The United States Federal Government is being petitioned to remove internationally illegal legislation that places industrial Cannabis cultivation under the control of the Drug Enforcement Administration and Office of National Drug Control Policy. Industrial Cannabis is not a drug and should only be controlled by agricultural policy administrations, farmers and the populations concerned. International law on this issue exists for the benefit of humanity and should be respected.

As Buddha said, "Three things cannot be long hidden; the sun, the moon and the truth". To which George Orwell rightly added, [yes Buddha, but] "In a time of universal deceit, telling the truth becomes a revolutionary act".

Thank you for being part of it.

www.hempconspiracy.com

www.ingramcontent.com/pod-product-compliance
Lightning Source LLC
LaVergne TN
LVHW021233080526
838199LV00088B/4337